Amelia Marriette

WALKING

into

ALCHEMY

The Transformative Power of Nature

Mereo Books

Mereo Books 2nd Floor, 6-8 Dyer Street,
Cirencester, Gloucestershire, GL7 2PF

An imprint of Memoirs Book Ltd. www.mereobooks.com

Walking into Alchemy: 978-1-86151-947-4

First published in Great Britain in 2019
by Mereo Books, an imprint of Memoirs Books Ltd.

Copyright ©2019

The address for Memoirs Books Ltd. can be
found at www.memoirspublishing.com

Memoirs Books Ltd. Reg. No. 7834348

Typeset in 11/15pt Century Schoolbook
by Wiltshire Associates Ltd. Printed and bound in Great Britain

Dedication

For Katie: wonderful as it is to walk,
coming home is even better.

inspirations

'Only ideas won by walking have any value'

Friedrich Nietzsche, Twilight of the Idols, 1889.

'The true alchemists do not change lead into gold;
they change the world into words.'

William H. Gass, A Temple of Texts, 2006.

CONTENTS

Acknowledgments
About this book
Introduction

Note: The photographs which appear at the beginning of each chapter were taken by the author.

ACKNOWLEDGEMENTS

I would like to thank Claudia Kronlechner for her initial encouragement, and for arranging for me to read extracts of my book to members of the local English-Speaking Group in the nearby town of Wolfsberg.

Myriam Robveille for her constant support, and for reading excerpts and providing feedback.

Kerry Carruthers for her astute observations.

Local journalists Julia Wurzinger and Martina Schmerlaib for their coverage of the walk and the book in the press.

Bing Hobson for her help in identifying birds.

Gabby Jensen, for her help with the geological information in the chapter entitled Stone.

Michiyo Kato for her help with the final chapter, Kintsugi.

Rachel Dorian, an ace proof-reader, and Gabi Ginsberg who suggested that I should think of a new title for the book which opened up new avenues of enquiry.

Most especially, I would like to thank Tali Silberstein for reading my manuscript in draft form, for providing invaluable support and advice and for always being kind, patient and insightful. And, I mustn't forget Paul and Charlene Murphy, who asked me to look after their dog, Jasper, and in so doing changed my life forever.

ABOUT THIS BOOK

The central theme of the book is my personal journey following redundancy and financial problems, depression and ill health and my fortunate relocation to Austria. The book has three other main areas of interest: a love story; a nature story and a book about art, culture and the wider world. The love story is one concerning my chance encounter with my now partner Katie which led to our relocation to her home town in Austria. I was surrounded by the stunning scenery of the Carinthian region, and my love of nature was rekindled. I sought repair and rejuvenation through the completion of fifty-two thirteen-mile walks in the span of one calendar year. This act of repetitive walking enabled me to study the changing seasons and explore the flora and fauna of the area; I was able to return myself to health by considering and reconsidering personal experiences, emotions, ideas and memories. I also returned to my love of photography. As the weeks passed, I began to find my sense of place and my new path in life. I realised that I was walking into alchemy, mining for gold as I went. It was then, as a former curator, of both the Holst Birthplace Museum in Cheltenham and at Torre Abbey in Devon, and as Shakespeare scholar, that I began to see connections everywhere. I began to invest my walks with meaning from paintings, musical passages and lines of verse.

I hope that Walking into Alchemy will inspire you the reader to find your own path in life, wherever that might take you.

INTRODUCTION

Five o'clock in the evening; a bitterly cold November day in Torquay, Devon. I lock the ancient back door of the museum with great gratitude. I have managed to survive another truly terrible day at my new job. In trying to shelter from the horizontal, driving rain, I drop my keys in a puddle, and the security light flickers for a moment and goes out. I fumble with the wet keys trying to find the right one, but it is so dark I can't see my hand in front of my face. When at last I find the right key I have run out of time, and the alarm refuses to set, so I begin the whole weary process again.

I phone the security people, and after some delay I set the alarm and eventually, thankfully, I manage to get away. I cross the road to reach my car, my umbrella blows inside out, and a blast of icy-cold grainy rain hits me face on. I take shelter in the local shop, and for some inexplicable reason I buy a bottle of Southern Comfort – I had never even tasted it before, but comfort, Southern or otherwise, was sorely needed.

Back at the car I carefully lay my new purchase on the passenger seat, but in the few seconds it takes me to struggle with my umbrella I hear a smash and the bottle is in the gutter. An aroma of sweet, peaty, spicy liquor fills the air and then is gone. I bend down to pick up the shards of glass from under my car tyre, cut my finger and feel cold water drip down my collar from the car roof.

I was miserable, broke and lonely that day. Such was my life in 2009.

Seven o'clock in the morning; June 9th 2015. We are waiting on the slip road to board the car ferry to Calais. We are leaving Devon, the UK and everything behind to begin a new life in Southern Austria.

1
REKINDLING

My life changed on a cold and dreary day at the dawn of the New Year of 2012. At the Christmas party at work I had offered to look after a colleague's dog should he ever go on holiday, but in the way of the English I had only said it to be polite and I never thought that I would be asked. But on 30th December the phone rang, and I heard a pleading voice begging me for help. 'I'm so sorry that it's such short notice but could you look after little Jasper, just for a couple of weeks? We've been let down, and we are really in a jam. You can stay at our cottage; it's really beautiful at this time of year.' I felt obliged to say yes, but I cursed myself when I put the phone down.

I was in a bad mood when I eventually arrived to pick up the keys from the neighbour; the cottage was almost impossible to find, lost in fog and mist in the middle of Haldon Forest near Exeter. I drove through hard-to-navigate lanes, and the whole area was dark and forbidding in the winter light and made more so by towering pine trees. My colleague had told me of the beauty of the forest, but one can only see beauty if one is inclined to see beauty, and I did not feel so inclined. It was also lunchtime, and my boss was of the opinion that no one needed to take a lunch break, so when I finally arrived, I was short of time and short of temper.

As instructed, I knocked on the neighbour's door. A petite, attractive woman answered. Her adjoining cottage was small, and my six-foot frame filled the doorway, making it necessary for me to stoop to prevent from hitting my head on the lintel. She urged me to enter, and I heard her speak for the first time, her voice rich and sultry; her accent – French perhaps? I wasn't sure. She introduced herself as Katie and gave me the keys to her neighbour's cottage. I collected the little dog from next door, and I was about to drive off when I heard her sultry voice again this time calling after me: 'Would you like to come for supper on Saturday?' I only agreed because I was too tired, busy and stressed to say no.

Saturday came; I wasn't looking forward to having to be friendly and polite, but I forced myself. I had been living alone for quite a while; after the breakdown of my most recent relationship, I had stopped socialising because I had begun to fear any company but my own. But surprisingly, the evening was enjoyable. Feeling too tired to drive home, I let myself into the little cottage next door. The little dog was delighted to be back on home turf; I smiled at this, envious of the happiness he took from so simple a pleasure. I slept very well, better than I had slept for many months.

The next morning I found Katie wrapped up in a large coat and a huge scarf and pottering about in her garden. I told her that my own garden in Newton Abbot was in a bit of a state and that I had once been in control of it, but that now it was in control of me. Immediately she offered to help me get it back in order. I was taken aback by this kind offer, which she implored me to accept. Over the next five weekends Katie drove over to my rambling Victorian apartment, with its shady and rather bleak garden, and we began cutting back and weeding, then trimming the old laurel bushes and large bay trees into shape. Katie worked tirelessly, bringing me plants from her garden, cleaning and sweeping up, and even buying paint so that I could restore my old octagonal summer house that was just about salvageable, which I had once used as my writing den but which I hadn't stepped foot in for years.

After the third weekend, I realised that I was beginning to feel alive again. An awakening began - why had I forgotten about nature and turned my back on it? I had once taken solace in it, but I had not ventured out into my garden or been for a walk for in a long time. As the foggy winter months began to turn into spring and the first signs of green shoots and buds began to appear, I knew that I loved Katie. One day as we worked alongside one another in my garden in the pale sunlight of a winter's day, it was suddenly blindingly obvious that the feeling was mutual. Neither of us had planned for this to happen; it was a joyful surprise. We did not need to speak about it; it just was. It just is. With this dawning realisation, we also felt the embers of our love of life beginning to rekindle.

2

Austria

During our gardening weekends, Katie told me about her life, and I discovered that despite her rich, French-sounding accent, she had been born in Austria. Over the ensuing months, Katie told me more about her home country and a little about her childhood. I began to see Austria as a place that I longed to visit; it sounded so beautiful, so majestic, with mountains, acres of pine woods and forests, deep lakes, open spaces and vast skies. I fell in love with the idea of it long before I visited.

My working life had not improved but become steadily worse. In the years when I had been working as a Keeper of Art I had been involved with two major refurbishment projects, amounting to nearly fifteen million pounds in total. With the barest minimum of staff available I was forced not only to curate but to hang off ladders and scaffolding to get several hundred paintings, some of them weighing two hundred pounds or more, displayed. With a team of just three, we had mounted over eight hundred objects ranging from medieval stone fragments to glass to textiles and more. I had also curated thirty contemporary exhibitions. The two most significant involved working with internationally acclaimed artists, namely Antony Gormley, Damien Hirst and Richard Long, and liaising with both the Arts Council Collection and Tate Britain. These years had been filled with action and excitement but also with an unacceptable level of professional heartache and strain. The workload was not the most significant problem: there had always been an unpleasant atmosphere at work, underpinned by an element of homophobia and the fact that some members of the old guard suffered from isolationist tendencies. Then, when I did not think that things could get any worse, more sinister happenings came to light. A long-standing member of staff was arrested and taken from his desk on a bleak Wednesday afternoon. The rumours, stories, and accusations were very dark indeed. We were forbidden to talk about it. He never returned, was not replaced, and now I had even more work, his and my own. I felt completely trapped.

It became increasingly apparent that my work was making me feel unwell. I was suffering from stomach pains, headaches, and food intolerances. Katie was worried about me and thought I needed a holiday; she also wanted me to see Austria in the summer. I was very keen to oblige, as I had not been able to take any more than a few days here and there of my holiday entitlement and had only been functioning because I had eventually gone to the doctor's and been prescribed anti-depressants. Finally, in July 2014 I managed to negotiate, or perhaps the word is beg for, some leave.

Austria did not disappoint; it was better than I had ever imagined it would be. I was not prepared for the glorious warmth or the lush beauty of the countryside. As we drove towards the

Carinthian region, wildflowers were everywhere abundant and the greenest grass I had ever seen. I was captivated. One morning I stood in the garden, cradling a cup of coffee and looked towards the nearby hills and mountains. Suddenly, I felt compelled to lose myself on a long walk, a walk that would take me out of my comfort zone and right up and into the hills, where I could see the mountains, and experience the feeling of being surrounded by trees and open countryside.

I dressed quickly and walked into the nearby town of Bad Sankt Leonhard and bought a map for one euro from the tiny tourist information office. On this map, several long walks were already marked out. I pored over it and finally chose, quite randomly, walk Q3.

The next morning the sky looked black, and rain seemed likely, but at nine o'clock I set out. As I walked, I breathed in the clean mountain air, and after about an hour I began to feel better. A few more hours of walking brought me to one of the highest points, where I stopped to marvel at the scene before me: a deep valley of undulating green fields, surrounded by pine trees and in the distance a range of mountains. Beside me, a beautiful apple tree stood by proudly, the everyday guardian of this beautiful view. I took out my phone and snapped a few photographs of the tree with the view forming a magnificent backdrop beyond.

I walked the full thirteen miles and it took me well over five hours. I was elated but exhausted when I returned. I fell asleep in the cool of the late afternoon and did not wake until the next day. When I finally awoke I was so stiff that I could hardly walk, and had to get downstairs by descending the staircase on my backside. But my mind felt quieter, and I felt much calmer.

A few days later we returned to England. I went back into an even busier and an even more stressful period at work, but the final stage of the redevelopment process was, at last, limping towards completion, and finally, in July, the museum re-opened. I began to see the light at the end of the tunnel. For a few months, I enjoyed seeing the public coming to see their favourite works of art newly displayed. I began to feel that my working life might become a little easier and even perhaps enjoyable. But, I still felt wounded by the events of the past six years, I was no longer a healthy or happy person, and I was always afraid that bad news was just around the corner.

I was right to be afraid. In December 2014 there was talk of redundancies. I was merely shocked at first, and then I felt outraged. Katie encouraged me to take a step back and consider my options. After a few weeks of difficult deliberation, I decided that rather than spend my Christmas holiday worrying I would volunteer to take redundancy. My request was accepted, so I began to map out a long list of work targets – updating museum documents, clearing up loose ends, and spring cleaning my office. On March 31st 2015 I was released. Amazingly, I did not feel afraid; I felt nothing but relief.

3

LIMBO

We decided that it was time for me to rent out my apartment, which would relieve me of my mortgage commitments, and Katie invited me to move into her cottage in Haldon Forest. I was very pleased about this, and it felt it was absolutely the right thing to do. I had also, at last, begun to recognise the beauty of the location of Katie's cottage: her extended 'garden' was three thousand five hundred acres of woodland. Entering this wonderland never failed to make me feel better when, on a Friday evening, I left work and headed out for the weekend, feeling a sense of relief when I crossed the bridge over the Teign estuary to wind my way through the narrow lanes to my destination. As I travelled deeper and deeper into the forest, it became increasingly overgrown and dense with trees, and it always felt as if I was leaving my troubles behind.

I arranged to store most of my belongings, but felt that I

needed to have some of my books and music around me, so on moving day I arrived laden with boxes. The cottage seemed to fill up very quickly; suddenly it looked much smaller, and we felt closed in. Furthermore, after a few weeks the realisation that I had no income and absolutely no idea what the future held started to weigh heavily on me. I felt like I was suspended in time, stuck in limbo.

One rainy morning I looked out onto a dripping, winter scene and after several hours of job searching online and updating recruiting websites with my current details, I began to feel panicked. It's notoriously tricky to get museum work anywhere, and in the South West of England it's almost impossible. I felt unanchored, and inevitably I was missing the routine that work brings. I began to think about our holiday in Austria and summoning up images in my head of all that I had seen. My long walk seemed like nothing but a figment of my imagination, but I longed to walk it again, imagining the route in deep snow, or hoar-frosts, verdant spring or a topaz autumn. Austria began to take on a mystical quality for me. I started to dream about it, and my dreams were filled with gigantic pine trees, leaf-strewn avenues lit by dappled light, waterfalls cascading and brooks babbling. I was always moving, never still, and as I climbed higher and higher the trees gave way to open vistas and far-reaching views and there I was standing in a silent, world of calm and feeling nothing but a sense of peace.

One evening I fell over a stack of my books that didn't as yet have a home, banged my head on the ceiling and stubbed my toe on the coffee table. Partly in jest and partly in frustration, and without even meaning to, I blurted out, 'I don't see why we can't go and live in Austria.' To my utter amazement, Katie simply said: 'I don't see why not. It seems like the perfect solution.' Following a fall, Katie's ninety-seven-year-old mother in Austria was no longer living in the house and had moved into a nearby, and extremely good, nursing home; this was a relief, but it meant that Katie could no longer call her every few days to check on her, as she was now often talking with friends or having her meals. So many things seemed to be coalescing - Austria seemed to be calling to us.

As soon as we realised that we were in complete agreement, the decision was made swiftly and effortlessly; everything began to happen very quickly. We worked exhaustively, and I felt at last that I had something to grasp onto – something to look forward to. We began by writing long lists in large black writing on the back of rolls of old wallpaper which we stuck to the kitchen door in the little stone cottage. We did this so that we could not possibly forget or ignore anything crucially important: the lists ranged from making our wills (which we still haven't done) to organising roadside recovery in Europe and decorating the cottage ready for renting out.

We started packing up Katie's cottage and found the task difficult and challenging, but we tried to make it as stress-free as possible, and in this we were mostly successful. Katie is a goldsmith, jeweller and artist. She is the kind of person who picks up pieces of metal from the side of the road, be they bent nails or rusty bolts and once they have become part of her collection of materials, they can never be relinquished. So packing up her workshop was the hardest job of all. Hundreds of tools, drills, bits of metal ('I need that.' 'But it's a broken screw.' 'I know, I need it, put it in the box') all had to be itemised and boxed up. Metal, precious and base; jewels, valuable or costume; beads; wire; soldering equipment and an immensely heavy rolling mill – all were treated equally, wrapped and labelled. It was a slow process.

Eventually we were able to send Katie's worldly goods to lodge with mine in storage ready to be sent onto Austria. After a few weeks of intense activity, I looked around the now almost empty cottage, and inevitably began to feel doubts about our impending move. I retreated into the forest to take succour from the vast array of conifers growing there, the Scots pine, the Lodgepole pine and the Douglas fir, and breathed in deeply. I stood under a long row of Sitka spruce trees, and just stared up at them; they reached up to the heavens, towering above me at over one hundred and thirty feet. As I looked up, I felt an extraordinary sense of calmness and well-being wash over me. Everywhere in that forest in Devon, I could see an immediate and concrete link with Austria, beyond language, culture or politics. I realised that I could live happily in a place where I could see the same trees every day; that many things would be as familiar as they would be new. Leaning back against the spruce tree, running my hands along the ridge of the bark I immediately saw that the move would be a positive one for both of us.

We organised a party for my fiftieth birthday in April 2015. Friends and family came to help us celebrate, and we announced that we were going to go and live in Austria for a few months. We didn't want to admit to ourselves or commit to the idea that we might never return. But soon we found tenants for Katie's cottage, which meant that we had a deadline. We could not turn back now.

At the beginning of June a huge lorry slowly made its way down the narrow lanes, already with our items from storage on board, and the rest of our possessions were loaded. I had to write a cheque for £6,000 – all my redundancy money – immediately, which worried me greatly – would we ever see our stuff again? We watched as our belongings left, feeling nervous but excited. I had already loaded our old satnav with new European maps, crossing my fingers that they would work, and placed a box filled with snacks and bottles of water into our beaten-up Land Rover Freelander, for which I had swapped my much sleeker grey saloon to rid myself of the burden of the car loan.

We drove first to London, to say au revoir to family there, then to Folkestone to make the short ferry crossing with our car to Calais. We travelled across Belgium and Germany, with one night in the aptly-named Rainbow Motel in Pforzheim, to arrive finally in Southern Austria after seventeen hours of driving. I had expected it to be a tough 'Ice Cold in Alex' affair and thought we would need to steal ourselves for an ordeal across deserts and over mountains (my geography is not that good.) But in fact, the journey though long, was surprisingly easy. Nevertheless, when we finally arrived at eight o'clock on the evening of June 10th 2015 at what was to be our new home in Bad Sankt Leonhard, we were more than a little euphoric to have arrived safely.

4
ASSIMILATION

As soon as we took possession of the house we began to re-live the origins of our relationship, and immediately we started the process of taming the too-large acre of garden. We coaxed the thirty-year old petrol lawnmower back to life and attempted to turn the lawn into something other than tatty grass with weed-filled borders. Katie's mother had once seen the garden as her pride and joy, and we were determined to restore it. We dug spiral and crescent flower beds, sowed wildflower seeds to make meadow flowerbeds, and planted new fruit trees to stand in miniature isolation next to their more mature relatives. On her almost daily trips to the nursing home, Katie was able to tell her mother about our progress.

We soon realised that we couldn't possibly afford to buy the number of plants that we would need to create the show garden that would return it to its former glory, so we might as well turn some of the garden into a place to grow food. Finding the only completely flat area of the garden, we created raised high beds out of old railway cargo crates – much to the amusement of the staff at the garden centre, who could not fathom why we didn't buy ready-made, easy-assembly ones. We had both separately harboured a desire to have a vegetable garden but had not had the time, the space or the knowledge to make it a reality. We grasped the opportunity zealously, possibly even foolishly. We did manage to raise some simple crops – but every tomato in that first summer must have cost us at least five euros a piece, so much did we spend on organic compost, seedlings and plants. The garden, once established, would become more cost-effective, we told ourselves. Luckily, with the excellent, neutral soil and with good weather and hard work, by summers' end we got better results: our beans grew so high that we couldn't reach the highest ones even with a ladder, and we grew abundant crops of potatoes, beetroot, lovage, parsley, endive, courgette and chard.

Heartened by our progress, and having shipped my curator's toolkit to Austria, I used my too-fine tools to make compost bins, potting stations and garden tables out of old pallets that we cadged from a local plumber. It was hard physical work, but 2015 was the hottest summer for over two hundred years, and I especially enjoyed the balmy weather, it reminded me of 1976, when I was eleven the best summer of my life. The heat of the summer and the hours of gardening did much to heal me. The high temperatures also meant that evenings were long and warm, so we were able to cook our evening meals outside – we had inherited a store of old seasoned wood that had lain in the cellar unused for over twenty years, so it burnt fast and furiously. We were able to pluck our homegrown courgettes and tomatoes straight from the high beds and place them immediately onto the wood fire. On occasion, we shared a few glasses of white wine or made up Hugos, a popular local recipe consisting of white wine, elderflower cordial and sparkling water. In a happily exhausted state, we sat unwinding, watching the sun sink behind the mountains. We began to feel restored, even full of vigour, and we both started to look disgustingly healthy. But the time ebbed away in a whirl of activity, and soon summer was over.

When the weather turned colder, and we were met every day by morning mists and fogs, the crops dwindled and the grass stopped growing, we moved indoors. We hung up our art and bought bookshelves, and I began the Herculean task of sorting out my library, the only job that reduced me to tears. The books just kept on coming, and I couldn't face seeing them any more. Katie began to sort out her workshop, decorating and finally unpacking her tools. Moving indoors, we had to face the fact that we wouldn't be able to live with the 1970s orange and brown swirly carpets, so we called a local carpenter, and he came over and covered the old carpets with new wooden flooring.

In the evenings we began the task of redecorating the living rooms and our working days increased from eight to ten hours a day, but we felt so vital during those first six months that we were buzzing with life.

5

Archive

Our cellar, like most of those in Austria, was made up of a series of rooms, one housing a huge boiler, one a cold storage room with a soil floor to overwinter vegetables, and four other rooms to store wood, skis and the like. Just before Christmas, we decided to make a stab at clearing the cellar of decades of clutter; we found boxes of old jam jars, yet more books, photographs, toys, a cache of twenty old radios and boxes of files and documents. We had stumbled upon the family archive.

One evening Katie hauled up some of the boxes, and on opening them, we found document after document, all beautifully catalogued. Katie had previously told me some of her family's history, but I was not sure of all the details. She began to piece the story together for my benefit. Katie's maternal great-grandfather, Jakob Lang, had had to make a new life for himself at the age of fifty-five. He had been forced to find a way to recoup the money he had lost in the First World War; he had invested heavily in Government Bonds, with the expectation that the Austro-Hungarian Empire would be the victors. Instead, Jakob and his wife Gisela (née Schmidt) lost nearly all they had. Jakob had risen from a humble waiter to become the owner of hotels in Switzerland and Czechoslovakia. The documents told their story – but when we opened a box file and saw a small, blue silk ring case, and found two rings, one nested inside the other, engraved with the words 'Gold gab ich für Eisen, 1914' (gold I give for iron), neither of us spoke. We were very saddened to know that Katie's great-grandparents had even given up their gold wedding rings for the cause in exchange for humble iron ones.

After their financial collapse, the Langs first became hoteliers in Vienna and then looked for new opportunities and ventures outside the city, finally alighting on Bad Sankt Leonhard[1]. Probably through a connection with a Viennese doctor who had bought the rights to a sulphur spa in the town at the turn of the century and was looking to sell. Bad Sankt Leonhard lies about 160 miles south west of Vienna but although small – the population even today is under 5,000 – the area around it has always been famous in Austria for its medicinal waters, so it's likely that the Langs had heard of it. There are two main medicinal water supplies in the area. The one with the oldest documented reputation is the curative Preblau spring, which is just six miles from Bad Sankt Leonhard and has long been used to treat bladder and renal diseases. The ancient Romans and the Celts knew of the positive effects of the Preblau water, and by 1233 the natural hydrogen carbonated water was being supplied to the bishops of Bamberg in sealed clay jars. In 1538 Paracelsus, the infamous Swiss-German physician, declared the water to have 'excellent medicinal powers'[2]. By 1612 the Preblau spring was marked precisely for the first time on a map of the

Carinthian dukedom. It is still sold commercially from the tiny hamlet of Prebl under the name Preblauer[3]. The second healing water source is found in Bad Sankt Leonhard itself, as the prefix 'Bad' of Bad Sankt Leonhard denotes; this refers to the fact that the town is officially designated as a spa town.

In 1927, as soon as their purchase of the sulphur spa was complete, Jakob and Gisela undertook a major redevelopment. They had bought the rights to the waters, and with them came ten small wooden chalets. Ambitiously the Lang's demolished these and erected in their stead a sizeable new structure of brick and render. They chose to make it homely and welcoming, painting it creamy yellow, adding attractive wooden detailing and carving, a pitched roof of slate and pretty six-paned windows. A large balcony which ran around the front elevation was filled with trailing geraniums in summer. Although it was built to a traditional design, their vision was ambitious. The property was on three floors, with seventeen bedrooms for paying guests and patients. Rooms on the ground floor offered state-of-the-art treatment facilities. They also incorporated a separate wing to act as their accommodation, and this was reached by a rather grand sweeping outdoor staircase made of stone and adorned with a carved balustrade. Much of the building was embellished with trellis, and red climbing roses grew abundantly for most of the year until the arrival of the first frosts. The extensive grounds were filled with shrubs and mature trees, and several immensely tall Noble Tannenbäume were incorporated into the scheme. Beds full of seasonal bedding plants were created, and a lake was dug out and stocked with fish.

In the difficult years after the First World War the Lang's new incarnation of the Sulphur Spa - or Schwefelheilbad - was one of the most expensive and grandest buildings erected in the immediate post-First World War period in the town. It was perhaps for this reason that in 1935 Jakob Lang was the first to petition the local authorities to add the prefix Bad to the town's name and thus firmly establish the town's credentials as an official spa town.

Perhaps it was fortunate that Jakob and Gisela lost much of their money after the collapse of the Austro-Hungarian Empire. It was their business interests in Bad Sankt Leonhard which would provide them with a legitimate escape route from Vienna before the atrocities of the Second World War.

In 1948, the Schwefelheilbad was turned over to the Langs' daughter Christine Wolf and his granddaughter, Katie's mother, also called Christine, and her Hungarian husband, Katie's father, Stefan Katai. Katie, born in 1950, grew to adulthood there. By all accounts, she had a wonderful childhood, playing with her sister and brother in the large, park-like garden and swimming in the lake. As Katie became more independent, she was able to roam in the hills and dabble in the streams, collecting berries and foraging for mushrooms.

But when it came to her turn to take over the business, she had no interest in it. Katie did not want to pursue a life in the health spa business, with its emphasis on clinical and medical treatments and the ever-present smell of sulphur. Likewise her siblings lacked the calling. So in 1973, the Schwefelheilbad was sold to the local council. After many years of neglect, it was finally demolished to make way for a modern health spa. It was the proceeds from the sale of spa which enabled Katie's parents to retire, buy a plot of land on the sunnier side of the town and build their own house, the house that Katie finally, thankfully, inherited.

Many extraordinary circumstances had made our current move to Austria possible. We found a photograph of the Langs buried in a box, and hung it on the wall by the front door as a reminder of the events that had led us here.

6
ANXIETY

22ND DECEMBER

We had thrown ourselves into our new lives with complete conviction, but as winter approached and our daily tasks began to grow less urgent, we were able to relax a little. My tenants in the UK decided to move on, and I sold my flat. This had been another happy event, another financial burden lifted. But as

Christmas approached – a time of year that I cannot abide – and the long, hot summer days seemed far behind us, some of my energy and recent good health started to evaporate. My old anxiety started to return. In the middle of December I received an email to say that after all, the contracts on my house sale would not be exchanged before Christmas. Bitterly disappointed, I fell into a blue funk and could not rouse myself from beneath its pall. I felt embarrassed, but forced myself to get up every day and look for purposeful distraction.

As soon as I had one anxiety, others began to crowd in. I began to feel worried about my obvious lack of language skills. I had learnt little or no German, finding the process very hard, and I worried that this would mean that I wouldn't be able to get any employment. I tried not to obsess. But when I found a strange mole on my stomach and rather ridiculously thought that I was going to die, immediately if not sooner, I was beyond worried. It was three days before Christmas, so I didn't want to mention it. Instead, I dressed up warmly and told Katie that I was going for a walk.

* * *

I walk and walk, unthinkingly, with no idea where I am going. After two hours I reach the tiny village of Schiefling. I try the door of the small pristine 15th century church, and when it gives, I decide to enter. I was not expecting to see so much bling – a wondrous over-the- top opulence, most unlike the modest, simple whitewashed churches of England built at a similar time, but stripped of their decoration by Protestant zealotry during the Reformation. This church was obviously rebuilt in the baroque style in the 18th century, so the early frescoes have been obliterated by extravagant ornamentation.

Behind the altar, an overlarge reredos – an ornamental screen which covers the wall – entirely fills the tiny apse. It is made of ornately-carved gold-leafed wood and adorned with so many flourishes that it is overwhelming. The ornate Corinthian pilasters, supporting an almost naked, bearded Jesus, has two chubby putti angels either side. The Virgin Mary, complete with an elaborate gold halo and a golden dress with long flowing sleeves, sits in a niche and appropriately holds centre stage. A wooden dove, hanging from a simple hook in the ceiling, recalling Christ's baptism by John the Baptist at the Jordan River, is also covered in gold leaf and sits on a bed of fluffy golden cumulus clouds surrounded by golden crepuscular rays. The lighting is ornate but much more to my liking - a delicate circular glass chandelier, held together by five rows of glass beads, resembling ice droplets on leaves. I feel as if I have entered a dream world from the ancient past or a film set. I have no feelings of transcendence, but I do leave the church feeling charmed by it as a piece of living art. My mood lifts a little.

As I reach the path again, I see a purple way marker with 'Q3' written in a clear, white font. Of course, I am on the walk that I completed last year and loved so much, but I have approached it from the opposite direction. I feel compelled to continue and walk the whole route. I walk for another hour, my stomach cramps beginning to ease. The sky is mainly clear - an exquisite blue at the highest point, but paler where it meets the rim of the mountains. There is an occasional patch of curdled cirrocumulus clouds, a mackerel sky. For December the sunshine seems to be bewilderingly dazzling. As I climb, I become hot from the exertion and have to carry my coat. I peer into the distance through a summer-like haze but am pleased to see that the mountains are snow-capped. I am happy not only because of the beauty of this sight but also because it indicates that cold seasonal weather is at least apparent, even if only in the far distance and on higher ground, and I love snow.

I look around at the several peaks that surround me which I have learnt to name since last year: the Saualpe, the Zirbitzkogel, the Koralpe and the magnificent range of the Karawanken in the far distance. The Saualpe, west of the Lavant River, is part of the Lavanttal Alps and runs through both Austria and Slovenia. The Zirbitzkogel rises to 7860 feet above sea level and is the highest point of the Seetal Alps, which are also part of the Lavanttal Alps. The Zirbitzkogel stands between Carinthia – the region that I now call home – and Styria, the county that borders Carinthia. I first supposed that the Zirbitzkogel must be named after the Swiss pine tree the Zirben, which grows abundantly there, but in fact it takes its name from the Slovenian word 'zirbiza', which when translated becomes 'red mountain pasture'. This is a reference to the red-petalled wildflower alpenrose, known locally as the Almrausch; it grows profusely there and is a member of the rhododendron family. Almrausch translates as 'alp delirium,' indicating that this pretty wildflower is toxic.

The Koralpe is a constant presence in our lives and dominates Bad Sankt Leonhard. It is the range which separates eastern Carinthia from the adjacent region of southern Styria. Its highest elevation is the Große Speikkogel, at 7020 feet above sea level. We can see the Koralpe from our house, and we now have a daily relationship with it. When I first arrived, I was excited to find out more about the folly or ruin which I imagined must be standing on the Koralpe's highest point. I thought that one day I would hike up there and inspired by the poet William Wordsworth, write 'Lines Composed Atop the Koralpe'. However, I was laughed at by Katie's brother who told us that the attractive shape that provides a pleasant punctuation mark on the peak from a distance is, in fact, a node for military radar airspace surveillance.

I was greatly disappointed, but I have overcome this by merely continuing to believe that I am looking at a delightfully sinister and decaying Gothic ruin. It is my very own Castle of Otranto[4].

I peer over towards the Karawanken mountain range, one of the longest ranges in Europe, with a total length of seventy-five miles. Since last year's walk, I have driven through the mountain pass – known as the Loibl Pass – that cuts through the Karawanken chain dividing Austria and Slovenia, so as I walk I visualise the vertiginous peaks, the highest of which is the Hochstuhl, which rises to an impressive 7335 feet above sea level.

I feel tired and stop for a short rest before I have to climb to reach the highest point of the walk, which will take me to just over 3280 feet. My stopping point once again is by the apple tree overlooking the expansive view that I admired last year. I take another photograph. The steep climb and the exertion restore me, even though it's quite arduous. I will myself on, but allow myself to rest to look at a stunning silver birch tree, with its crop of golden, Klimt-like leaves, standing proud and erect against the blue sky. I scold myself for wasting precious time worrying and feel a little better. I hear the two-tone call of a great tit and the constant cheeping of a blitz of blue tits and wend my way home.

I now feel able to tell Katie about my worries and my mole, and she looks at it, puts me in the car and takes me to the doctor's. I get an immediate appointment to have it removed, and a few days later it is gone, but I have to wait for the test results.

7

REALISATION

29TH DECEMBER

I get through Christmas with the help of Katie, her old school friend and her husband who come and join us for the holiday period, and this helps me tremendously. But, that weird, soggy time between Christmas and New Year is nearly upon us, and it is a black hole that I don't want to fall into. As a distraction, I reach for my new diary, thinking to transfer across important dates and plan some projects for the coming year. But I haven't got anything planned; this alarms me, for as long as I can remember I have had projects to work on, and of course, I have always had work, my studies and my hobbies, so my days have always been full to bursting.

I look at the blank page and there written in tiny letters are the words 'WEEK 52.' For the rest of the day I potter about aimlessly, but in the evening I think about those tiny little letters and they fly into my head like one of those shots from old movies where a spinning newspaper announces a new development in the plot. I'm not entirely sure what this means.

When I awake a few days later on the 29th December, it's a cold zero degrees, but it is a bright, crisp day. Over breakfast, I suggest that we go for a walk. Katie is busy with new jewellery commissions and must work, but I decide to go anyway. I'm not sure where to walk, and I don't have time to dither, the days are short, and darkness falls fast, so I must leave before noon at the latest. It seems sensible to stick with the walk I know rather than try and find a new one. I dress up warmly, and by late morning I am ready.

When I get to the stream that runs through meadow land, instead of hurrying past it this time I try to take more notice of where I am walking and what I am seeing. To my surprise, the stream is completely iced over, so there must have been a very cold frost in the night. It is rare for rivers and streams to freeze in England, so I find this unexpectedly enthralling. I peer in through the green-tinged, crystal surface to admire the bright green leaves trapped in their icy prison; I tap the surface to see how thick the ice is, and it does not yield. It seems utterly miraculous to me that life is being partly supported by this layer of ice which is acting like an insulator helping to prevent the water from freezing solid, which would result in the loss of all life therein.

Feeling suddenly chilly I move on, but I remember to look out for the two mallard ducks that I vaguely noticed last week, a handsome drake and his mate. I hear them before I see them, as they come waddling towards me, following a narrow track which they alone must have made. They reach their destination, and begin to grub around contentedly (I have never seen a duck that seemed anything other than happy, they always seem to be playing and taking great pleasure in skimming across the water as they land, and teasing each other – I might come back as a duck). The female is always close, but she often walks a few paces behind her mate. He has a magnificent green head; her wing feathers match his, in the same dark blue. They live near another small stream, but so far I have not seen them in it. I hope as the days and weeks go by that I will see them swimming and frolicking, and smile in anticipation at the thought.

Climbing further, I notice an old decaying tree stump, eroded not only by wind, sun, rain, frost, and snow but also by a pest infestation. I take several photographs and look for a broken fragment, and after a little searching I find a sharp, jagged, elongated piece of bark; it already looks crafted. I pocket it for Katie, feeling sure that it will appeal to her. I had not even noticed the tree stump last week.

I have long been fascinated with the study of clouds, so I turn my face to the heavens and look carefully. Dark grey cumulonimbus has cleared to reveal a blue sky littered with a few pale cirrus clouds. One of my heroes is the British pharmacist, Luke Howard, who presented his Essay on the Modification of Clouds to the Askesian Society in December 1802. Howard was the first person to classify clouds, giving each type a simple Latin tag name: cumulus, Latin for pile or heap, cirrus, Latin for curl, and stratus, Latin for layer. Howard painted delicate pencil and watercolour sketches of the different types of clouds to record his findings accurately. In turn his work inspired John Constable, who was one of the first artists to go out in nature armed with small sketchbooks and record in them cloud studies based on his observations. Constable's work is lauded for its naturalism in this regard, and in 1821 he wrote to his friend John Fisher: 'skies must and always shall with me make an effectual part of the composition.'[5]

It's impossible to have a favourite cloud type, but cirrus is certainly one that I always look out for – I love its wispy, dreamlike delicacy. I watch and walk as the few curling clouds slowly transform and alter their shape. They are resting at

20,000 meters above sea level, and are made of ice crystals. By this simple but concentrated observation of the sky, I take my mind off my worries. Cirrus clouds sometimes indicate a change in the weather, but I am not concerned; I have a raincoat.

As I climb higher, I get warmer and warmer, and the weather looks sure to remain fair. I reach a bench and rest place. Today the apple tree is in silhouette, because shining directly on it and through the skeleton of the branches is a blindingly bright white ball of a sun. Its shadow cuts across my path, and for a moment I feel at one with it. I snap a quick photograph and move on.

I rest again and take a moment to consider a spinney of twelve tall silver birch trees; they are still clinging onto the last of their yellow leaves, a symphony of silver and gold against a blue sky. Despite the thick ice I admired in the stream at the beginning of the walk there is no snow today on the high peak of the Koralpe, and I am really surprised; I felt sure that there would be white-capped peaks at this time of year.

I feel a little weary, so I speed up and hear a great tit calling and calling, his shrill voice piercing the air. Rooks and sparrows join in the chorus. A constant barrage of bird sound accompanies me on the final leg of my journey. Happily fatigued, I return home at 3.25 pm.

I go to my study (for the first time in my life I have a proper work room of my own) and begin to enter some of the details from the walk into my diary. Once again the tiny letters spelling out 'WEEK 52' grab my attention. My mind clicks and whirs: it's the 22nd December and it happens to be the fifty-second week of the year. Maybe I could do the walk every week for a year – fifty-two walks in fifty-two weeks. But what kind of venture would this be? How should I approach it, and what should I aim to produce at the end of my year of walking?

Over the next few days, I began to feel much better as my

embryonic idea starts to take shape. During my years working as a Keeper of Art I had learnt a great deal from working with contemporary artists. Previously I had only worked with art and objects created by long-deceased artists, who don't argue or offer any advice. All my studying had led me to believe that most artists, and indeed writers, tend to work within a tradition or genre, being watercolourists, landscape artists, portraitists, and so on. In my family my great-grandfather, my great-uncle and my grandfather painted watercolours, and almost inevitably my father and his twin brother followed in their footsteps. I didn't inherit their skills. But contemporary artists tend by and large to shun this model and are happy to take on projects that might not immediately accord with their skills or experience.

When I was newly appointed in my last post, my experience was limited, so when I was approached by an artist and asked if she might be able to apply for Arts Council funding to become our artist in residence, I looked at the form that we had to complete together and asked her the standard sort of questions: 'What medium do you work in normally? What constitutes your usual body of work?' She politely and firmly refused to answer, not wanting to commit herself or be backed into a corner. She explained to me patiently: 'If I knew now what I was going to make right at this moment I could just go and make it today, but any ideas that form during my three months here as an artist in residence would in that case be fruitless, don't you think?' I felt embarrassed; I had been thinking in narrow terms. She got her funding, and over the next few months she peered at the museum art collections, made notes, took photographs, found her way into the craggy, unused parts of the medieval building, and found hidden wonders that we had not known existed. At the end of her tenure she produced some simple but exquisite documentary photographs, was inspired to create an excellent audio piece, and eventually, in collaboration with a playwright, she created a short theatrical work. All of this came out of her three months of observation, and none of it had been planned. I learnt a great deal from her and from many others during my time there. It made me understand that the process and the planning stage are critical to success and that not knowing all the answers is a crucial part of the process.

Perhaps I could approach the walk in this way, looking at it as a contemporary artist would? Rather than know at the beginning of a procedure what the outcome would be, I could explore my ideas and allow the process to unfold organically. Nevertheless, I felt it necessary to set myself two main ground rules: I must aim to complete my recurring walk fifty-two times within a fifty-two week period, and I must photograph the apple tree every time. If, in the end, nothing creative came of my efforts, then at least the completing of them would afford me an opportunity to explore my new homeland, and if I was flexible and open about where this might lead me artistically I might open up tangential avenues and take myself out of my comfort zone.

I made a few notes and felt a surge of adrenalin at the birth of this new idea.

8

understanding

With a sense of renewed energy, I rise early. I feel ready to begin. My first goal is to understand more about the walk and where exactly I am walking. The Q3 walk that I have chosen – or perhaps the walk that chose me – rightly begins in the centre of Bad Sankt Leonhard. Because we have been so busy establishing ourselves and making a start on the garden, I have never explored the town in any meaningful way; this seems like a good task for today. It's bright and frosty, so I wrap up warmly, grab my notebook and walk into the town.

I find plaques on buildings and read the tourist information signs. I visit the small library and consult the few books they have in English. Bad Sankt Leonhard gained its charter in 1325, relying throughout much of its history on the mining of precious metals, until iron ore mining was discontinued in 1876. Even after this it seemed that the town would have continued to thrive, but it suffered a decline in the 14th century, when in September 1348, the plague known as the Black Death struck[6]. The outbreak began in Venice and spread first to upper Italy and then to the Carinthian region.

I had wondered why in the centre of the town there is a tall and impressive stone monument, known as the Virgin Mary column. I venture outside to look at it for myself. It consists of a tall column on which stands the statue of the Virgin Mary; below there is a four-cornered pedestal on which stand statues dedicated to St Rochus and St Sebastian. A Latin inscription states that the monument is for 'The inhabitants [so that they] may always be protected under the care of Maria, Sebastian and Rochus'. In 1348, despite the fact that all around the plague raged, St. Leonhard was spared because of its high encircling wall which enabled the gates to be locked and guarded to prevent anyone leaving or entering the town during the epidemic. When, inevitably, the plague drew nearer, a cross – Pestkreuz – was erected in the Höllgasse and the elders of the town vowed to organise a votive procession to Hirschegg every year if the inhabitants were spared. Still, to this day on the Sunday before Pentecost, some of the Leonharders make a pilgrimage by walking the twenty-two miles to Hirschegg, in neighbouring Styria. The pilgrims are met by the town band and a market and an atmosphere of celebration prevails. In 1732, as further proof of gratitude that no mortalities were suffered, this large and impressive monument was erected in the main square.

I also look around and take note of the well-maintained buildings. Most date from the sixteenth and seventeenth centuries and are painted in hues of blue, cream, bright yellow and light and dark orange, with the result that regardless of the season the town invariably looks cheerful and friendly. Even the fire hydrants are painted in cowpat shapes of lilac, purple, orange, yellow, red and blue. The high street is tree-lined and has a large and impressive town hall, three banks and a range of quirky little shops – a jeweller's, a gift shop, a charming old pharmacy with original fittings, a large furniture store, a hardware shop – selling absolutely everything – and even a first-class restaurant, initially established in 1790 and now of Michelin star quality.

I follow the sign to the church, taking a narrow alleyway that leads away from the high street. The church is almost cathedral-like in size. This is the Kundigundkirche, first mentioned in 1591, and initially built to a Gothic design. As seems popular here, it was rebuilt between 1740 and 1750 in the Baroque style. It sits just below the looming and magnificent castle ruin of Gomarn, built around 1300 but reduced to a ruin by fire in 1762. Opposite the ruin is the Renaissance palace of Schloss Ehrenfels, built in the 14th century, altered in the 16th century and renovated in 1945, having suffered from bomb damage in an air-raid. It is still almost complete but is badly in need of repair. Its series of small windows and grey stucco give it a slightly stern appearance, but nevertheless it is an impressive addition to the town and its history.

I trace my footsteps back towards home, and my route takes me towards the official church of the parish and one of the most beautiful ecclesiastical buildings in the region, the Leonhardikirche. Dedicated to Saint Leonhard and placed at the foot of the Erzberg hill, it sits high up on open ground and dominates the town as you approach it from Wolfsberg. It dates from 1320-1380 and has a vast basilica – 157 feet in length and 69 feet wide. The church has many windows, with 130 coloured glass panes in total. These were provided for by the Fugger and Chropf families in the 14th and 15th centuries, and are very splendid indeed. Most remarkable is the characteristic chain which loops around the outside of the church at a height of about 20 feet. It dates from the Turkish invasion; the original chain encircled the church twice and was a visual reminder of a period of enforced occupation. At the end of the 18th century, the chain was removed. 1n 1910-12, however, it was finally replaced, at the expense of Dr Schnerich, with a smaller and more attractive chain. The church suffered from a fire in 1885 and again in 1917, but today it has an imposing central spire, with four smaller spires surrounding, which were erected after 1929 and lend the church a fairy tale, castle-like appearance.[7]

As I leave I make sure that I have spelt Leonhardikirche correctly, and as I am forming the letters I immediately think of my father, who was called Leonard, but I push the thought down as it upsets me to think about him and I don't want to be unnerved today. I mark the page in my notebook with an asterisk and write: 'What can the walk tell me about my father, if anything? Explore.'

9

snow

5ᵀᴴ January

It has been snowing steadily for twenty-four hours; the landscape is hidden beneath a stunning coat of winter white. There is a vivid blue sky and no wind, so it is perfect walking weather, and I am beyond excited. I have an idea which I have not yet voiced – I wonder if my project might interest Katie. She would look at the walk in a completely different way to me and a collaboration with her could bear some symbiotically rich fruit. I decide not to explain this fully, but I do encourage her to accompany me; she isn't sure that she has the time, but when Katie looks outside and sees how stunningly beautiful everywhere looks, she agrees.

At first we both feel very cold, and we begin to wonder if we should continue. However, after only a short while we start to climb. We immediately become overheated, and hats and scarves come off. We are also too captivated by what we are seeing to turn back. Against the white of the snow coppery beech leaves shine in the sun and golden-brown bracken peeps through the whiteness, green lichen on trees glows, path verges are encrusted with orange larch needles; dark pine trees are occasionally and suddenly illuminated by beams of sunshine. The sun warms the snow-laced tree branches as soon as it touches them, and a faint gossamer of melting snow begins to tumble down in vertical shafts, like icy confetti, momentarily glistening in rays of sunshine. To appreciate this fully we walk with our heads slightly tilted towards the sky, which requires quiet and concentration and offers a rare opportunity to be entirely enthralled and in the moment. Walking attentively requires focus, so we don't even speak.

Travelling and holidaying demand this kind of attention; perhaps this is why both are such beloved pursuits. Being away from home renders us vulnerable, thus focusing the mind for the duration of the walk or journey. All you own you have to carry, and if you are thirsty, hungry or ill, you have to rely on your wits or the kindness of strangers. Walking in harsh conditions is dangerous, but perhaps for that very reason, it is invigorating.

Once we are through the woods, we take more note of the world around us; we hear cowbells chiming and a bellowing bull. On my first two walks I met no-one, but today we see half a dozen people, taking time to enjoy being outside in the fresh snow, or working the land. We see a young family sauntering along slowly, parents patiently holding the hands of their small children. We see a farmer and son, their heads almost touching as they work in studied concentration with a noisy and dangerous looking bandsaw. We see two more men, one older and apparently in charge as he instructs his young apprentice. They are felling rotten pine trees to make firewood. It begins to turn colder, so we hurry on. We see animal tracks criss-crossing the fields and realise that there must be much more wildlife here than we know about or see.

The apple tree today is laced with a fine layer of snow, but otherwise it is utterly bare. With the snowy landscape as its backdrop, I can note its form: the main trunk has a slight tilt to the right, from where the two main branches spring, and has a distinct gothic sway[8]. Katie and I both see at the same moment the remains of a wizened rotting apple lying on the snow, the colour of hot lava - a fiery orange and black. We look at each other, and without hesitation, I stoop to collect it. I now have two 'found objects', our new acquisition and the fragment of wood that I gathered from a rotting tree stump on the 29th December.

The sky is a bleached white, the exact colour of the landscape. Indeed sky and land merge but for a crack of bright amber light on the horizon: the day is already beginning to die, and we must head for home. As we near the end of our journey, Katie becomes very tired and cold, and her hip suddenly starts to ache. We walk more slowly, inching our way home. We see in the distance an elderly man standing outside his driveway; I am worried that he will delay us and it is now bitterly cold, dusk is upon us and Katie's hip will not be helped by a spell of standing still in the cold twilight air. As I knew he would, he beckons us and says half smilingly 'it costs a hundred euros to pass by my house.' Katie laughs and offers to pay him five schillings, referring to the old Austrian currency before the introduction of the euro, but he does not smile, he just nods his head in uneasy acknowledgement.

Katie and the old man speak in German for some moments. I am aware that Katie is in pain and I am concerned about her, but I am also aware that the man might well be lonely and want to talk. Inevitably, as elderly people like to do, he tells us his age. 'I am 90 years old,' he says, but then without any encouragement, he launches into a tale about the Second World War. I am only partly listening. My German is not yet that good, but I do hear the phrase 'Waffen SS'. I look up in alarm. Katie looks at me and asks in English 'what did he say?' I reply 'he said Waffen SS' and whisper 'Hitler's henchmen.'[9]

He tells us that he is one of eleven brothers and that they had all been in the SS, and that they all had to prove that they were strong and of pure race and each received an Aryan certificate, he smiles at this. When he finishes his story he looks at me, perhaps hoping for some encouragement, but I am restless and feel very uncomfortable. I do not speak. Katie explains that I am English and tries to break away. But he is delighted that I am English. 'Ah, the English saved my life!' he says. He goes on: 'at the very end of the hostilities the Americans arrived and were going to shoot us, but when the moment arrived an English soldier appeared and asked if anybody was from Austria, particularly from the Carinthian region or the Styrian region, so I raised my hand immediately, and I was rescued.' He explained that he was of course not Austrian but German and that he had never heard of the Carinthian region, but he had realised that if he raised his hand, he would most likely be spared. He goes on to tell us that his life in Austria has been a happy one. Stunned, we manage to extract ourselves. We walk home in silence.

It is extraordinary to think that as I write this, I can see the back of this man's house from my study window. I am perhaps most alarmed not because I have met somebody who was in the

Waffen SS, but that I have met somebody who was proud to be a Waffen SS officer and seems to have found it unnecessary to reconsider or feel ashamed by the association. The long tentacles of the terrible suffering that total war brought, indeed any war, continues to spread a dark stain across time.

This encounter left us feeling amazed and shocked, even a little bereft. Katie's family was, like so many others, deeply affected by the Second World War. Katie's family on her mother's side had to flee from Vienna, due to their Jewish ancestry, and her father left his Hungarian homeland to become a soldier and would never return, seeing his Hungarian family very rarely. My uncle was killed in action.

This latest encounter has made me very fearful. The UK is holding a referendum in June, and for the first time it occurs to me that perhaps people in the UK will vote to leave Europe. I feel that it's crucial to remain a part of the EU, because if nothing else it helps maintain peace. My concern is not lessened when I consider that there is a genuine possibility that Donald Trump may soon become the President of the United States. Katie reminds me that here in the country that is now my home, the far-right candidate Norbert Hofer might well be voted in as the Austrian President. I am worried.

The third walk started majestically in white beauty but has now been marred by ugliness, dragging us both down an avenue that we did not wish to travel down. The terrors of the world cannot always be avoided, even if your quest is to find beauty. I make another mark in my notebook and write 'use the walk to seek out beauty and avoid ugliness.' Then I carefully pluck the apple core 'lava' from the plastic box in my rucksack and place it next to the piece of bark that I previously collected. They both have a raw splendour. I simply write in my notebook 'found objects? Explore.'

10
wire

13ᵀᴴ January

This time I don't even have to ask Katie if she would like to accompany me; she is ready before I can even suggest it. We leave at 11.45 am. It was -4.4°C overnight and it is now about zero degrees, but the air is dry and there is little wind, so it does not feel cold. There is also sunshine and as ever a blue sky, which aids us on our way.

The frosty night temperatures have had a transformative

effect on the landscape. The many barbed wire fences that line our route have bundles of horsehair clinging to the barbs. Frozen mist has rolled in and encased them in ice, turning them into tiny pure white sculptures that shine out brightly. I look more closely, and in some cases minute, blue-white ice droplets hang from the hair ends. It is strange to see these fragile and delicate ice sculptures clinging to something so brutal; I ponder on the incongruity of the juxtaposition.

The first patent for barbed wire was issued in 1867 to Lucien B. Smith of Kent, Ohio, and the wire was used to restrain cattle. Very soon after its invention barbed wire was used for the purpose of encaging people, in the Spanish-American War of 1898, and by all combatants in the First World War (1914-18). It is also associated with concentration camps, having been first used by the British in the Boer War (1899) then famously used by the Nazis in the Second World War on border perimeters, along with the more deadly razor wire. Its use to encage people, especially refugees and asylum seekers, looks likely to increase as arguments over borders and boundaries intensify. I have always detested barbed wire, seeing it as ugly, bellicose and warlike, no more than a necessary evil.

I remember buying a small book about the First World War Artist Paul Nash when I was only in my early twenties. His war paintings had a profound effect on me, especially his 'Wire' of 1918 – a monochrome of grey, brown mounds of exploded earth and stagnant water and broken tree stumps shrouded in curls of savagely hacked barbed wire, reaching to the sky. It looked as if the limbless tree was growing barbed wire instead of branches; the war had made nature as savage as man. Nash himself wrote to his wife from the front line: 'I am no longer a painter interested and curious, I am a messenger who will bring back word from the men who are fighting to those who want the war to go on forever. Feeble, inarticulate, will be my message, but it will have a bitter truth, and may it burn their lousy souls.'[10]

For the first time in my life, actually seeing the delicate angel-hair-like icy fragments of animal hair and frozen foliage clinging to barbed wire and lit by bright sunlight makes me re-evaluate this harsh material. Even this can become a conduit for beauty. Furthermore, without its invention the countryside would be marred by fences, especially since the uprooting of the hedgerows that once divided fields. At least barbed wire enables the walker to see vistas far into the distance.

Katie finds, growing from a wall opposite the tree, a clump of annual honesty.[11] It has sprouted out from an ugly breezeblock wall. In spring and summer annual honesty bears white or violet flowers, and these are followed by light brown, disc-shaped seedpods, the skin of which falls off to release the seeds, revealing a central membrane which is white with a silvery sheen which persist throughout the winter in a silver seedpod form. The botanical name of the plant, lunaria, derives from the Latin word for the moon, and refers to the shape and appearance of the seedpods.

As I suspected Katie is seeing things that I would not. As a metal worker and jewellery maker she is attracted to the metallic appearance of these silvery seedpods. I photograph them in situ and carefully collect a few silvery, flimsy pieces of 'moon' to take home.

I notice that the owner of the farm is nearby and urge Katie to approach him. I have been very keen that we speak to him as it seems only polite to ask his permission for the project and I would like to know more about the apple tree. He seems puzzled at first, but after a bit of head scratching he recalls that the tree was there when his father owned the farm, and even before this when his grandfather owned it. He is not much interested in the crop but he tells us that it has yellow-golden apples and that they are early fruiting. We conclude that it is probably a Klar apple tree.[12] We shall not know for certain until it begins to fruit. He seems bemused by us, but he is amiable and friendly in a quiet way and soon makes his apologies and departs.

We thank him and bid him farewell and head for the snow-trimmed pine wood. We stop at what has already become my favourite bench and eat Scottish shortbread and drink water. We sit in companionable silence for a few minutes; as we do so it starts to snow very lightly, but the sun is also shining. We share a wonderful precious few moments of peace, but become cold quickly and have to move on in case the weather worsens before the light fails.

At just over 3,200 feet above sea level we come into snow-topped trees. There is a clear line where ice and snow have painted the trees with a white impasto, whilst the rest of the trees, mainly pines, remain their usual dark green. As we approach this ice line, we immediately feel a drop in temperature and have to put on hats, scarves and gloves. As soon as we begin to descend the snow line disappears, and the sun becomes warmer; we allow ourselves to watch the snow melting from the trees, catching the sun as it does so. As it falls it throws up a thin mist of sand-like powder like ground diamonds, then as it dissipates the snow powder turns to yellow becoming glowing crystals in the sun, just like a lighting effect. Snow also flies off on the wind and melts immediately. Underscoring this sight there is a rhythmical drip, drip, drip sound of snow-melt, which grows increasingly louder and becomes faster and faster.

We move on, instinctively quickening our pace on hearing this tattoo of water-drumming percussion. As we pass through a shady patch of young pine trees the trees start to drip in stereo; bass notes resound when large clumps of snow fall from the trees and these notes are echoed by high piccolo notes as icicles fade and crumble. The string section of the mountain stream gushes sotto voce in the background. I can't resist leaving the path to find a deep patch of snow to crunch in – I have a childlike love of the sound that boots make on icy snow – but the sky has turned to pewter and is tinged with yellow, heralding, perhaps, more snow to come, so we hurry on, and by 3.15. we are back home. In the week that follows we will both be free from physical pain. The walk is having a tangible effect on us, and we feel healthier and fitter.

I fetch my found objects from the past weeks, the bark and the apple core, and place them next to the lunaria seedpods. I see Katie looking at them and I feel sure that she will feel inspired and will create some magic in her workshop; it looks like I have found someone to collaborate with.

Later in the evening I force myself out of my comfort zone. I am a very poor map reader, but I go in search of maps of the area. I look in cupboards and on bookshelves and eventually find an old but decent one in the cellar. I am not even sure exactly where the apple tree is in relation to where we live, but I would like to use it as my seasonal barometer. I feel that this task is necessary, as this is my home now and I need to understand the area better.

I find St Leonhard's Church, the Leonhardikirche, easily. I compare the old map with the less detailed one that I bought and find the path waymarked Q3. To the best of my ability, I trace the walk and manage to draw out the shape of it, but it looks to me like nothing more than a long-snouted mouse stiffing the air, its nose turned up to the sky. I am disappointed by the apparent inconsequentiality of the line; it doesn't help that I have little understanding of the topographical detail in the map. All the same, I keep my sketch – perhaps something will come of it – but I don't think my topographical map reading skills are likely to improve very much.

11
ice

20TH january

Our house is cold; the heating system, a huge bright orange monster of a boiler in our cellar provides water and heating, is over forty years old, but I imagine it sounds like the boiler room of the *Titanic* when it fires up. We realise that it is inefficient, but we are sensibly waiting for better weather before we replace it. We have not installed our loft insulation as yet either, so the house is rather like a bird cage in winter: draughty.

I feel that to keep well I really do need a day wrapped up

warmly but outside in the cold, clean, fresh air. Katie opts for an uninterrupted day in her workshop instead. I manage to leave before my not-too-strict midday curfew at 11.55 am. I have set myself a curfew in a false attempt to give my endeavours some kind of discipline, but Katie finds this amusing, pointing out that I perhaps I am institutionalised. She may well be right.

It's a beautifully sunny, windless day. Although it was -6°C overnight, the temperature is now hovering at around zero, but it's a dry cold, very unlike the much damper climate of the UK, so it feels pleasant. There is a pale blue sky with only some small patches of cirrus clouds to interrupt the heavens. To begin with, the walk is hard going, but then something seems to happen, the rhythm kicks in, and my blood begins to flow, and as always, my progress becomes easier and more enjoyable.

I reach the path by the stream, bordered by wild scrub, and the whole field resembles a mini glacier shining in the sunlight, a tapestry of white rivulets on an opaque grey background. Beautiful but treacherous. I half-walk, half-crawl around the edge of the field where it is much less dangerous to traverse. That done, I move on and reach the river, realising that it is utterly silent: just a white ribbon of ice and snow, I cannot see or hear a drop of flowing water. The footpath widens into a mass of ice, a glassy monochrome Monet-like lake.

I have to traverse virginal snow to reach a place where I can jump the icy stream at its narrowest point. As I do this I meet two walkers and in my broken German explain that up ahead it is 'sehr gefährlich' (very dangerous). They seem most untroubled by this news, but thank me all the same. I am sure that they think it may be sehr gefährlich for an inexperienced English woman, but not for them; however they smile politely and bid me farewell.

I arrive at the wooded area, and I am immediately cheered by the sound of a banditry of great tits, not seen but certainly heard, housed in the branches of a thick belt of pine trees. There is a constant cacophony of high-pitched chattering all around me. Sparrows sound like kindergarten kids, but great tits sound like noisy teenagers before a football match. Periodically and without warning, the noise dwindles to a murmur, before rising again in pitch and volume. If only I spoke 'Greatitian' or 'Sparrowegian.' These birds are definitely communicating something, but who knows what?

I rest from my exertions for a few moments on a nearby bench and sip my icy water. Some snow from a previous fall lies in the shade of a forested area next to the path, and there is a trail made by some large footprints making a new route directly through the forest – this affords me an opportunity to follow a tangential avenue. Carefully I place my feet into the much larger prints, but soon I have to climb into ditches and over frail-looking fences, and I have no idea where I am. I start to feel afraid. Initially, I had felt safe because I was following in someone else's footsteps, but I begin to worry that the owner of them ultimately came to harm. I feel foolish; I undertake these walks on the understanding that I do not put myself in danger. But soon I see a way back to the footpath ahead, and get back onto it. It's a little icy, but it has the comfort of familiarity. A feeling of relief comes over me. I will never be intrepid, but even a taking a small risk seems like progress – leaving my known route feels like progress. Perhaps I am getting my self-belief back?

After the biting temperatures last week and the icy start to today's walk, I am pleased and surprised when the sun makes an appearance. It becomes almost pleasantly warm, but this is deceptive, as there is much snow on the high peak of the Koralpe, and although shrouded in a thick haze the Karawanken range shines like a white gash in the bright sunshine. As the daylight begins to fade the temperature suddenly drops and I am now keen to be back home. Expecting to see little of great interest as I descend, I am delighted to find that a water pipe, one that drips perpetually the whole year round, has produced wonderful ice babies, of gorgeous shapes, created merely through the process of thawing and refreezing. I spend some time looking at them but it suddenly becomes icy cold, and with dusk approaching, I force myself to move on. But the last images of those icy forms remain as the lasting memory of the day; I blow on my hands to ease the numbness and hasten my speed by setting my sights on home and warmth.

When I return, Katie shows me her day's work; she has turned the piece that I collected on my first walk from the decaying tree stump into an unfussy brooch. By means of simple sanding, polishing and the application of a little gold-leaf she has allowed the beauty of the wood to shine out. I am delighted with it and gather it up, carefully placing it with the other found objects, but as I am putting it down, I think that the shape of the brooch looks oddly familiar. I lay it over the drawing of the route that I sketched out last week; it shares almost the same outline as my long-snouted mouse, with which I was so disappointed. Perhaps I didn't waste my time plotting the route after all? In some strange way, I see this as auspicious.

12

DNA

I already begin to see that my walk may be part of a much bigger idea, and modest as my final accomplishment might be, I feel as though I might be able to walk my own spiritually-renewing path, just as our greatest predecessors walked their own diverse, invigorating physical journeys. For more than two thousand years, from antiquity to the present day, from Plato to Virgil, Jesus to Mohammed, Chaucer to Coelho, philosophers and artists have been inspired by walking their own progressive tread.

Writers especially seemed to have gained from the experience, not only in their personal lives but by using walking as a catalyst for change in the lives of their characters. Stories of travel and pilgrimage are well represented in early texts. In the late 1300s both William Langland's *Piers Plowman* and Chaucer *Canterbury's Tales* were in various ways exploring the mysteries of walking more than simple physical progress. In Cervantes' *Don Quixote* and Henry Fielding's *Tom Jones*, it is the movement through time and space that provides not only plot and excitement but discovery and personal enlightenment. The road, the path and the outdoors force examination and protagonists are permanently altered by their journeys.

Tom Jones is an example of Bildungsroman, a novel that focuses on the psychological and moral growth of the protagonist from youth to adulthood: Henry Fielding knew that his eponymous hero could never become an enlightened individual by merely staying at home. Fielding sent Tom out, not only into the world but more importantly into nature, exploring and enlarging upon the age-old debate that surrounds town and country. I have always preferred the country to the town, so in this regard I expect little to change. But do I really understand it? I have mainly admired the country from the comfort of my own home, safe and warm within. I have no idea what it feels like to be part of an ever-changing landscape and to watch it increase and decrease across a calendar year. Perhaps I too will achieve some personal enlightenment, perhaps I too will be permanently changed?

* * *

One of the earliest investigations of the town and country debate was written by the ancient Roman poet Horace. In his *Satires*, he relates an old wives' tale - the story of the sophisticated town mouse who travelled from Rome to visit his mouse friend who lived in the country.[13] Despite being offered oats, raisins and tasty bacon scraps, the town mouse has little appetite; he cannot abide the roughness of the hilly countryside all around him. The town mouse persuades the country mouse to leave his home, and they depart together to Rome and to the town mouse's beautiful house which is full of gorgeous furnishings: crimson textiles, and ivory and marble decorations. But no sooner have they seated themselves to begin to eat a lavish feast than they are interrupted by a pack of large dogs. The country mouse runs away in fear and returns to his hole in the ground to live a life of peace.

Ever since Horace first explored this debate, writers and artists have been mining the dichotomous tension between town and country. This theme reached something of an apogee when the Romantic writer Johann Wolfgang von Goethe merged fact and fiction. So inspired was he by the curative wonders of nature and the outdoors that in 1779 he abandoned city life to hike through the Lauterbrunnen Valley in the Bernese Oberland in Switzerland, in the guise of one of his own fictional creations, Werther, a melancholy Romantic young poet. Goethe even dressed the part in order to immerse himself in the fiction, wearing an outmoded blue tailcoat and buff waistcoat and trousers just as his hero had.

Ten years later, in 1789, nature writing as a non-fiction form came into being with the work of an English country parson, Gilbert White. White's pioneering nature diary opened up the study of the 'manners' and 'conversation' of both animals and plants; he is also credited with being the first person to 'watch' birds. The greatest English nature poet John Clare, a farmer's son born without great privilege, came to his poetry not only through working the land for long days but by taking long walks in his native Northamptonshire. Even Charles Dickens, perhaps one of the most celebrated writers of city life, was in reality an obsessive wanderer through not only the streets of London but beyond to the suburbs and out into the regenerative countryside. In A Christmas Carol, Dickens' description of Scrooge's nephew could only have been written by someone with an intimate knowledge and love of walking. 'He had so heated himself with rapid walking in the fog and frost, this nephew of Scrooge's, that he was all in a glow: his face was ruddy and handsome; his eyes sparkled, and his breath smoked again.'

* * *

My desire to walk is also beginning to feel instinctive and right; for most of my life I have lived near hills and mountains, and there has always been a dull ache in my stomach, a feeling that I should be outside, out there, up there – walking. Perhaps this seed was sown in North Wales, the place of my birth. In the early 1960s, after seeing an advert in *The Lady* magazine, my parents left London and bought a huge stone manor house in Llanbedr with its own lake and acres of grounds, eleven bedrooms and a leaking roof. It was incredibly cheap; this really ought to have rung an alarm bell. It was a strange and crazy thing to do, as my father was born in Surrey and my mother in St. Helens, Lancashire, and Wales was at that time very remote and hard to get to. My father gave up his good job as a commercial artist, and with three children and no income, off they went and opened a hotel.

My father had fallen in love with Wales during his time in the war when at the age of eighteen he had been posted to the North Welsh town of Pwllheli. He had never seen a mountain before and there he was, away from the bombings and the night-raids, and the deaths, a brilliant artist with lots of time and a handful of sketchbooks, surrounded by the most beautiful countryside. Snowdonia was only a forty-minute drive away with its eight hundred square miles of mountains and glaciers, a hundred lakes and countless craggy peaks. From the summit of Wales's highest mountain, Mount Snowdon, he could look across the sea to

Ireland. Irrational as the decision was, I can understand why he wanted to return there and make it his home.

He had married his RAF sweetheart, but was cruelly widowed at the age of thirty-four. He was distraught; he had two children and a stressful job. He then married again quickly, and I suppose that with his new, much younger wife he retreated to a world that he remembered as mythical and splendid. It was a disaster, as he should have known it would be. My father didn't like people very much; he only liked art, nature, birds, food and opera, and he didn't believe in small talk, but somehow he thought that he could run a hotel. What he actually did was put on a tweed suit and tie and go out and sit on the seat of his tractor and sketch the stunning views that could be seen from every angle of the house.

I was born a few years later, and for the first five years of my life it was the Welsh scenery that informed my universe. Eventually, however, my parents gave up waiting for the guests that never came, and could no longer face fighting with the sitting tenant they had unknowingly inherited who lived in a cottage in the grounds and who switched their water off whenever he felt a grievance. They moved on again, once more seeking out hills and beauty, but this time in a much more sensible location, Malvern in Worcestershire, an area of outstanding natural beauty right in the middle of England. The Malvern Hills dominate the surrounding countryside, and from the highest summit of the hills you can see the panorama of the Severn Vale, the undulating landscape of Herefordshire and the Welsh mountains and three ancient cathedrals, those of Worcester, Gloucester, and Hereford.

So my universe was once again informed by hills and grandeur, and as a family, we occasionally traipsed across one of the many commons, but we never walked far from home. My real introduction to the pleasure and pain of walking came when I was eight, and I stayed for a week with the family of a school friend of mine. His family lived high up in a place called Old Hollow, in West Malvern, in an almost inaccessible house which clung to the hillside like a limpet. I had never been in a split-level house before, and the expansive views from the living room window took my breath away. My friend had five brothers and sisters, and his parents didn't own a car, so they walked everywhere, which meant that while I was their guest, I too had to walk everywhere. We walked to go and buy food from the tiny shop, we walked two miles into Great Malvern, the town centre, and back. I had never walked four miles in my life. I found it gruelling, but, on my last day with them, we went for a walk apparently just for pleasure, walking over six miles up to the summit of the Worcestershire Beacon and back home. I was reluctant to go – I would much rather have stayed at home and watched the Sunday afternoon film – but even as an eight-year-old I couldn't help myself from feeling a vital and visceral connection to the ancient rocks under my feet, 680 million years in the making. I enjoyed the walk, and this was a revelation to me.

I remembered that walk for a long time - for about two years, I talked of becoming a mountaineer. But oddly I did not venture up the Malvern Hills again until I was in my late teens and struggling with my increasing awareness that I was gay. I felt a desperate need to have some time alone and to escape from my physical environment. I thought my sexuality must at all costs remain a secret forever, so I wanted to avoid people as much as possible. I bought a second-hand Zenith camera, plugged myself into my Sony Walkman and stomped about on the hills, trying to come to terms with my tragic life.

* * *

I have not thought about those walks in Malvern for years, but now I wake and find that I have been dreaming about them. Often through the day my head is full of them, and most of all I remember that even though I still had all my problems when I returned home, I at least felt more able to deal with them.

I decide that nothing is going to stop me from completing my fifty-two walks. I need to do this because walking, I realise, is in my blood and hard-wired into my DNA.

13

Heart

28TH January

Despite my recent resolve, I am a little sluggish today as last night Katie and I went on a long moonlight walk, organised by the local Gemeinde. We found ourselves amongst a group of very hardy and experienced Austrians, all wearing miners' lights on their helmets and wielding proper snow sticks; we had none of this equipment and really looked like amateurs. Before we started there was the obligatory speech and word of thanks for the organisers, as we stood about in the mighty cold of the evening. There were many warnings about falling and what to do if someone was taken ill, so when we set off we felt more than a little nervous.

When we reached 4200 feet above sea level, we were walking in very thick snow and it was frighteningly dark, but then a dazzling moonbeam came out from behind a cloud, and the snowy landscape was suddenly illuminated. As we moved along, the many lights on helmets and the torches being held aloft lit up ice crystals which glowed on the snowy ground like buried fire. The moon became even brighter, and it became so light and clear that we could even see delicate deer prints on the path.

After about an hour of walking, we were given refreshments served by candlelight in a remote pine cabin; hot, sweet Glühmost (apple cider mulled wine) and cakes, all cooked to regional recipes and, for some unknown reason, provided free by a local bakery. By this time we had numb legs and numb lips, but the hot liquid restored us instantly. It was a truly magical evening.

I worry that my walk today won't be half as enchanting as last night's lunar hike. But I receive good news just as I am leaving: our glamorous post lady arrives to deliver a letter informing me that the mole that I had removed in December was, after all, completely benign. I am so relieved! I am well, and thanks to my walks, I am feeling much stronger than I have for a long time. I suddenly feel very hungry, so I return to the kitchen and eat a proper hearty breakfast, which I haven't done for many months. Finally I head out.

The weather matches my mood: it is a very pleasant eight degrees, the sky is beautifully clear and blue, and there is only a little haze. I decide to walk the route the opposite way: I will reach the stream at the end of the walk, but I will get a chance to spot more birds as they always gather at this time of day by the small garden that is adjacent to the Leonhardikirche. It is full of easily-recognisable birds. The man who looks after the churchyard also tends this little garden; I have seen him on occasion and he is obviously an avid birder. There are feeders of various shapes, sizes and types hanging along the entire perimeter of the stone wall by the church. I was delighted to discover when I moved to this area that most people feed the birds here, especially in the snowy winter months. The piles of bird food in the shops dwindle quickly, demand outstripping supply because so many people feed the birds. Katie's mother did it all her life, and outside our kitchen door the patio tiles have large dimples caused by the pecking of the many bird beaks, because for forty years birds have landed there, sure to get the food they need. We do not intend to replace the tiles; it's a lovely memory of her loving nature. Because of her persistence we are on a feeding route, and the birds will always come to us. Small birds especially cannot risk reaching a destination and finding the cupboard bare.

Britain and the United States are the nations that are most obsessed with bird watching and bird feeding. The first person known to have fed a wild bird is the 6th-century monk Saint Serf, who lived in Fife in Scotland. He was not, however, feeding his bird, in this case a pigeon, in order to allow it to live its free, wild life more efficiently; he was attempting to tame and domesticate it. Feeding wild birds for their own benefit is a relatively new phenomenon. The exceptionally cold winter in Britain which lasted from the 25th November 1890 to the 22nd January 1891 caused national newspaper editors to call on people to put food out for the birds. So successful was this campaign that by 1910 the feeding of birds had become a national pastime. In the 1950s a brand of bird food called Swoop was the first to corner the domestic market. The habit of feeding the birds then spread internationally; in the United States today, more than fifty million Americans spend a billion pounds on bird food annually.

If I approach the small garden by the church quietly and carefully I am often rewarded by the sight of a few birds swinging on these feeders, attacking the fat balls and pecking at peanuts. I usually spare a happy few moments to be with them before I am seen and they fly away. I especially love to see a charm of goldfinches rise as one entity; they twitter and bob as they flee, their song sounding like the gentle dropping of shards of glass as they go.

The European goldfinch is wonderful for the untutored birdwatcher because it is very easy to recognise. The male has brighter markings, but both the male and female have the distinctive red face mask, which gives way to white, then black, then again to white on the nape.[14] They have brown upperparts, white underparts with buff flanks and breast patches, and the wings are bright yellow and black. Essentially, they look as if they have been put together by a child from an identikit. Goldfinches were once seen only rarely in gardens and urban areas, but the ready availability of niger seeds, bought and put into bird feeders, has led to a significant increase in this birds' fortunes. Niger seed is high in energy and an excellent food source for birds in winter, and goldfinches especially love it.

About fifteen years ago I had my first real success as a bird lover when I bought a long cylindrical bird feeder and a large bag of black niger seed and installed it in my garden on the fence post opposite my kitchen window. I was the curator of the Holst Birthplace Museum at the time and was living in Cheltenham, and my small house stood adjacent to farmland and a footpath bounded by trees on both sides, so the birdlife was fertile and abundant. My sudden fit of enthusiasm was fortunately timed – I must have accidentally bought the seed at precisely the right time of year. I was rewarded after a few weeks by a male and female goldfinch visiting my feeder, one sitting on the left perch and one on the right, facing outwards and not conversing, like a typical married couple. I very rarely had time to go home for lunch, but one day I happened to pass my house at lunchtime, having been out of the office on a research trip. I called into my home to collect something, and looked out from the kitchen window to see the fledging of six tiny goldfinch babies. If I had been five minutes later, I would have missed them. I was as pleased as any proud parent. It was only then that I realised that goldfinches are not born with the distinctive highly-coloured markings; the juveniles are called 'grey pates' as they are almost entirely monochrome, having only a dash of a yellow wing stripe.

Before my success at raising a goldfinch family (I don't take all the credit), I had known this exquisitely marked bird more from art than from life, having seen many depictions in Italian Renaissance paintings. The ornithologist Herbert Friedmann, in his book *The Symbolic Goldfinch*, discovered that the goldfinch has appeared in nearly five hundred works of Christian art.[15] Traditionally, it is seen as a symbol of the Resurrection of Christ. Medieval theologians saw the bird as an allegory of Christ's return from the dead. Other legends are also associated with it: when Christ was carrying the cross to Calvary, a small bird – sometimes depicted as a goldfinch and sometimes a robin – flew down and plucked one of the thorns from the Crown around Christ's head, and some of Christ's blood splashed onto the bird as it drew the thorn out.

Sadly, due to their distinctive and attractive markings they have too often been kept as pets, and owning such a bird was once seen as a sign of the owner's high status. In such cases there was very little consideration for the needs of the birds. In the eighteenth century they were kept in elaborately ornate gilded cages and taught tricks, and were often chained by the leg to prevent escape. A favourite trick was to train the birds to dip a bucket on a chain into a cup of water and bring it up to drink.

Happily we now rarely see birds and animals as mere decoration and are much more content to see birds living wild and free. I realise that I have spent too much of my life looking at the natural world as envisaged on a flat, two-dimensional canvas, or consuming it passively through the written word or a television programme. I have sympathy for a captive bird or a captive anything; I am intensely grateful for my new-found freedom.

I raise my face and bask in the warmth of the sunshine for a few moments. I was not expecting to be walking in January in sunny, warm weather; I imagined that I would be struggling through snowstorms and thick ice. The romantic part of my soul is disappointed, as I believed that this would have been enjoyable in a perverse way, but in reality I am pleased to be walking effortlessly in mild winter weather. I was even able to eat my meagre picnic on the grass overlooking the Koralpe with the sun burning down. I am amazed to see a wasp and, flitting hurriedly by, two orange and black butterflies; it is almost spring-like. I can see only a little snow on the Koralpe, and even less on the Zirbitzkogel.

The warm weather brings out many more walkers than usual. Mothers with children in prams and pushchairs stroll about contentedly and several dogs scuffle about, impatient for their owners to hurry along. I was, as I always am, sad to see that the road and path waysides have been cut, and rather savagely, by an unforgiving machine. I am amazed that this has been done so early in the year, as I would have expected it to have been done nearer to springtime.

I reach the apple tree as the sun is beginning its descent, and everything looks different in the low sunbeams of late afternoon. I am just in time to see that a kink in the barbed wire fence opposite the tree which is caught in the last golden rays of the day and its rusty form has created a misshapen heart. Just as before, when Katie and I first saw frost laced barbed wire, I am forced to modify my view of this industrial material.

14

DAD

4ᵀᴴ February

My sister and her daughter are visiting us in Austria and can't decide whether they should accompany me today. They are a little disappointed as they had wanted to find Austria in deep snow, but none has fallen recently. I point out that the Koralpe is snow-capped and the Karawanken will almost certainly be so, and that once we have climbed high enough, we will be rewarded by stunning views.

They are convinced, and we depart at 11.30 am. It is a chilly -1°C but feels colder, as it is very blustery; however, we are heartened by the sight of a beautiful blue sky. As we rise higher, we do indeed see the Karawanken Mountains, which are extraordinarily clear, snow-capped and magnificent. I explain to my companions that they are eighty-three miles away and that they separate Austria from Slovenia – with Slovenia to the south and Austria to the north, and with a total length of seventy-five miles in an east-west direction, the Karawanken chain is one of the longest ranges in Europe.

When I was jotting down some tentative ideas about how I might use the walk to explore tangential avenues back at the beginning of January, it occurred to me that my project might help me to explore more about my father, because by a strange coincidence he was stationed in Austria from 1946-1948. Immediately after the conclusion of the hostilities of the Second World War, my father was posted to RAF Klagenfurt, which lies only forty-three miles from my new home. RAF Klagenfurt is less than an hour away from Bad Sankt Leonhard. Moreover, Klagenfurt airport is the one we always use to travel between here and the UK – it is sited approximately on the same spot where RAF Klagenfurt once stood. Immediately after the cessation of the hostilities of the Second World War Austria had been split into zones of occupation and controlled by Britain, France, the United States and Russia. Reg Herschy outlines in his book *Freedom at Midnight* the problems that the Allied Military Governments of the four powers had to address: the immediate problems not only of hunger but of dealing with the 'Thousands of refugees that had fled from the advancing armies and great numbers of anti-Tito forces who had been driven over the frontier into the Carinthian region.'[16] My father was one of the military personnel sent to Austria to help administrate the repatriation process.

The year before he died I realised that although he had travelled extensively in his long life, he had never returned to Austria. Suddenly it seemed vitally important to me that he should return, so on his 89th birthday I asked my father if he would like to visit once again. He readily agreed, as despite the awful circumstances he had enjoyed his time in Austria and had been left with a life-long love of the Austrian landscape. The short trip was planned for October and was a success, and during it, my father spoke more about this formative and early part of his life than he ever had before.

After the visit and within an hour of us returning from Austria and having got my father safely home to Malvern, my father quietly left the living room, went upstairs and came back down with a small box containing his diaries from 1943-1948. I had no idea that they existed. I am sure that I would never have seen them if we had not made the journey back to Austria. Later the same day, I remembered that years before I had seen an old suitcase in the loft marked with a sticky label with the word 'ART' scrawled across it. Climbing carefully up the ladder and into the attic I found the suitcase, opened it and there I saw a neat stack of unframed but completed watercolours, all dating from this period of my father's life. Later, I was able to match them to the diary entries. As a curator, this was a dream come true.

* * *

I feel that today, as my sister and niece are with me, this is an ideal opportunity to tell them about my father's early experiences. I point out that the Austrian Karawanken motorway (the A11) runs from Villach to the Karawanken motorway tunnel, and explain that father had arrived in Villach before reaching his final destination at RAF Klagenfurt in June 1946. While en route to Austria my father had celebrated his twenty-first birthday in Naples by climbing Mount Vesuvius and lighting cigarettes from the hot volcanic earth beneath his feet. He and his pals, as he

always called them, billeted in Villach in the Austrian Province of
Carinthia on 5th June 1946 before reaching their final destination.
His diary entry for that day reads as follows:

Wednesday 5th June 1946:

*At six o'clock on a chilly morning the train drew in at
Villach, and we emerged with kit feeling tired, fed up
and cold. We arrived in a transit camp – part army and
part RAF 59 PTC [Personnel Transit Camp], set amid
magnificent wooded hills and tall mountains, the higher
peaks I noticed were snow-capped even in June. I was
refreshed by a good meal during which time I heard on
the wireless the favourite tune of myself and Daphne.*[17]
*Up to now I have been feeling tolerably contented, but to
hear that tune sets me to thinking of happier days and in
consequence I became disinterested and even depressed.
I spent the day lounging upon my wooden comfortless
bed, finding it difficult to keep awake. I went out after
tea; probably against my better judgement, with Stan,
Doug and the rest. We enjoyed a pleasant walk in the
sunshine on this lovely evening. We perused the small
town of Villach, which is quite an attractive little place
set in a charming setting. Though the village and trees
reminded me of home – even to a blackbird singing –
the atmosphere is distinctly Austrian, this doubtless is
caused by the attire of the people.*

I feel pleased to be able to tell my sister and niece more about
my father's life in Austria. During the last two years of his life
I began to talk to my father about his memories of this time, at
first he was reticent, but when I had the idea of recording him
as he spoke he immediately became more fluent, as he addressed
the machine and not me personally. It was during this process
that I began to understand why he was reluctant to talk about

the war and why he had not wanted to tell anyone about his war diaries. For my father the great betrayal of the twentieth century was Total War. As an artist, he wanted to create, not destroy. He was appalled and amazed to recall that so many millions of people across Europe were so easily persuaded that war was more honourable than peace, especially as the war that he was personally involved in came so soon after the horrors of the First World War. He was dismayed that governments are often over-zealous and too dependent on war and that it is often accepted as without question the best and only option. He hated the fact that being a proud nationalist was for him and his peers the only real option available. He felt that to speak against war and killing was, and is still, to make oneself at the least an outcast and at worst a criminal. His consternation at the idea of wearing a uniform or firing a gun in anger was very real, but something he did not feel he could talk about. He could never comprehend the impulse to cheer or become excited by a bomb being dropped. He never articulated his moral objections in so many words; he merely avoided answering specific questions. He was often evasive, or even more tellingly he would contort his face into a rictus of disgust, which, of course, spoke volumes. Remembrance Day was for him especially trying and difficult. The War Memorial with the name of his elder brother etched on to it, in his hometown was a constant and painful reminder, which he did not like to visit.

Remembering those who served and died in conflicts is problematic; in many cases, there is a genuine need to be admiring and thankful of individual acts of bravery. However, my father was not convinced that the causes of war are always altruistic; governments have vested interests, and we are not privy to the political machinations that lie behind many decisions that cause conflict. The more I have studied the two world wars of the last century, the more I have come to doubt the efficacy or justness of war. Like most rational people I am wholeheartedly anti-war, or perhaps more accurately I am pro-peace, pro-discussion, and pro-non-violent intervention. But war and warmongering is still sadly part of the political landscape.

I have to thank my father for encouraging me to consider the issue thoroughly to reach my own conclusions. I think this was the most active parenting he ever did.

* * *

My sister and my niece listen to my account of my father's time at RAF Klagenfurt attentively. Now, less than a year after his death, we miss him and feel his absence keenly. Surprisingly, it is much easier to talk about his life knowing that he too saw what we are now seeing, that the Karawanken Mountains that he was awestruck by are substantial and real before us. Instead of looking inwards at each other we look out towards the pale blue sky. This makes the conversation flow a little more naturally, and a sense of catharsis comes over us.

We walk in companionable silence for much of the way home, feeling a little closer to each other. When a small plane appears as if from nowhere and starts buzzing around us we all accept that despite his huge reservations about the armed forces we can still take this as a nod to my father's five years of enforced service in the Royal Air Force more than seventy years ago.

Leonard Eason, in RAF Uniform, Algiers, en route to Austria, May 1946. Author's private collection.

15
weir

9ᵀᴴ February

I make a good start and leave the house at 11.20 am. It is a very good temperature for walking, a balmy (for winter) 3.8° C, with only a light wind. It is partly cloudy, but as I have come to expect now there are sunny patches and I am certain that they will become more prolonged as the day proceeds. The stream is no longer covered by thick ice but is almost completely melted, the ice crusted around the edges leaving gaping holes. To peer into the dark water below is to experience a world in miniature, imagining being on the edge of a huge precipice. I anticipate the sound and sight of great tits as I pass by the river. I have no fear for the future of this beautiful bird, as they are very abundant in this part of Austria. The great tit seems to have adapted very successfully: they are very widespread and common throughout the whole of Europe, the Middle East, Central and Northern Asia, even inhabiting parts of North Africa.[18] Great tits can thrive in any kind of woodland, and there are several places where I am sure to see them, and they are welcome companions, as appreciated in fact as any friend would be.

Birds have always been a feature in my life, and I have always been aware of them and sympathetic to their needs. I have a suspicion that my father preferred birds and plants to people. We would often be silenced when we were out if my father happened to hear a chiffchaff or a stonechat call, even if it was through an open car window.

I think he was fortunate in that his passion for ornithology began early for him and he was fortunate to have an identical twin brother and therefore a birdwatching ally. My father was twelve when the first affordable book for the amateur birdwatchers came out in 1937. He shared his copy of the *Observer's Book of Birds* with his brother. It had excellent illustrations by Archibald Thorburn, and these greatly inspired my father and uncle. They would roam around the fields and woods of their home county of Surrey and watch birds, taking it in turns to use a pair of field glasses and using the book to identify the birds they saw. Thanks to that early hard work and devotion, recognising any bird, by its call or its markings was very easy for them. I still have their copy of that little book; it is very tatty, held together by tape and water stained, with sand and grit embedded in the tan-brown canvas cover. A small printed bookplate on the inside front cover proudly announces that the book is owned by:

Ex Libris
Leonard & John Eason

This example of their shared library seems poignant and illustrates that their relationship was not a competitive one, but an equitable one of shared interests. They shared their love of birds, nature and art. They shared a bedroom; they sat next to each other in school producing artworks which they were encouraged to show to their school friends. Their artistic talents eventually became so evident that at the age of sixteen both left school on the same day to take up places at Epsom Art School. Then on July 6th 1943, at the tender age of just eighteen, much to their horror, for both were pacifist by nature, they were called up to serve in the Royal Air Force; their service numbers were one digit apart. But neither ever lost their love of birds or their ability to identify them, and this passion sustained them throughout their war service.

My father, not gregarious by nature, and not by any means a natural teacher, did provide me with my first very vivid bird sighting memory. When I was no more than six years old, he took me to his favourite nature haunt, an extraordinary place called the Knapp and Papermill Nature Reserve in a tiny hamlet called Alfrick in Worcestershire, a place filled with old valley meadows, woodland and orchards. We walked for some time and then suddenly my father stopped and knelt quietly beside me, encouraging me to watch and wait patiently for the bird that he knew would appear. We waited beside a weir; I vividly remember hearing the crashing of water and being aware that the water above was an odd dull green, still and clear and without a single ripple. It was not long before I saw a bright blaze of blue and orange more like a flash of light than anything substantial. It really was for the briefest moment, but I had seen my first kingfisher, that famous unsurpassably beautiful and colourful bird of rivers and streams.[19] I was beyond excited, and I have never forgotten it. It was all the better for the fact that it seemed to me that my father had willed the bird into existence. I think of that day whenever I walk by the weir at the beginning of my weekly walk.

I have only seen a kingfisher on two occasions since, once on a holiday in South West France, and once on my thirty-eighth birthday (which made my day). I have no idea why it is so magical to see birds, even fleetingly, and moreover recognise them. In my case I think my father's love of birds transferred to me by osmosis, and probably it was that first shared moment in my childhood that sparked something in me. Sadly, I am not the knowledgeable and talented bird-watcher my father was, but as part of my quest to see beauty in the ordinary, I am more than content to look at the birds I know; the everyday bird is beautiful to me. For example, if one forgets for the moment the ubiquity of the great tit, and looks at it afresh, it is a gorgeous bird: a splendid black head and neck, prominent white cheeks, olive upperparts and yellow underparts. I am always pleased to see one clinging expertly to a branch, hopping to and fro and finding insects to eat. I also like its distinctive call (probably because I can recognise it quickly). In fact, it has many calls, and perhaps the species as a whole has as many as forty. A single bird has a repertoire of up to eight separate calls or songs. These varied calls are perhaps to give the impression to predators and enemies that many birds and not just one protect the territory. The most familiar call, however, is the metallic 'tea-cher, tea-cher', likened to a squeaky wheelbarrow wheel, which is most commonly used to proclaim ownership of a territory. I always smile when I read this description, and imagine an old wheelbarrow squeaking along lamely. The descriptions of bird calls in any book on ornithology are always, thankfully, more a combination of the poetic and the imaginative than the scientific. These descriptions are much better for a novice like me, and besides, they betray the deep affection that we all - scientists included – have for birds.

During the past weeks, I have become fascinated by the great tit and have been avidly researching as much as I can about this little bird. I found a scientific study completed in 2015 that found that great tits would rather feed with their mate than alone. Ten mated pairs were tagged with identical tags so that they could be identified visiting feeding stations and feed together, and seven pairs with incompatible tags, so that one of the couples would be locked out of any visited station. Birds fitted with incompatible tags would not be separated. One bird would patiently wait for the other outside, although they were completely free to go and find out other food sources.[20]

I move on and as more great tits dart in front of me, it is impossible not to think about my father. I know he would have loved to see so many happy birds here and I am saddened that he cannot. It is now some months after his death, so I am able to take great comfort in the fact that as a young man of twenty-one he fell in love with Austria. His love of birds never diminished, and when he became a professional artist he still always made time for birds in his life.

Being posted to Austria was not easy for my father, separated as he was from his fiancée, his parents and his beloved twin brother, but it was a paradise after living on the periphery of bomb-damaged London throughout the Second World War. My father did not just dislike war but authority, and he despised ceremony. As he became older he hated any mention of the war because he had lost his brother, Dennis. Dennis was the complete opposite of his brother, a tough, strong and rather brusque character. He was very quick to volunteer, and after his gruelling training, he became a Marine. In 1942, when his ship was part of a convoy taking food and supplies to alleviate Malta, his ship was strafed from the air and he and many others were killed. Dennis was twenty-one years old. Thankfully his craft was able to limp into port.

My father did not volunteer; he was conscripted into the Royal Air Force and became a not very able airman. He was in no way technically minded – it was a struggle for him even to pass his Morse code exams – but he was a very talented artist, most likely inheriting the gift from his father or grandfather. Had my father been able to utilise his skills in the RAF, he could quickly have rendered a mountain, lake, or building with perfect precision, but this was not his role. Occasionally my father did work hard during his service years, but only when the need arose (which does not seem to have been very often, according to his diaries). He was never given any real work to do and was shamefully underemployed, which he found frustrating and depressing. Understandably, at every opportunity he would take to the hills around Klagenfurt, swimming in the lakes and watching the birds. He often painted *en plein air*, which very much interested the local Austrian population, who attempted to speak to him in what he called 'their unintelligible language.'

Painting and drawing certainly helped him, but I am convinced that it was bird-watching which saved him from the becoming horribly home-sick and bored. His diary entry for July 7th 1945 refers to the importance of bird-life to his health and happiness during this terrible time of global and personal uncertainty: 'What an integral part of my daily existence is the observation of bird life. I am forever conscious of their presence, a dull life it would be without them and their songs and their habits.' I think it also helped him to mourn the death of his older brother, a subject which was rarely if ever, referred to in his family. I think his sentiment is correct; life would be much duller without the presence of birds.

* * *

To prevent the memories of my father seeping like water into every part of my brain, I make myself look up to the mountains. The wind is picking up a little, and the cloud cover is becoming thicker and greyer. I reach the apple tree, but I do not loiter, taking my photograph quickly. It feels cold now. I cannot see the Koralpe, Karawanken or Zirbitzkogel peaks today, but where the sky is blue it is a deep indigo, and there is definitely rain on the horizon, so I begin to look forward to getting home.

As there is little in the way of flora and fauna to see and the mountains are obscured, my eye seeks out other wonders: it is then that I notice for the first time two murals on a derelict farm building. I step beyond the boundary fence to take some photographs of these fading but colourful works of art. They depict the three roles of Archangel Saint Michael. In the first one Saint Michael acts as the defender of the Church defeating the dragon. In a companion to the first another mural shows him with scales, weighing the souls of the dead; as sin is heavier the scales tip accordingly and sinful souls are consigned forever to hell. Above the whole is the Eye of Providence, or the all-seeing eye of God, which is a symbol showing an eye surrounded by rays of light and enclosed by a triangle, the eye of God that watches over mankind. In the second mural, Archangel Saint Michael is shown as the chief opponent of Satan; only a flourishing tail remains, but once there must have been a dragon or snake. My imagination runs riot: the commissioning of the work, the craftsmen on a rickety ladder toiling away diligently, receiving little or no monetary reward, but believing that through their art eternal salvation will come.

I enjoy the rest of the walk, thinking not of my past but the distant past and especially considering those who live their lives while continually striving to improve the quality of life through their dedication to artistic endeavour.

16
opaque

∀

18ᵀᴴ February

The whole landscape is snow covered, but it is a surprisingly mild day, with temperatures reaching 0.5° C, with only a light wind. It does feel, however, a little oppressive as the sky is engulfed in thick grey altocumulus opacus clouds which completely obscure the sun's rays. Opacus is the Latin word for opaque, and it very aptly describes these cloud formations.

A few weeks ago I took a few days' break and flew to Berlin.

On the flight back to Austria I was offered a masterclass on the wonders of these impressive cloud formations. The engines roared, and we rumbled down the runway and took off. For a short time, I could see the whole of Berlin from above under acres of pure white, fresh snow. Then we climbed up and through the very dense altocumulus opacus clouds, which now lay below us, a complete, solid mass of white, looking precisely like the downy insides of a duvet. I could even imagine that I was looking down at the South Pole, Shackleton or Scott of the Antarctic sledging past below us. Before we had taken off all we saw above us was a total white-out, but once above the clouds, we were flying through a beautiful blue sky. Flying offers us not only a bird's eye view of the world, which we take for granted, but a chance to understand the sky in a way that was only dreamt of by our grandparents.

As I walk today, I tell myself that although I cannot see them, bright sunshine and blue skies are above me, and I find this comforting. Having been under the weather for the past few days with a stomach bug, I was afraid that I would not be able to walk, so I need encouragement. This thought, combined with yesterday's fall of snow, has inspired me, and I begin to feel much better. The snow is already thawing, and the temperature fluctuations shroud me in fog, added to which a ground mist begins to rise. I am faced with a snow-laced, foggy landscape which is entirely denuded of colour, resembling an old black and white film. Wooden fences and gates stand out black and stark against the monochrome landscape and white snow. There is no view of distant mountains and horses, and cows appear like ghostly apparitions from the gloom. It is deathly quiet, because snow absorbs sound, but pausing to listen, I can hear a crump like distant thunder as a load of snow falls off a nearby barn roof. Another fall of snow this time from nearby trees is more gentle, the branches below catching the excess and breaking the fall. A large shower of snow falls from a nearby tree, but luckily it lands just in front of where I am walking. I stop and watch as a strip of snow several yards long tumbles from a long phone line, to reveal in certain places the black wire beneath. The cable now seems to be speaking in Morse code as a dot, dot, dash, dash black and white pattern has emerged.

The toneless nature of the landscape is not total. On closer inspection, I see that life and colour continue to break through: green-yellow catkins hang forlornly like mouldy fingers from their branches, dripping their drops of thawed snow like crystal jewels. The dark green fir tree branches act like large plates, offering up platters of immaculate undisturbed white snow. The cut wood of the woodpiles, although topped with snow, shows bright orange-yellow edges where the timber has recently been cut. These edges shine out, bright patches of colour in this newly-created monochromic world.

I am very thirsty, but instead of struggling to get my rucksack off, I walk over to a snow-laced branch which is at head height and eat snow from it; it's delicious and very refreshing. High up on the approach to the apple tree there are two tiny ponies, which I have never encountered before: one creamy white, the other dark brown. Against the brilliant white of the snow they look like they have stepped out of a sepia photograph.

When I reach the apple tree, its branches are skeletal against a misty, white backdrop. Tyre marks around its base indicate that the farmer has already shovelled away the worst of the snowfall, and a mushy brown pile of snow lies at the base of the tree. I realise that as the farmer rises so early, it is unlikely that I will ever see the tree surrounded by virginal untouched snow, as I would have to walk for two hours in the dark to arrive early enough. The view that I usually see, against which the tree proudly stands, is all but obscured: only the power lines, scratched across the sky like music manuscript paper, stand out above the white mist.

For a few short moments the cloud clears, and the mountains in the distance rise blue-black with pure white snow pooled in hollows and forming a beautiful bright contrast to the shrouded misty landscape below. The two roads, little more than footpaths, which lead down from the tree have already been cleared of snow. They stand out like grey ribbons, lacing their winding way across deeply snow-covered fields. They are much more prominent and graceful than I realised, although the one which snakes itself down towards Schiefling on an alternate route that I have never taken looks today as if it may lead to the dangerous Wild Wood of Kenneth Grahame's *Wind in the Willows*.[21]

Some bulky shapes which I at first mistake for bales of animal feed prove to be cows. They are standing still, alone or in groups; I am surprised that some are even lying down in the snow, apparently untroubled by the cold earth; I feel chilly just looking at them. I quickly eat some dried apricots and a bit of chocolate, button my jacket up firmly and set off for home. On the way back I notice a beautiful farm building, against the snow, I note the texture of the stone walls; a woodpile stacked half the length of one side, the roof an untroubled white; I have never thought it noteworthy before, but it is picture-postcard pretty today. Each time I walk this route, something I have merely glanced at before I now see in different conditions, and new finds appear. Today's found object is a simple three-windowed one-chimney barn with fine stone lintel-topped doors. Its patched walls and broken window panes look picturesque, and it shines out clearly in the toneless scene.

Requiring a little colour to brighten my walk home, I collect a russet-red flower from a vinegar tree, such a gorgeous, deep colour to see on such a colourless day. At home, I set it in a vase in the window to act as a foil to the muted landscape.

17
PEARL

24ᵀᴴ FEBRUARY

An earlier start today, leaving at 10.35 am. In complete contrast to the last walk, it is 1.5° C, very sunny, and there is a vivid blue sky, but mounds of snow still lie against walls like recumbent polar bears ready to rear up and roar.

Since I began the walk last December, I have mostly had fair weather, only once being caught in a terrible storm. I was expecting the climate here to be much less kind to me; perhaps I am even a little despondent that I have not had to battle through horizontal snowstorms and wade through drifts of snow. It is a strange fact that humans seem to thrive on a certain amount of controlled discomfort. It may be that at such times we are forced to live in the moment, able only to focus on our immediate problems and the decisions we must make to ensure that we are able to return home to safety.

There is little to see but brown-green grass, so I pause to contemplate the clouds. Cumulus humilis clouds drift at an altitude of about 20,000 feet and they are happily scattered across a cheerful blue sky.[22] Such clouds denote fair weather, so once again I am going to be lucky. My love of clouds stems mainly from my father's obsession with them. When I was about ten, I was given for my birthday a pack of illustrated cards explaining cloud formations. I remember that I loved everything about this gift: the feel of the thick card, the neat small print, the detailed coloured drawings, even the smart plastic cover that it came in. I had these cards for many years and often consulted them. But I don't think that an academic understanding of clouds can offer a true appreciation of them. The science of clouds is fascinating but is also limiting in many ways, utterly failing to convey the sensation of clouds.

In 2007, when I was at the beginning of my foray into the world of contemporary art curating, I began a different kind of self-discovery, one that would open up new worlds to me. I had just applied for a new job which would not only involve me in the curating of old masters and delicate watercolours but afford me the opportunity to work with living artists who make it their business to deal in ephemeral concepts and ideas. In preparation for my new post, I searched for exhibitions both near and far that I could visit, and every weekend for the few months when I was serving my notice period at the Holst Birthplace Museum I attended as many contemporary art exhibitions as possible. On a warm overcast day in July I made my way to London by train to visit an Antony Gormley exhibition at the Hayward Gallery. I did not realise then that this visit would lead me to beg the Arts Council Collection, whose collections are based at the Hayward Gallery, to exhibit Antony Gormley's installation 'Field for the British Isles' in my new post at Torre Abbey in South Devon some while later.[23]

Primarily, I had gone to London see 'Event Horizon', the thirty-one erect fibreglass figures that Gormley had created, modelled on his own body and dotted around the roofs of buildings next to the River Thames[24]. Like many people I was enthralled by this and walked into a fair few lampposts as I looked up at them.

What I was not prepared for was the installation called 'Blind Light', essentially a large glass box filled with mist or cloud, designed specifically to offer an opportunity to experience being inside a cloud.[25]

I waited patiently to enter the box; only twenty-five people could enter at one time. Once in there, feelings and sensations became exacerbated. I felt nervous, and became more so, as lost in fog inside the box, I knocked into the glass walls. I felt claustrophobic, and with hands outstretched I bumped into someone coming towards me. I was at first embarrassed, but then as I heard the stranger laugh, I too laughed. As people left I remained, and I began to feel as if I was walking, really walking in a cloud; I felt light, free and euphoric. I was new to the power that brilliant contemporary art can have, but at that moment it became clear.

Ephemeral art which cannot be hung on a wall or even

photographed, one that makes the viewer the subject of the installation, has untold power. I was the figure in the cloud; I could not only see the art but feel it as well. It was as if I was suddenly standing inside Turner's seminal oil painting 'Rain, Steam, and Speed' rather than merely looking at it. Turner's painting, a vortex of steam, mist and fog, is a whirlwind of movement, full of sound and fury. Centre stage is a black train emerging from a murky grey-white world, which Turner created by applying the paint with a palette knife in thick impasto. A rabbit, hitherto the fastest thing that could be seen in a British landscape, scampers away, now surpassed by mechanised speed.[26]

As I stood in the cloud created by 'Blind Light', I became the steam of the speeding train, and I felt as if I was experiencing the engulfing rain, as the passengers in the open carriages would have experienced it; I had become the rain pouring from the cloud. That work held me spellbound.

Since that day I have looked more to artists and poets to understand clouds than to science. My plastic pack of cloud cards evaporated into thin air long ago, and no matter how many books I consult on the subject of meteorology I feel no more informed. Since that July day, I have sought out exhibitions and art installations that help me understand clouds better. In the year when I first spent a prolonged period in Austria, a cultural trip to Vienna led me to the Leopold Museum and the 'Clouds: Fleeting Worlds' Exhibition. There I encountered Andy Warhol's 'Silver Clouds': twenty-five metallic silver pillows, or clouds, filled with air and helium, just enough of the latter to allow them to float, as they danced around the gallery space we the onlookers were allowed to interact with them. As they rose up and swirled around us, defying gravity, the effect was mesmerising and joyous. 'Silver Clouds' introduced me to one of the most attractive features of contemporary art, humour, while offering an opportunity to indulge in a child-like fascination for something so simple yet so awe-inspiring.[27]

Today I wish that one of the high-borne clouds would descend and encircle me, but they stay firmly in their sphere, and I trudge along looking down at the brown-green grass, scorched by both heavy frost and the recent snowfall. The bright sunshine, the beautiful clouds and the tree silhouettes that cast long shadows where the snow has not thawed prevent the walk from becoming a melancholy experience. And when I reach the apple tree, by sheer luck there is at the very moment of my arrival a tiny pearl of water from a melting drop of snow illuminated in a ray of sunshine, suspended from a low branch of the tree. It is a thing of pure beauty, but I only have a few moments before it will fall. No fence divides the tree from the path, so I move forward in a trance-like state to try and photograph the pearl of water before it disappears. I hold my breath as I focus the lens and capture two shots, and then it is gone. I wonder, is this where the idea of fairy lights on Christmas trees comes from?

The sun disappears and I walk in dullness for a prolonged period, but when another ray of sun appears I am delighted. As it lights my way it highlights a bank littered with pine needles and bright russet copper beech leaves, decaying in the winter sun. Tiny self-seeded conifers fit for a fairy kingdom are growing haphazardly; saplings of wild elderberry force their way ever heavenwards. Looking even more closely, I see a network of glistening cobwebs which are only occasionally visible as they flutter and catch the light. They lace through the entire length of the bank, stretching 150 feet or more, a rivulet of ice-covered snow sparkles by the side of the footpath.

Then, as quickly as it arrived, the sunlit vision disappears. Those cumulus clouds that I love so much close over and the beauty of the entire scene dissolves. As I make my way home, little earthbound clouds in the form of the first snowdrops of the year mark my way.[28]

All in all a beautiful walk filled with snowy-white clouds, a crystal drop of melting snow, topped off by the sight of the first pearly-white snowdrops of the year.

18
YELLOW

1ST MARCH

It is 4°C and very sunny, but there is a cold wind. I am joined today by Katie, her sister-in-law and my brother, who is visiting from England. We set off at 11 am after a hearty breakfast.

I am very glad to have Katie's sister-in-law with us as she has a wonderful ability to recognise and name wildflowers. Almost immediately she spots the first sighting of a spring flower of the season – the coltsfoot.[29] It has medicinal properties, as its

Latin name 'tussilago' implies, deriving from the Latin *tussis*, meaning cough, and *ago*, meaning to cast or to act on. Nearby, I spot the first pale yellow bud of a primula and its soft leaves bursting through the cold earth. The primrose,[30] although native to western and southern Europe, happily flowers in the cold harsh conditions of the Ukraine, the Crimea, the Balkans, the Faroe Islands and in Norway, and in hotter climes from Algeria in northwest Africa to southwest Asia.

I remember choosing as my first photographic project, when I was fifteen and had my first camera, a patch of primroses growing in our garden. The garden was built into a hill, and was extremely hard to cultivate. This inevitably led to it having a wild, natural, some might say unkempt, appearance. It was March and I was very frustrated that there was very little in nature to photograph. But taking my life in my hands, as there was a sheer drop to the patio below, I bravely scaled the terraced garden to find anything of interest. In the absence of any other colour or life I was very drawn to the little pale yellow primrose buds and the little leaves that emerged from the earth like tongue-tips. After that day I often went to look at them and chart their development, watching as the leaves became large, soft and ever more rubbery. I still have those photographs in an album. One of them is out of focus as I had not yet learned how to work the camera properly, but I still put in the sequence. It has a 'helpful' sticker on it from Boots the Chemist who developed the film: 'this photograph is out of focus.'

I think back to those teenage years as I take my primrose photograph today. I am now far from that place, not only geographically but mentally. At fifteen I would not have thought of Shakespeare and Hamlet as I do now, without even meaning to; as I muddy my knees to take a better photograph, Ophelia's words of warning to her brother Laertes, which I always think of when I see a primrose, come to me:

Ophelia: *Do not, as some ungracious pastors do,*
Show me the steep and thorny way to heaven,
Whiles, like a puffed and reckless libertine,
Himself the primrose path of dalliance treads,
And recks not his own rede.[31]

Ophelia is so clear-sighted in this exchange. She is completely aware of the double standards that exist in Elsinore; whilst she must be remain chaste, her brother is allowed to be a 'reckless libertine.' The 'primrose path of dalliance' is such a wonderfully wrought line – as Laertes skips up the path lined with the innocent yellow flowers he is in danger of crushing them, but this is of no concern to him. Shakespeare never misses a trick. A flower rarely appears in any play that is not there to make some kind of moral point or act as a means to point out some obscure truth. Moreover, Ophelia is the character most associated both in life and death with flora. The Royal Horticultural Society notes:

Rosemary is particularly associated with remembrance of the dead, and pansies get their name from pensées, the French for thoughts. Fennel represents marital infidelity and columbine flattery or insincerity. Rue, also known as herb of grace, is very bitter and stands for regret, repentance and sorrow. Daisies are a symbol of innocence and the violets, now withered, mean faithfulness.[32]

There are many, many daises today and my brother is surprised to see so many. Later we research this little flower – which is often erroneously referred to as the English daisy in England – to realise that the first flower to appear here, the bright yellow coltsfoot, the white butterbur and the common daisy are related.[33] I love the daisy; it is such a cheerful flower, bright white, with a tiny hint of pink on the outer petals, and that sunny yellow centre. It brings in the spring and remains throughout the summer; it's easy to picture a hot day and a lawn dotted with daisies. Perhaps spring is after all just around the corner, although it is hard to imagine, as the ground is brown and looks far from alive.

In the beehives of the garden where the owners sell honey from their homes, there are many bees buzzing around their hives. It seems to me too early for such activity, and I fear that a cold snap will come and be fateful. But the bees flicker past us, their 'pockets' full of bright yellow pollen, and I smile and think of Shakespeare's play *Twelfth Night* and of poor Malvolio and his cross-gartered yellow stockings.

I rarely rest for long when I am on my own, but today we all sit down and share cheese sandwiches. Katie, I think wanting to impress my brother, and her sister-in-law rose early and baked Gugelhupf. We stop and eat thick slices with some coffee from a large flask. The Gugelhupf is a large cake baked in a 'form' which gives it grooves and a distinctive hole in the middle (which is there to ensure uniformity in the baking). The word 'Gugelhupf' derives from an Austrian myth. Local lore claims that young Capuchin monks, when joining a monastery, were given a pastry called 'cuculla offa.' Cuculla is the Latin word for the monks' hood, shaped not unlike a Gugelhupf. This word was translated to 'gugele' in Middle High German. With the addition of the suffix 'hopf,' meaning yeast, the word Gugelhupf was born. It has been popular in Austria since the Middle Ages, but it was Emperor Franz Josef's fondness for the cake that led to its adoption by the Viennese.

Whatever the origin of the word, its soft, airy deliciousness is always a delight. We set off rather too full of cake and I point out the snow-capped Zirbitkogel and Koralpe, both looking slick with ice and brilliant in bright sunshine. As usual, the Karawanken can only be seen in blue silhouette.

I hang back towards the end of the walk as this is a better time to see birds, when they need their last feed of the day. I will not see any unless there is quiet, and I think a few moments on my own will do the trick. I sit quietly and in only a few short minutes I hear an odd grating sound, then see half a dozen long-tailed tits. Their tails are ridiculously long, much bigger than their bodies. They move around together, sometimes in flocks of more than thirty, and whiz from tree to tree. The long-tailed tit is sometimes called the 'silver-throated dasher' because they constantly dip and dive as they chatter. They have always been much loved and popular; this is illustrated by the number of alternative common names that refer to this bird in particular: long-tailed pie, mumruffin, bottle tit, bumbarrel, bum towel, oven bird, bag and hedge jug.[34] It is not only their long tails and distinctive shape that make them easy to identify but their distinctive colouring; their pink and brown backs are offset by the long tail which is black with white edging, and a black and white badger striped head. I find it impossible not to feel a lifting of the spirits when I encounter this bird.

I am so happy with this sighting that I hurry to catch up with my walking companions. I do not expect to have any more excitement today, but out the corner of my eye something flares. I detect movement and see a tiny goldcrest.[35] I have never seen a goldcrest before. It is small, weighing only 0.2 ounces and only 3.5 inches in length. The little gold-orange flash on its head makes it easy to identify. It thrives here as its thin beak is designed to be able to pick out insects from between pine needles, and in this extensive pine forest the pickings must be excellent. Despite its small size, the goldcrest is sometimes referred to as the king of the birds. This is perhaps because it is part of the kinglet family, but it may have more to do with the flash of gold in its crown, which looks monarchical.

I did once see a firecrest, which looks almost identical to the goldcrest but weighs an ounce or so more.[36] The male firecrest's blaze is yellow-gold with a dramatic orange flame at its centre. Appropriately when I saw my first firecrest, in my garden in Devon, I was tending a bonfire, I became so excited and kept so still that I did not notice that a log had become dislodged and my trousers had caught fire. I ended up in the accident and emergency department with bad burns on my leg and hand; I had used my hand to put out the fire, not one of my best decisions or one of my most glorious moments. Looking back I was more excited about telling my father about the sighting than I was for myself: I couldn't wait to tell him that I had at last seen a firecrest. But today my goldcrest sighting is a personal victory. Although I would dearly love to be able to tell my father about it, I am happy to add this spotting to my own list of achievements. I hear a thrush singing atop a very high larch tree, in the absolute quiet, which I savour for a few minutes; standing with my eyes closed, I simply listen.

Walking hastily I catch up with the other members of my party, who are already a little impatient and asking about supper and how quickly we can reach home. We do not delay further and arrive back in record time, to drink hot tea laced with just a smidgen of rum.

19
BRUEGEL

9TH MARCH

We awake to a thick, thick blanket of snow covering the entire countryside as far as the eye can see. It is always a remarkable sight to me, and Katie cannot resist coming with me. By the time we leave is it just after 10.30 am.

Before we have walked even beyond the front gates, I spy a large solitary jackdaw perching on the power lines outside the house. I put my finger to my lips and signal to Katie to be quiet and to watch for a moment. He is like a statue: completely still, his body stiff, his blunt, square, motionless tail feathers clearly visible; he creates a black exclamation mark on a pure white paper sky. As we watch, he begins to move his short neck, twisting slowly to survey the opaline heavens, which are lit by a bright orb of a sun which is shining brightly, although obscured behind a pall of pearly white clouds. Above these clouds hang elongated lens-shaped (lenticular) clouds, creating an oval of pearl grey above the crisply shining, brilliantly white snow-covered Koralpe.

We turn away from the golden sun momentarily and walk north-west towards Reichenfels through a sea of low cloud and mist, but this clears so that in the distance we can see that the small town of Reichenfels is also wholly snow-covered. We pass the Leonhardikirche and the bare skeleton of the immense lime tree looks magnificent. Ever since moving here I have been struck by the wondrous changing colours of its millions of leaves, in summer lime-yellow, in autumn russet gold, often contrasting against a vivid blue sky of unsurpassable beauty. But today not a single leaf remains, which makes us look more closely at the cracked, gnarled texture of the ancient bark. We even steal a few moments to feel the immensity of the tree, wrapping our arms around it, a simple moment of childlike pleasure, which makes us both laugh.

There is no way that we can manage to span the probable thirty or so feet of the tree's girth. This tree is, according to records held at the local Gemeinde, three hundred and fifty years old. I look up into the branches and think of our short little lives of eighty to a hundred years (if we are very lucky) and marvel at the antiquity of this tree and how it will long outlive us.[37]

The hills all around are dotted with trees: the bare branches and trunks of the deciduous trees are outlined in an ermine of white, while the dark green pine trees are a uniform sea of icy silver. Even the once bright orange of the autumn larch trees, which only yesterday were a dead brown, have become a monochrome of white. Spaces where whole areas of trees have been felled are suddenly bright and obvious – they are white motorways of virgin snow.

As we climb, the delightfully named village of Mondschein Siedling (which translates as 'moonshine dwelling') lies below us and we can see glowing lights from window panes and wispy smoke from chimneys, indicating warmth within. A mosaic of pastel colours, the yellows, reds and greens of the painted houses are enhanced today under their snowy roofs and radiate chromatic cheeriness. There is little activity; most people are sensibly seeking refuge indoors. Looking back towards our town of Bad Sankt Leonhard we see that it is equally beautiful and also dressed in a new white winter coat.

I cannot view a snow-covered townscape from a high vantage point without recalling Pieter Bruegel's *Hunters in the Snow*, a small replica of which my parents always had hanging in whichever house we had just moved to, so it is an image that I can quickly recall to mind. On one of my first visits to Vienna, I was thrilled to discover that the original painting hangs in the Kunsthistorisches Museum, walking into the gallery it took my breath away to see it, I sat admiring it for a long while.[38]

The winter of the year that Shakespeare was born, 1564-5, was bitterly cold, one of the most penetratingly cold winters of the millennium. Bruegel was completing his twelve small landscape scenes depicting the twelve months of the year. Of the twelve landscapes, *Hunters in the Snow* is the most exquisite and most famous of them all, so much so that it is has become part of our shared lexicon of winter images; it is the most used image on Christmas cards in the western world. But the painting not only records the harshness of winter; it also manages to capture its excitement and beauty. Originating from the Low Countries, it is clear that Bruegel saw this scene with its craggy snow-capped mountains as exciting, even perhaps exotic. It is doubtful that he ever saw the exact view that he offers, and maybe he never experienced snow at first hand; instead, he painted the scene that he wished was there. Looking closely, it's clear that the snow he paints is impossibly beautiful. Bruegel does not, for example, include any brown, slushy, clumpy, or dirty snow – it is all pristine.

Further, he romanticises reality by intentionally drawing our eyes away from the hard labours of the hunters, who enter bottom left, directing our gaze to the right side of the piece, and there we see playfulness: happy people, sledging, skating, dancing and slipping on the ice. The grey-green sky, the exact colour of the icy ponds, shows a single long-tailed magpie soaring happily over the joyous scenes below. Yellow-red buildings glow warmly under their snow-covered roofs. The cold of the winter is more easily tolerated if there is a warm fire, a cosy inn, and some hot food to eat.

Even though we have several hours walking ahead of us I am already imagining the hot pumpkin soup that we have already prepared and the candles that we will light and the fire that we will kindle.

* * *

There is so little colour around us that when we turn a corner and see several alder trees sporting bright Orange Jelly Fungus, the presence of which indicates that the trees are rotting internally, the little jabs of orange and yellow pierce the eye. I've never seen jelly fungus, so we stop and admire the vibrancy of the colour and gently touch them to feel their odd rubbery texture. Katie tells me that the fungi are edible, but as they taste like soil, we shan't bother to collect any, so I don't argue. The trees are cloaked in bright green furry, moist moss. Katie makes a quick note in her sketchbook and I feel that something will emerge from her workshop in due course.

Approaching the apple tree we pass through the wood and under two boughs which meet over the path; they are completely encased in snow and we walk under them as if under a pergola of white roses. The tree holds in its branches copious amounts of snow, and at its base clouds of pure white caress its trunk.

As we pass houses on our return, we see that where the sun has begun the thawing process and the snow has refrozen, it has begun to metamorphose, transforming itself into ice, which shines crystal clear in the last bright white light of the day. As we descend, passing buildings, we see that the long ice crystals on roofs are becoming water once more and the drip and tinkle of ice falling into gutters or plunging into soft snow is all around us.

We agree that today's walk was like no other. For much of the way, we walked under a strange milky sky which melted into the snowy horizon so that no division between heaven and earth could be determined. And we were accompanied by a mysterious suspended pale orb of a sun which haunted our every step.

When we finally reach the house the jackdaw is still there; he has moved his position, but only to reverse his view. I look at him one more time, nod to him respectfully and close the front door to entrap the warmth within.

20

BUTTON

19TH MARCH

We have had a few days in Vienna, which we enjoyed very much. But I feel even more appreciative of the beauty, stillness and majesty of the countryside of Carinthia. I am very keen to be out walking again. I leave just after noon; it is a lovely 8° C and very sunny. I feel relaxed, but I am still not able to walk without feeling that I must be using the time more industriously. I have managed to pick up some work with the British Council and have a short deadline; they want me to offer some explanatory notes on *Hamlet* to accompany the 400th anniversary celebrations in Vienna of Shakespeare's death. It seems like walking and listening might be a great solution, so I begin to listen to an audio recording of the play. But it is very hard just to be doing one thing well; this is a problem that we all face as we multi-task our way through our lives, but perhaps it was always so.

The Humanist scholars of the 16th century, notably the fiercely hardworking Dutch scholar Erasmus, advocated that no time in the day should be without industry; reading, studying or exercising. When I was working full time and studying for my first degree with the Open University, every moment was filled with activity, and after that intense period of my life, I was never able to break the habit. But in all honesty I am neither really concentrating on the play nor enjoying the walk. I begin to have the odd sensation that I am merely filtering my walk through the eyes of a fictional, suicidal Dane, as imagined by a clever Warwickshire lad. I do, however, manage to extract a nugget of information from my dual act before I finally give up. Even though I know the play well, as I am listening certain things come into focus and seem new-minted. Shakespeare knew and understood nature, and he must have paid very close attention to it. A passage jumps out at me as it never has before: 'The canker galls the infants of the spring / Too oft before their buttons be disclosed.'[39] I have never noticed that Shakespeare refers to a bud as a button and at first I find this a strange choice, but it makes complete sense. The word bud comes from the Old French *boton*, which became in the 12th-century *bouton* and then finally button. In French the rosebud is sometimes referred to as *un bouton de rose*. It is typical of Shakespeare to use the domestic word 'button' to describe a new 'infant bud of spring'. As the son of a glove-maker, he was well aware of the similarity between a finely-worked glove, adorned with expensive bud-like buttons, and a new bud of spring.

I finally realise that I have to stop listening to the recording and begin to seek out some 'button buds' of my own, so I pack away my headphones and look about me. I immediately see a small yellow clump of coltsfoot – in fact, the more I look, the more of them I see bursting into life around me.[40] I spot a clump of white butterbur, a plant related to the coltsfoot, and growing abundantly by the stream there are tiny buds curling into wild roses, their leaves already a healthy dark green. Even the apple tree has, at last, small vivid green 'button' buds. There are drifts of creamy yellow primroses that must have been planted by gardeners as they are outside farmhouses, but I can see that they are slowly but surely encroaching into the wilder areas, spreading their buttery-yellow beauty far and wide. In the unkempt garden of the derelict house with the wall paintings of St Michael which I first noticed on the 9th February, crocuses festoon the bank which rises from the path. They have forced their way through the hard ground, and their pale heads are just above the surface. Mauve and purple petals offset by the bright glow of orange offer a vibrant splash of colour.

Tomorrow it will be the Vernal Equinox and day and night will be approximately the same length; it will officially be spring at last. The indicators of this are all around: dozens of white snowdrops are apparent as I climb and I count at least eleven Brimstone butterflies.[41] They are the first species to be seen flitting about in early spring. The luminous yellow-green common Brimstone may even be the originator of the word 'butterfly', a corruption of 'butter-coloured fly', a term which may have been applied to the Brimstone by early naturalists. It is a beautiful insect and a grand master of camouflage; the pale greenish underside, raised wing-veins and wing tips combine to disguise the butterfly as a leaf, making it near invisible when at rest under bramble or ivy. In flight its bright colour is almost fantastical in its intensity until it alights on the early flowering primula to feed, then with wings folded once again, it becomes virtually undetectable. I follow one of them as far as I am able and am captivated by it.

The welcome warmth of spring has also encouraged the Peacock butterflies out of hibernation.[42] The Peacock is happy here in this environment; there are plenty of old buildings where it can hide over the long winter. Two beautiful specimens flutter by me, their gaudy red, blue and purple colours dazzling in the spring sunshine.

I see a robin; I'm sure I would have missed him had I not been watching closely and giving my full attention to the walk.[43] I am delighted. Is there a more loved bird than the robin? I'm sure there is not. He is both easily recognisable and friendly. The slender bill, the fragile stick-like legs, the wonderful plump red breast, which the male and female alike share. The large, pretty, intelligent dark brown eyes. They always look healthy, and they are jaunty, gregarious and unafraid. The robin is a bird that takes every advantage of our willingness and desire to provide food, but he doesn't just take advantage, but actively seeks contact with humans. We have recently been pruning our plum trees, hoping this year to get more than three plums from each tree, and making new beds for vegetables and shrubs, and invariably Herr Robin appears, sitting territorially on the cut branches, puffing himself up and hopping into the thicket. When I hear a robin singing I am always struck by it; it is my favourite birdsong, and the marking of the passing of winter as the robin welcomes the early spring is a delight. The nature poet John Clare wrote lovingly about the robin in his poem *Autumn Robin*:

The far-famed nightingale, that shares
Cold public praise from every tongue,
The popular voice of music heirs,
And injures much thy under-song:
Yet then my walks thy theme salutes;
I find thee autumn's favoured guest,
Gay piping on the hazel-roots
Above thy mossy nest.[44]

Today the Koralpe is bathed in sunlight and looks like dark blue marble, with the snow running in marble-veined lines across the summit; much has melted since last week. The Karawanken Mountains are as usual, lost in haze, I am viewing it as if through a gauze. As I rise I see its dark brooding presence in the distance, but instead of looking oppressive and forbidding, it always appears to be sitting in a halo of light. This is due to the Rayleigh light-scattering effect. No matter what the weather, the hills in the distance will always look lighter the further away they are.[45] The nearby hills and trees are always noticeably darker than those in the distance. From this perspective the hills become lighter and lighter the closer you go to the horizon because of the accumulating density of air. Rayleigh scattering is named after the British physicist who was the first to study this fully. Lord Rayleigh, or more prosaically John Strutt, published his theory 'On the light from the sky, its polarization and colour' in 1871 in the *Philosophical Magazine*. I find the theory comforting, as the hills in the distance will always appear lighter. Even my small grasp of the scientific allows me to trust in the reliance of certain things. It not only gives me a sense of security but it also creates a very beautiful effect: hill upon hill, mountain upon mountain becomes lighter and more dreamlike than the last. My father was once commissioned to paint a watercolour of the

Malvern Hills, and I remember a discussion with the purchaser, and some doubt about the payment being made in full, because 'the Welsh Mountains in the distance would surely be darker wouldn't they, as they are further away?' My father was never able to explain a single thing to anyone about his art, and in reply to this unfounded criticism he merely waved his hands around, squinted and said 'um' a few times. I wish I had known about Lord Rayleigh's theory then; I would love to have come to my father's rescue.

* * *

An extremely vocal great tit, convinced that spring is here, calls and calls, and I wonder, not for the first time, how such a small bird can make so much noise. I hear workers in the pine wood and see that they are in the process of felling. It makes me feel melancholy, but the smell of pine sap rings out pungent in the air, and despite myself I enjoy the aroma.

The final moments of my walk are enhanced by large white stratocumulus clouds which offer the perfect retreat for the sun to hide behind. Before long I am admiring a splendid display of crepuscular rays shining brightly from the behind the clouds.[46] They appear to be radiating from the sun itself, but in actuality, the rays are columns of sunlit air separated by darker cloud-shadows. The rays create near-parallel shafts of sunlight so that the scene before me seems filmic and unreal. In the 1930s crepuscular rays were called 'sunburst designs' and became a trope; from Lichtenstein to compact cases, radiograms to garden gates, the sunburst design was everywhere. I can recall the coloured glass on the front door of my paternal grandparents' house. It was the interwar design that spoke of hope, a hope sadly dashed by the Second World War. But despite this, today I cannot imagine a more pleasant coda to the day.

21
crocus

24TH MARCH

Having spent the morning creating high beds in the garden so that we can grow even more vegetables this year, time is against me. I have never begun the walk so late. I eventually manage to leave at around three o'clock. It's a pleasant 8° C, but rather windy. I realise almost immediately that my walk will take much longer, as at last the beautiful spring flowers are beginning to appear and I must make time to stop and admire them. It is many years since I took the time to really inspect a flower. Today I see an especially bright purple crocus with a bright orange stigma. While I have always been happy to see crocuses appear as a blaze of colour in the cold of late winter, I have looked on them as a momentary pleasure, seen and soon forgotten. When I was thirteen, I planted some bulbs in the front lawn of our house, spelling out my name with them, but we moved house before I ever saw them flower. I have sometimes wondered whether they are still there and if they have spread over the intervening years filling the lawn up with colour.

The word 'crocus' comes from the Greek *krokos*, while the word 'saffron' is from the Latin *safranum*, which in turn derives from the Arabic word *za'faran*, meaning golden yellow, light, lighting or revealed wisdom.'[47] Saffron is more expensive than gold because harvesting it is so laborious. For the commercial production of saffron, the flower of the plant *Crocus sativus* is used. This yields three stigmata, which are picked by hand and then dried to create saffron strands. A mere gram (0.035 of an ounce) of saffron sells today for up to £75, so it is very lucrative. Saffron has been used as a medicine, in perfume, as a blusher for cheeks, as an aphrodisiac, and as an expensive yellow dye, but is now most commonly used in the flavouring of rice dishes. The earliest extant depictions of a saffron harvest can be found in the palace frescoes of Minoan Crete; the Blue Monkey Frescoes, dating from c. 1500 BC, show elegant vividly blue monkeys carefully picking out the stamens. [48] In his *Metamorphoses* (8 AD) the Roman poet Ovid re-tells and popularises the Ancient Greek story of Smilax, a nymph who was loved by a youth named Crocus, but she did not return his love and Crocus pined away feeling hopeless for lack of the love of her. Perhaps it was a blessing that he was turned into a crocus flower. Her fate was to be transformed into flowering bindweed, which seems a less happy one. Every flower tells its own story. Modern saffron production centres on Iran and Kashmir, but in the sixteenth century, the small town of Walden in Essex was renamed Saffron Walden when because of the climate and quality of the soil, it became a centre for saffron production. It is still so named and happily in 2014 crocus production was re-established there.

I kneel to try and get a decent image of the purple crocus. In so doing I am reminded of my fifteen-year-old self and my desire to find beauty to photograph and my very first images of pale yellow primroses. I was the proud owner of an over-heavy Zenith camera, which I had sent off for via mail order. This was the early 1980s. I worked for the Ministry of Defence at the time, and many of my colleagues thought that owning a Russian camera was both decidedly odd and reactionary. I was probably ear-marked as a communist for owning it; there may still be a note on my file somewhere to this effect.

Sadly, after some years I traded in my Zenith for a somewhat inferior Japanese camera, also 35 mm, which I gave away to charity when I relocated to Austria. I wish I had kept my Zenith. Wet photography is not something I am likely to pick up again, but digital photography is much more affordable and accessible. This project has made me long for a decent camera again, so on a recent trip to London, I picked up a second-hand Nikon D5300. It has a shiny, dark red body and I am already very fond of it; using it today, I find that my enjoyment of the world around me begins to increase. I once again start to see the world through the tiny aperture of the camera, which enhances the experience of looking, like Alice in Wonderland spying gorgeous gardens and palaces through keyholes. Close-up photography focuses the mind and blocks out everything else, and I find it an excellent way to live in the moment. Capturing a good image defies time or at least arrests it; there is always a desire to try and defeat the worm in the bud. This walk sometimes feels a little like work, but today because of my new camera, the beautiful weather and the appearance of more spring flowers, the walk is nothing but a pleasure.

Suddenly I have a spring in my step, and I feel a forgotten childish happiness. I tuck my walking pole into my trouser belt and rest my hand on the handle, as if on the hilt of a sword. I allow my mind to wander, and suddenly think that I am a swaggering pirate or swashbuckling cad, perhaps Errol Flynn in *The Sea Hawk* or my favourite heroine Hannah Snell, the woman who borrowed a suit of clothing from her brother-in-law, James Gray, stole his name, became a sailor and went in search of her deserter husband. Snell was born in Worcester, and as a ten-year-old girl I was taken to the Swan Theatre, also in Worcester, to see a play about her life. I will never forget the moment when the actor playing Hannah lay groaning on the floor, unable, for obvious reasons, to ask for help in removing a bullet from her groin. The experience of seeing this play in 1975 had a profound effect on me. I had no desire to run off to sea, but I admired her courage in escaping the confines of the life that had been mapped out for her as a woman, but which she re-charted. Those few hours in the theatre made me realise that gender issues were more complicated than I had been led to believe, and I have been attracted to theatre ever since.

I am alone in a very secluded part of the forest, and I feel very free, so I indulge myself and play. I imagine that in living here in Austria I am playing a part, that I have a new role to learn and have taken on another mantle. I feel a lifting out of myself; a lifting out of my exterior skin. My innate and essential feminine self is of no consequence here when roaming free. I am also living in a country in which I presently cannot even name the words with which I would need to navigate the complex tributaries of gender politics; this too is strangely liberating.

Being alone in nature allows for imaginative role play – nature does not judge. I became aware of this when I was first coming out in the early 1990s; a gay friend told me how vitally important nature was in allowing him to go out on a walk with his partner and walk hand in hand without having to check himself at every given moment, fearing judgement or worse. I think of this conversation now as a bittersweet memory. I am happy that he felt able to share this with me, but wonder how much the world has or has not moved on since then. I allow myself to interrogate this theme more deeply, and let my mind wander. It's true that I have been led to believe that some of my interests ought more rightly to appeal to the male psyche than the female, which I have never understood. Many people still cling to these gender perceptions. Indeed, my mother found it impossible to cope with me as a muddy, grubby, penknife-wielding, welly-wearing tearaway of a child who liked to stamp in puddles and climb trees to find conkers. She finally banned my carefully curated country attire.

My renewed love of walking in the hills and mountains, especially in harsh wintry, snowy conditions, seems less than feminine to many people. Added to this I love gadgets, technology, watches, compasses, rucksacks, pens and good walking boots. I also like books and old libraries, so what does all this mean? I have often felt unable to raise this subject, which I find endlessly fascinating, but seems to be a taboo subject, However in 2014, Professor Alice Roberts, who has made so many complex issues accessible, presented a Horizon programme on television with Dr Michael Mosley called 'Is Your Brain Male or Female?' The programme concluded that men's brains and women's brains are identical at birth. I watched this programme feeling vindicated. The clothes we wear and the objects we own ought to be completely irrelevant factors in determining who we are, but we are too wedded to the false and oversimplified dichotomy of male and female. Perhaps to escape the issue, I have always explored the space in between, and increasingly androgyny intrigues me, and over the years has provided me with some leeway. I shall continue in my quest.

I have walked for too long; the light is failing me, and the temperature has dropped. So much so that as I approach home the path becomes slick with black ice and I have to pick my way carefully and delicately with total concentration, as I fear that I may fall and am very relieved to reach home in one piece. I am studying the ground so intently that when I spot an old, cracked piece of flooring, 1970s linoleum is my guess, looking for all the world like an arrowhead, I think it is auspicious in some way and with my pole-as-sword in my hilt, I return home tired and happy, for this walk has returned to me my muddy, grubby, nature-loving boy-girl, inner child.

22

Anemone

3ʳᵈ April

Over the past few days we have completed the installation of further high beds and will grow melons, sprouts, aubergines, cucumbers, tomatoes, parsnips and yet more runner beans this year. We've added trellis to the back of our high beds, not only to hide my row of homemade, rustic compost bins but so that we can use it to stake up any rambling and climbing vegetables. Once the long days of summer are here the pace of growth will be alarmingly fast, and this will offer us a quick fix.

It took us a long time to choose exactly the right trellis design. At the garden centre Katie picked out one that she liked, and when I asked her why she chose it, she replied: 'because it's tantalised - it will last longer.' I began to laugh, explaining that the word she was going for was Tanalised (a wood preserving treatment to protect against rot). Laughing loudly, we turned to see that we had brought the garden centre to a standstill, the same garden centre that already thinks we are crazy for buying their stock of old cargo crates to plant our vegetables in instead of lovely new bespoke, plastic ones. We are affectionately known in the town as the 'lustige paar' (the amusing couple), an epithet that we are most proud of.

But I must forget about the fact that the high beds need another coat of paint and leave the garden work behind me if I am to complete all fifty-two walks in the time limit I have set myself. I feel guilty, but because I became institutionalised over my years of working, it is helpful to me that it's a Sunday, and a day of rest. I would feel much guiltier if it was, say, a Wednesday. Katie waves me goodbye. She is happily planting seeds and listening to a podcast (she is still addicted to BBC Radio 4), and she is very unconcerned that I am not working in the garden. For this I am very grateful.

I depart at 11 am on the dot. It's 10° C and expected to reach 20° later. It's sunny and a little breezy, but I do not need a coat, and this feels liberating. A grey wagtail, his long tail feathers twitching like a pianist flicking up his tailcoat to begin a particularly tricky piano recital, busies himself along the verge.[49] In the silver birch trees by the stream, a bullfinch in his pinkish-red and pale grey livery sits statue-like, his chest plumped up proudly.[50] Nearby, a brambling, equally smart with his orange and white breast feathers ruffling in the wind, is feeding; he finds food quickly in the rich brown earth of a newly-ploughed field.[51] I watch, unseen, as a female blackbird hops along the stream bed, feeding and drinking happily, her pale yellow beak glowing slightly in the sun, the water shimmering in the sunlight.[52] Pockets of pale blue forget-me-nots with egg yolk yellow centres dot the landscape, a dazzling display of colour and more than welcome after weeks of walking in a colourless landscape.[53]

The Greek name for this wildflower is Myosotis, which translates as 'mouse's ear' both a poetic and literal description of the shape of the flower's small delicate petals. The main origin of the common name forget-me-not, however, comes from a medieval German legend: Rudolf the warrior was walking by the River Danube with his girlfriend Belta when she saw the flower but could not reach it. Rudolf, wanting to oblige her, jumped into the river to fetch it, but the river was flowing too fast and although he managed to retrieve the flower he was drowned in the process. Realising that he would not survive, he threw the flower to her with the words 'Vergissmeinnicht!' (do not forget me!) One hopes that Belta did not forget him, but in any case, the name and the flower have been remembered ever since. The legend may partly have come about because the forget-me-not is poisonous, so a story associated with death is appropriate and acts as a reminder not to taste or use any part of this very invasive wildflower.

In the shade of the wood, nestling in dappled sunshine amid lush blades of long grass, is an abundance of the sultry pink drooping flower heads of hollow larkspur, and underneath bright lime green florets of wood spurge bubble up.[54] All gardeners know its large cousin, euphorbia, in its many forms; it is an essential addition to a perennial border, and as necessary as the magnificent and tall garden favourite delphinium, which in its turn is related to the small hollow larkspur.[55] After the monochrome of winter both the bird sightings and the colourful flowers are very welcome sights.

I walk past a summerhouse which is set up over a pond-cum-wild-swimming pool, where a pipe continually circulates water, thus creating a constant pleasant sound of trickling water. There is a bench under a large fir tree and a little wooden fence. It looks like a perfect oasis for a writer and it is away from any houses. I imagine a 19th century novelist sitting quietly and industriously at a small desk and writing here – Mary Ann Evans, Elisabeth Gaskell, even Chekhov or Tolstoy. The owners have a well-developed sense of humour because bright yellow danger signs alert passers-by to the 'dangers' of the imaginary wildlife: 'Beware of the Camel!' and 'Beware of the Kiwi!' Even more bizarrely, since my last walk more quirky additions have appeared: there are now twelve bicycles of various shapes and sizes, all sprayed identically in a dark burgundy red: seats, wheels, tyres and handlebars. They are padlocked to the chain link fence. In the centre of the red bicycles is one small child's bike which by way of contrast is sprayed dark blue. It's an art installation that any significant urban gallery would be proud of, it's wholly incongruous and yet magnificent. It lightens my heart to see humorous, witty art out here in the landscape. I hope one day to meet the owner of this small plot of land and converse with the artists who have turned this space into a living art gallery.

I make the long climb up to Schiefling, but I am distracted by a bright yellow sign which reads 'Free Running Bull – Danger of Life' which has been erected on a new electric fence. The words are accompanied by a cartoon picture of a bull, stamping and rolling one foot while clouds of steamy breath protrude from his nostrils: precisely like something from a Beano comic. I walk over to the fence and peer into the field; it is bounded on one side by a brook, and the alder and young willow trees create a latticework tangle which is difficult to see through. I look for several minutes, but I cannot see a dangerous bull or even a friendly one. Then, as I am turning away, I see that lying on the muddy ground in the middle distance is a small, young bull with horns like those on a Viking helmet. He is chewing slowly and staring directly at me. Apart from the working of his mouth, he is entirely stationary. I look him straight in the eye and say 'hey, Johnny what you rebelling against?' he looks nonplussed – he's no Marlon Brando. I move on.

As I rise and survey the landscape from a birds' eye perspective, I see newly-ploughed dark brown fields standing out like luxurious velvet next to the tawny and scrubby fallow fields. Others are perfectly striated from meticulous mowing, almost too picture-book-perfect. There are farmers in most of the fields on tractors, both old and new. Red tractors seem to be the most popular, and many have names like 'A Farmer's Best Friend,' invariably written in English, inscribed proudly on their shiny surfaces. In truth, before the advent of the tractor, ploughing the land by hand or using animal power was time-consuming and exhausting. Neither an ox nor a horse understands reverse; the reverse gear is truly the 'Farmer's Best Friend.'

One farmer sees me and waves as he effortlessly transports over-large fence panels along the rutted path; another trundles past with an empty trailer and a gadget which is delicate enough to pick up even small twigs and deposit them into the container; he need never leave his seat. Everywhere I see activity. Each week as the temperatures rise, the blood is up, and there is a straining in the slips to be up and doing.

A brash and vocal blackbird sings so loudly that he drowns out the distant chainsaws and the throb of human activity. I stoop to admire a creamy yellow primrose, and as I snap my camera case open a small terrier launches at the fence. I have never been so affrighted! I jump so high that I in turn frighten the dog, so we are both launched into the air for a millisecond and my heartbeat is racing. After this I find a little calm by sitting on a bench and admiring the cirrus clouds gathering above me and the still white peak of the Koralpe.

I am on my descent home, and a usually dull and shady bank is filled with wood anemones. As I approach a very welcome ray of sunshine spotlights one for me, as if offering it up as a small gift with its six white petals open and pure and its myriad of yellow stamens, swaying slightly and casting tiny shadows onto the petals.[56] So welcome are these spring flowers, but I feel slightly tricked when I bend down to smell one of the leaves; I know that they are also called 'smell fox' and, yes, this is apt, the leaves do have a distinctly musky scent.

I return at just past three o'clock and get one coat of sage green paint onto our high beds before the day is done.

23
Asteraceae

11ᵀᴴ April

It's a wonderful day for walking, a warm 15°C. At last it feels spring like. There is a deep blue sky filled with cumulus clouds, and a fair but pleasant breeze. All my life I associated March with the first stirrings of spring. I need to adjust now, as spring comes rather later in Austria, but now that it is warm and April well under way, I hope that today there will be new flora and fauna to see.

Immediately I note that dandelions[57] are beginning to appear and wild elderberry, which is invasive here, is everywhere in leaf. Wild pansies dressed in yellow and white bob their heads in the breeze.[58] These pretty pansies are set off by blue-green lichen which is crusty enough to cast small shadows across the surface of the large stone that is their host. A non-stinging dead nettle with delicate white flowers stands tall, and the topmost and newest crown of leaves have a delicate reddish tinge. When Katie was a child she roamed these hills with her siblings and they used to suck the honey-like sap from nettles, occasionally getting some extra protein in the form of the odd beetle swallowed by accident.[59]

A decorative wizened hazel tree in the garden by the churchyard is a mass of beautifully hand-coloured eggs in yellow, green, blue orange and purple. They are left over from Easter and have, I think, been deliberately left – every opportunity to cheer up the landscape is grasped in this still not quite polychromatic world. Even the shrine by the church still has coloured eggs amongst the floral offerings. More yellow coltsfoot have sprung up, and the ground is littered with daisies. This suddenly makes complete sense to me as the daisy is from the same family as coltsfoot and butterbur – in fact plants with composite flower heads are amongst the most important and widespread of all plants. Yellow chamomile, daisy, marigold, marguerite, chicory, chrysanthemums, dahlias, zinnias, sunflowers, to name but a few, are all from the Asteraceae family. They are not only ornamental but important for the economy, providing products such as cooking oils, coffee substitutes and herbal teas.

A woodpecker screeches and jets past me in a fearful hurry, while an elegant elderly woman, dressed in a stylish burgundy coat, is exercising back and forth along the length of a narrow meadow just as if this was her own long gallery, such as those found in Elizabethan and Jacobean houses in England, which enabled the taking of exercise during the colder months.[60]

Peacock butterflies flit from flower to flower, and the din of insistent bird-chatter is constant and urgent. Bees are buzzing, busy about their hives. A kestrel hovers overhead, waiting to dive for prey.[61] His long tail is fanned out to act as a balance and his wings are flapping to keep him airborne, but his head is entirely still so that he does not lose sight of that vital prey. A jackdaw croaks and creaks as he rises from a decrepit wooden fence and is lifted onto a strong thermal, he drifts lazily into a temporarily sun-filled patch of blue sky.

As I reach higher ground I see patches of bright yellow, and at first I think I am looking at gorse – I remember many a spring holiday in Wales with gorse littering the whole countryside. But I am actually looking at the dark green leaves and the simple open sunny yellow flowers of the alpine potentilla.[62] They scale up the bank in low-lying clumps, standing out starkly in the still brown frost-bitten grass, which as yet shows few signs of new life.

Best of all, at last the apple tree is beginning to develop and bud on practically every branch, the first signs of life I have seen. There are even dandelions growing out of the concrete breeze block wall opposite the tree. New life is an unstoppable force. I am very keen to see how the tree develops over the next few weeks of early spring, but then I remember that very shortly we must go back to England for twelve days. I am surprised by my feelings: I realise, happily, that I have settled here so well that I have no real desire to leave Austria at the moment. But, spring in England is one of the most beautiful seasons because there will be daffodils, and the green, green grass of home. I laugh to myself, because now that I am happy and not worried about anything in particular I am anxious and afraid that it will all vanish into thin air. Such is the human condition.

I view the hard outline of the still snow-capped Koralpe through soft yellow triple catkin fingers that hang on the birch trees. The Karawanken is lost in haze.

24

UNSEASONAL

29ᵀᴴ APRIL

A few months ago, we spent many hours sowing seeds. We have a little wooden gizmo that forges my ever-increasing pile of read and unread *Guardian* newspapers into seedling pots. Every window ledge in the house is filled with these pots, and we are already growing aubergines, beans, cabbages, courgettes, pumpkins, spinach, tomatoes, night-scented stocks, nasturtiums and lots of geranium cuttings.

The geraniums we have taken from family heirlooms. For many years Katie's mother nursed them through the winter, and many of those we still have are either the originals or their offspring. We have even grown a pomelo from a shop-bought fruit that Katie managed to coax into life.[63] All the seedlings and cuttings are doing well, but they desperately need sowing outside, they are leggy and pale. In our eagerness, we started them much too early. When we seek advice about planting out our babies everyone looks at us oddly, and the reply is always short and to the point: 'but you must wait for the Kalte Sophie!' This is a reference to the 15th of May, a date that all gardeners and farmers here both mark and strictly observe. No one will plant their precious seedlings or crops before this date. The 15th of May is the feast day of the early Christian martyr Saint Sophia of Rome, who died around 304 AD. Relics from her martyrdom are buried under the church of Santi Silvestro and Martino ai Monti in Rome. Sophia is only one of the saints whose feast days are associated with the last possibility of frost in Catholic Central Europe. There are also four Ice Saints, or Eismänner: Mamertus, Pankratius, Servatius and Boniface, and they have their feast days immediately before Sophia on May 11th, 12th, 13th and 14th respectively.[64] By remembering both the four Eismänner and Saint Sophia and their respective dates, these dates are fixed in the hearts and minds of those whose livelihoods rely on this information. As it has been for many generations, this knowledge is handed down via the oral tradition. Sadly, we receive this knowledge too late to save many of our seedlings, which die for want of fresh air and warm soil.

* * *

On the 28th April I jump out of bed early; it's my birthday, and I have always loved celebrating it. I go to the window to look out on the world, and I am stunned to see that there has been a very heavy fall of snow overnight. Snow on my birthday? It utterly amazes me and takes everyone by surprise. Frost is expected well into the middle of May, but heavy snow at the end of April is a great shock to everyone.

The already cleaned and polished snow ploughs have to come out of storage, and we hear about the many people who have been stranded in railway stations overnight. The trees, which are already in leaf, cannot take the weight of the snow, and branches break, falling on cars in the streets – they have to be cleared immediately. There are long traffic jams and costly delays. Farmers are severely affected: the early spring buds are damaged, and many will not now fruit. I worry about my apple tree and hope that I will still get to see the green apples in early summer. Climate change is frightening, and today it seems much too real.

Katie's brother and his wife come over (they live next door) with presents for me and a bottle of Austrian Kupferberg sparkling wine, and even though it's only midday we take a glass each. They smile and embrace me, and I feel like I have another family now in Austria too. I decide to postpone my walk and enjoy a restful day.

Fair weather or foul, however, I cannot postpone indefinitely. By 29th April the temperature has risen to nearly 6° C, and I look on a cloudless blue sky which is host to a bright sun, but incongruously there is still thick snow everywhere. It remains on high ground as an even layer, but on lower slopes, it is melting very fast. I never expected to be walking in the snow in April. The small roads and paths that take me high into the hills are steaming in the bright sun. Snow melts on woodpiles which have top coats of white furry snow, and all around there is the sound of dripping water, with long icicle shards are melting, gleaming and refracting the light. The new lime-green leaves of spring glow through the snowy branches like little ears. The apple tree is an early fruiter, so it already has clusters of buds, but they seem to have survived and don't look burnt by the frost. Perhaps selfishly I hope that the new buds will bring forth fruit, not only for the farmer but also for my project.

I descend to the river and the meadow to find that the snow has almost gone, but there are hundreds of bright yellow dandelions poking out through the white blanket. In some cases, diamonds of not-quite-melted snow nestle between the yellow blooms. The hardy dandelion seems untroubled. I walk all the way back accompanied by the bluest of blue skies, the sun shining on a dazzlingly white landscape. But although it is beautiful, I cannot help but feel that this odd unseasonal weather is simply not right. I am reasonably confident that this unexpected fall of snow will be the last I'll see until the winter comes again, so I scoop up a fistful just so that I can feel it and study it. Because of the warmth of the air, it is already granular and loose; it feels like I'm holding a handful of freezing wet diamonds. I grasp the snow firmly so that it forms a clump in my hand and it soon becomes a crystal knuckleduster, turning from white to transparent. It starts dripping through my closed fingers. The pain from the cold shoots up my arm from my hand but subsides quickly. Despite this momentary coldness I feel warm, for it is not a cold day. I taste the piece of the now icy crystal enjoying the crisp, refreshing notes. It smells clean, like menthol; I am surrounded by minty air. I have never studied, touched or savoured snow. The occasional snow days that we had in England when I was a child were days of excitement, but I was either off school and bunkered in, or depending on where we were living at the time, walking miles to fetch milk and bread. There was no time to study the intricacies of snow, and the idea never even occurred to me. But this new strange, unseasonal fall of snow has afforded me with an opportunity to consider something that I have only ever thought of as a complete entity: as a thing of mass and majesty, now I have looked at it microcosmically.

I feel amazed by the unusually inclement weather and feel thrown by it, and besides, I am still recovering from the virus that I contracted in England; I suddenly feel drained. I know the last stretch of the walk so well that I walk with my eyes closed for a while. When I open them, I see, nestling in a patch of gently thawing snow, a beautiful piece of stone in the shape of a heart. I use one of my hiking sticks to prise it out of the ground. I see that the shape of a heart has been formed by the wet tyres of vehicles driving over the stone, cars which have had to move to one side at this juncture to allow oncoming traffic to pass. The stone is not heart-shaped at all but has a heart-shaped impression on it. We see the world through our own experience and our unique worldview. One of my main passions in life is Shakespeare, and this is the first walk I have completed since 23rd April and the 400th anniversary of Shakespeare's death. This, combined with my recent visit to the UK, has rekindled my interest, so as soon as I see the stone, Othello's words spring to mind: 'No, my heart is made of stone.' Othello, faltering just before the wanton murder of Desdemona, urges himself on, instructing his heart to become a thing of stone, no longer the seat of love but of hate, revenge and jealousy, a hard-heartedness that marks the climax of the tragedy.

I pluck the stone from the cold earth and take it home. As soon as I return, I show it to Katie, and within a matter of moments, we have together completed a design in which we can feature the stone accompanying it with other found pieces from previous walks: red glass and rusty metal.

Katie tells me that while I was walking today, she finished a piece inspired by the walk, a necklace of worked fine silver, which she heated and then beat out to forge it into a laminate of layers, adding feathery-gold detailing around the edges to complete the effect. Katie has the skill to transform a sliver of wild cherry bark, which was sloughed off as the tree outgrew its outer coat, into a something lasting and beautiful – she can achieve alchemy itself. I am awed by this.

25
Dandelion

It's a cool 11°C and somewhat cloudy. I leave just before 11 am. After the last walk, I contracted a terrible cold, and I am still not feeling entirely well. I am worried the walk will be more than I can manage, but my core fitness has very much improved in the last nine months, so I decide to try my luck. My legs feel shaky for the first twenty minutes, but I rest more than usual, and soon my progress becomes less difficult as I find the right rhythm. After the first climb I stop under a rich canopy of newly-formed leaves to enjoy the sound of cowbells, birdsong and the rushing of water in mountain streams, swelled by rain and snowmelt.

I reach the apple tree quite quickly; it is now surrounded by an electric fence, so I am separated from it. I am keen to return home and rest, but as I round the bend to look down on Schiefling, I see a sight that immediately lifts my spirits: as far as the eye can see the fields are filled with dandelions, hundreds and thousands of them.

I have been led to believe, along with almost everyone else, that there is nothing more pernicious and evil than a dandelion. Currently, even the Royal Horticultural Society's website, while briefly acknowledging that the dandelion is an important source of nectar for insects and bees, has a page of more than five hundred words on the chemical eradication of this 'weed.'[65] One of the first and most notorious organic compounds used as a pesticide on such weeds is DDT, which was created by Swiss scientist Paul Hermann Müller, for which he received the Nobel Prize for Physiology or Medicine in 1948. It was used extensively and indiscriminately during the Second World War, primarily by the US military. The mosquito was a key target, as malaria was a vital issue, not only causing fatalities but incapacitating whole battalions. In his book *The Long Road Home*, Ben Shephard relates that in 1943 DDT was used to disinfect typhus victims to eradicate the louse that lives on the body, the chemical having first been tested on inmates at Maison Carrée prison in Algiers and then on the local villagers. After this it was successfully used in Naples in January 1944 when 1.3 million people were deloused, and within three weeks the typhus epidemic was mastered, with almost no fatalities; this prevented a repeat of death by disease that occurred after the First World War, and in this regard, the benefits of DDT seemed miraculous. Newspaper journalists began to laud DDT, saying that it seemed 'almost too good to be true.'[66] This paved the way for the release in 1944 of DDT for civilian use, and this escalated exponentially. In the late 1940s images of smiling babies were used imploring housewives to use DDT on walls, floors, doors, and even kitchen surfaces to kill flies and mosquitos. The chemical industry and the world of advertising have altered our relationship to all manner of flora and fauna. Today, the dandelion especially is targeted: everywhere from Facebook to YouTube, adverts for Roundup pop up unwarranted and often accompanied by animated dandelions which are out of control and seem capable of driving the suburban gardener into a frenzy.[67]

Many of these poisons are lethal, radiating deep into the soil to eradicate even the root of this wildflower. Garden centres have row upon row of these harmful poisons, which are still bought and often applied without any consideration of harmful and drastic effects they have on the delicate ecosystems that our gardens are host to and their carcinogenic properties. In the 1980s I bought my first house and had a tiny garden of my own, and a colleague gave me a bottle of weed killer as a 'thoughtful' gift. I was very grateful, and agreed that of course I wanted my path and lawn to be weed free. My father and uncle, I remember, had other views about weeds which I chose to ignore, because in British suburbia one must live a weed-free life. The word 'weed' comes from the Old English word 'weod', which Chambers dictionary glosses as meaning simply 'a herb'. Sadly, the word 'weed' now has only negative connotations: 'a useless plant of small growth, any plant growing where it is not wanted by man... useless, troublesome... obnoxious.'[68] What's in a name, indeed?

However, to stand on a hillside and look on the stunningly beautiful sight of millions of dandelions stretched out as far as the eye can see is profoundly moving. I suddenly feel very foolish for having been so idiotic as to wish even one of them out of my life. The very name dandelion, from the French '*dent de lion*' meaning lion's tooth and referring to the jagged tooth-like leaves, ought to have afforded this plant a long-lasting place in our affections. In German, the name is equally adorable: *Löwenzahn*, also meaning lion's tooth. At one time, then, it is clear that this flower did have a more elevated reputation. In Christian art it was often used as a symbol of Christ's Passion, appearing in paintings of the Madonna and Child and the Crucifixion. Raphael includes the dandelion in his Alba Madonna of 1510; there it is nestled in the triangle formed by John the Baptist's chubby knee, the Christ child's delicate naked foot and the Virgin Mary's elegant sandalled one. Raphael adds other symbols and signs to heighten the drama and indicate that this is no ordinary child at play – not only the dandelion but the anemones on John's fur robe, the deep red centres of which are there to remind the viewer of Christ's sacrifice and his eventual awful fate.[69]

It is not only the sight of so many dandelions that has altered my perception. Since I moved to Austria, I have been reintroduced to the dandelion: Katie and I have taken to picking the new young tender dandelion leaves for salad when they first appear in the meadows around our house. When the gorgeous yellow flowers appear Katie makes dandelion honey with the petals, just as her mother used to do. It's a slow but simple process: the plucked petals must be boiled with water, sugar and lemon juice. We often have free range eggs from a local farm with fresh herbs and a selection of 'weeds' from the garden, all of which have health benefits. We pick them, chop them finely and sprinkle them on to our food, and include not only dandelion leaves but also young, tender Giersch leaves,[70] Gundelrede[71] and Tausendgüldenkraut.[72]

Dandelion roots are also useful because they can be ground up and boiled with water to be used as a coffee substitute; in fact this was a common practice during the Second World War. The dandelion has many beneficial properties. It is suitable when correctly prepared as a purifier for the blood and to normalise blood circulation, and helps to prevent rheumatism, gout and urinary tract infections. We haven't as yet used our dandelions for dyeing our clothes, but I perhaps even that will one day come.

Other than its health benefits, the dandelion is the only flower that represents the three celestial bodies of the sun, moon and stars. The yellow flower resembles the sun, the creamy-white puffball of seeds resembles the moon, and the dispersing seeds when they are blown away in the wind scatter like stars. The dandelion flower opens to greet the morning and closes in the evening to go to sleep. When rain is approaching dandelions withdraw, so they can be used as a warning of impending bad weather. Lastly, there is the dandelion horn: cut a flower with a long stem and remove the head, then blow down the stem, and you will be amazed at the volume and timbre of this little instrument. When I mention this to Katie, she is reminded that she used to annoy her little brother with dandelion horns, blowing them directly into his ear.

Having stood gaping at the sight of the sight of hundreds and thousands of yellow dandelions and white seed heads before me, I am reminded of reality when it begins to rain. It is the first rain I have had on any of my walks, another reminder that I am not walking in Britain, for surely there I could not have already completed eighteen thirteen-mile walks without being drenched a few times. Suddenly my tiredness returns; I search for my Pac-a-mac and walk quickly home.

26
RANUNCULUS

18TH MAY

It is a balmy 14° C, and this improves my mood. Today I am also much cheered because we have received an offer on Katie's cottage in Devon.

I leave around mid-morning. As soon as I begin to climb,

I come across fields and fields of a type of buttercup; they are much taller and leggier than the ones I know in England, but they still have that gorgeous glossy-yellow appearance.[73] They are very dominant and have mostly replaced the acres of dandelions that have accompanied my walks in the past weeks. Unlike the dandelion, all parts of this plant are toxic. The grass is now long and glossy, and there are a hundred different types of green to admire. Everywhere there is lushness and life.

My head is not racing at all today, and although it is not tranquil as it was when I walked in the snow, I feel as I walk a calmness seeping into me. I do not feel the need to plug myself into any exterior distraction; I have not downloaded any podcasts; I have nothing prepared. But it is easier now that it is late spring, and there are so many sounds to enjoy: birdsong galore, and the crickets' orchestra moves between a restrained classical score to one of classic rock. I imagine them as out-of-control rock stars with their own noisy thrill of fans. Insects are buzzing; meltwater, from the recent heavy snowfall at the end of April, tumbles and cascades over rocks; and underscoring all these brash sounds there is the pleasant sound of the leaves in the trees rustling quietly in the breeze. But the cows, at least, are very quiet. Most are lying with their young calves in the sun, seemingly happy and contented.

The walk soon becomes an absorbing experience, and my mind manages to enter a state of flow.[74] In 1975, the Hungarian psychologist Mihaly Csikszentmihalyi both recognised and named the psychological concept of flow. I am amazed when I realise that I have achieved this feat at last; I completely lose all track of time. By walking more slowly and rhyming my footsteps with the calling and singing birds I become fully immersed in an energized feeling of focus and involvement. I think it only happened by walking more slowly and rhyming my footsteps with the calling and singing birds. I did not realise before just how difficult it is to learn to live in the moment, but because of this project, I am beginning to unlearn bad habits from the past. This is not an outcome I expected, but it is one I would certainly have wished for.

There is snow on the Koralpe, and it is still a thick icing of brilliant white, but it only crowns the top. The Karawanken are also snow-capped but are lost in haze, which is quite usual. I watch for several long minutes, not daring to move, as a copper-red kestrel on a telegraph wire eyes his prey and then swoops to kill, flying to a more distant perch to consume his catch.

I reach the apple tree and discover that the apple blossom is now at its very best. Paying attention to the shape of the spring flowers, I begin to appreciate and understand that the apple tree is part of the rose family, and although short-lived the blossom flowers are truly as beautiful as any flowering rose.[75] I suddenly have the impulse to lean in and smell the blossom; it does smell like roses, with perhaps a little extra vanilla. It has never occurred to me to do this before. The apple tree is now a symphony of colour and fecundity, with tight dark pink buds, snowy-white petals, and in the centre of the petals the creamy-yellow, pollen saturated stamens, while around the blossom the luxuriantly green leaves sing out.

As I study the blossom closely, I realise that the whole tree is a throbbing mass of bees; it's so noisy that at first, I think there must be a moped in the vicinity. The blossom is offset by patches of yellow and green lichen which have wonderfully textured, erupting surfaces, and I touch them very gently so as not to harm them in any way. The lichen is especially apparent on the shadier side of the tree, where the trunk is facing the prevailing wind and rain, for lichen and mosses are moisture-loving and require this extra dampness. Although it has a firm hold it is not harming the tree; in fact, it indicates that the air here is clean, as lichens only thrive in clean, fresh air. Today I collect a small fallen branch from the apple tree, one that displays a fine example of the green lichen. I am hoping that Katie will not be able to resist forging and beating some metal, inspired by these growth patterns, perhaps adding verdigris to copper to try and mimic this magical mossy-green colour.

The farmers have mowed many of the dandelion fields, and this harvest will be used as animal fodder. In so doing they have left wonderful swathes of verdant green fields which look perfect in the late evening sun. The stripes of the newly-mown fields, in fact, look like a watercolour or a linocut, perhaps depicting manicured cricket fields, although a ball game would be difficult if not impossible due to the steep undulating nature of the landscape. The whole scene reminds me of the delicately pale, luminous watercolours of Eric Ravilious, who was a great inspiration to my father.

Ravilious was born in 1903 and died tragically young in 1942 when he was serving as an official war artist; the plane he was travelling in was lost near the coast of Iceland on September 2nd 1942, and his body was never recovered. His life is commemorated on the Chatham Naval Memorial, near Kent, a large stone obelisk which is reserved for members of the Royal Navy who died during the First and Second World War and have no known grave. By a tragic coincidence the very short life of my father's brother, Dennis Eason, is also recorded on the Chatham Naval Memorial. My uncle also lost his life at sea in 1942; he was killed on the 18th November at the age of twenty-one.

Ravilious grew up in East Sussex, and would walk across the South Downs, an area now designated as a National Park, the place which most inspired him. The South Downs, although quite low lying (rising only to 889 feet above sea level), provided Ravilious with the views he seemed to most favour; he loved to survey a scene from a high vantage point. I can imagine that both he and my father are standing next to me, admiring as I am now, the artful work of the farmer. While other artists shunned the everyday and the banal, Eric Ravilious recorded daily life: English harvests, or old and broken machinery lying abandoned in fields. He was also a master at depicting the tillage of the land, the striations made by the plough or tractor.[76] My father also found beauty in the simple furrows made by a tractor, and I have an early watercolour on which he has written on the reverse: 'A View from my Billet, Downham Market, April 45.' It's clear in this small piece that he spent as much time patiently painting the furrows and carefully mixing cobalt blue and burnt umber to get just the right brown earth colour, marking each ploughed line meticulously.

I have spent many hours looking at this particular Austrian landscape - nineteen walks already completed - and I am fascinated by the ever-changing states of the land. Watching it being perpetually altered and manipulated has served only to increase my fascination. Collectively we no longer have the vocabulary to explain all these different states, but such words did once exist and were in common usage. Take 'sillion', 'vores' and 'warp' as examples. 'Sillion' is a poetic term meaning 'the shining curved face of the earth recently turned by the plough.' 'Vores', originating from Devon, means the furrows made by a plough. Having lived in Devon, I can see how when spoken with a Devon burr, furrows easily becomes vores. And lastly, 'warp' is the soil between the furrows, a word, in fact, that originates from Ravilious' Sussex.[77]

I am normally happy to spend time taking photographs and I do not normally consider it to be a poor relation of the other visual arts, but today I feel that a paintbrush and paints would be able to render the scene before me in a way that the camera cannot.

27

LUPINS

25ᵀᴴ MAY

It is a very pleasant 16°C, sunny with a cooling breeze. The wildflowers by the stream are stunning today, a corridor of fecundity. I see farmers in fields both high and low stoically harvesting their crops to make animal fodder.

Winter has at last completely lost its grip on the landscape. Some of the dandelions are already in seed, but their egg-yolk yellow brightness is now provided by mouse-ear hawkweed, a shaggy version of the dandelion; the flower petals look raggedy, as if they have been bitten by tiny mice.[78] Pink field scabious are voluminous and their little pincushions of violet-blue (strangely not pink at all) flowerheads attract butterflies like magnets. Red campion and banks of high, yellow-centred, white-petalled marguerites litter and brighten the verges all along the route.[79] Wild lupins in burgundy, pale pink, pink and white mixed, and lemon fill the bank under my favourite row of silver birch trees. In the shade of the pine wood fiddleheads of ferns are beginning to unfurl their Fibonacci spirals; some are already large and strident, spooling out their teethed leaves high into the air.[80] The tall stems of wild horseradish stand out proudly, the blooms pure white and surprisingly delicate.[81] Grated horseradish root, the hotter the better, is very popular here and is used as an accompaniment to all cooked meats, not just served with beef as it is in the UK. At Easter, freshly-grated horseradish is mixed into chopped-up egg to make a pungent side dish to add to the Easter feast. The flowers can be used to create an infusion by simply steeping in boiling water for five minutes to relieve cold symptoms. Competing with the tall horseradish blooms, the cow parsley is winning, as it is already over a three feet high. Cow parsley is the one thing that reminds me of the hedgerows of England, but I do not feel remotely homesick. I realise that it is pointless to associate one wildflower or a particular wild bird with one distinct place; nationalism about nature is not a helpful emotion, although it is a trap I have fallen into in the past. If anything I prefer the abundance of variety here; cow parsley has become overabundant in the UK.

This abundance is so unlike the deathly silence of my first winter ice and snow walks, but it is not just the flora which I notice; it is also the sound. It's loud: noisy crickets; the swift clattering of a beautiful black squirrel, skittering up a tree with a hazelnut in his mouth. Fields of cows, their bells chiming out, create a constant tintinnabulation of clamour. My brain transforms the sound of the many cowbells merging it with Arvo Pärt's *Cantus in Memoriam of Benjamin Britten*.[82] I came to Pärt's music after I became the Curator of the Holst Museum. Gustav Holst's daughter, Imogen Holst, was Benjamin Britten's amanuensis; in other words, day after day she wrote by hand onto manuscript paper pages and pages of Britten's music as it poured from his 'genius'. During the composing of his major work for the coronation of Queen Elizabeth II, Imogen was transcribing twenty-eight pages a day, an undertaking for which she received very little credit or thanks.

In Pärt's *Cantus*, the striking of a tubular bell at regular intervals throughout the piece is a perfect accompaniment to the wonders of nature. As I replay it in my head, I can place the sound of the cowbells alongside the clanging of the tubular bells. The final bell strike of Pärt's piece resolves from A minor to A major, so that it ends on a note of resolution and hope; cowbells always sound melodious and hopeful.

When I was employed at the Holst Museum I was able to speak with a musicologist at length, and he was able to explain to me why a piece of music written in a minor key disturbs and agitates us. It is because music written in a minor key has a chemical effect on the brain, and the unnerving feelings are therefore beyond our control, but we continue to listen to such music because we know that it will end and that we will at its cessation be returned to a position of safety and comfort. Listening to music in a minor key or listening to atonal music, which flouts the natural laws of harmony, is much like watching a horror film or riding a rollercoaster. Access to controlled discomfort is life-affirming, which is why we crave it in small doses.

In 2013 I was involved with an art project led by the Philharmonia Orchestra which involved me interpreting for the public an installation involving one recording of a live performance of Igor Stravinsky's *Rite of Spring* replayed on thirty massive television monitors for up to twelve hours a day, on permanent repeat at an ear-bleedingly loud volume. I can confirm that to listen endlessly to a piece of music written to 'celebrate' a woman dancing herself to death for four days consecutively is not to be recommended. If I ever doubted the power of music before I was convinced by it after this project ended, because when I drove home after my last shift I felt unaccountably exhausted, confused and tearful.

Eventually the sound of the cowbells dies away, and it begins to rain very lightly. I am pleased, for the rain brings with it a drop in temperature and cools me. But I cannot help feeling thankful that after only ten minutes the rain ceases.

* * *

I am currently working on a lecture about Shakespeare's *King Lear* and feel that for the remainder of my walk I can combine work and pleasure, as with so much garden and house repair work going on I seem to be very short of time. Occasionally, BBC Radio 3 commission new recordings of Shakespeare's plays and currently their most recent stars Ian McDiarmid as King Lear. I plug myself into my earphones and begin to listen. I had not realised before how much it is a play about movement and the outdoors. Moving through nature as I walk, I hear the play as I have never done before. The whole experience is enhanced, because alongside McDiarmid's quiet, restrained performance I can hear an alternative and actual soundtrack complementing the action: water in streams, swelled by recent rain, gushing down ravines; birds singing; crickets screaming, wasps, bees, beetles and flies buzzing. Words and lines take on a new resonance, especially Gloucester's much-quoted line:

> As flies to wanton boys are we to th' gods.
> They kill us for their sport.[83]

I can hear birds of prey offering up their piercing cries, an echo of the predatory, cruel behaviour of Goneril and Regan. Gazing on nature as I walk adds a third dimension to my understanding of the work, and I am struck, not for the first time, by the power of both the play and of nature. When the recording finishes, I feel as I always do when I have experienced *King Lear* in any format – utterly bereft. I no longer wish to think or listen to anything, but of course the whole play debates the value of silence and nothingness, so this is perhaps a suitable response.[84]

As I climb to the highest point in the woods I do not want the bleakness of the play to seep into me, so I look around in the hope that I can connect with something positive. And there, after only a short while, a stoat scuds across my path. I stand fixed to the spot like a monument as he passes in front of me. I long to photograph him, but I remain still, and having nosed the air he scurries away. I am glad that I could not capture the moment digitally. I have had very few such encounters with wild animals, so I have a clear mental image which I can replay any time I choose.

The sun begins to drop in the sky, and I can see midges dancing in the air highlighted by the light from a golden sun which accompanies me all the way home. I watch dandelion seeds floating thickly in the air, occasionally punctuated by the appearance of buff-beige moths or colourful butterflies. The distant Karawanken and Koralpe are almost lost in haze, but I can see a slight crest of pure white snow on both.

I pass through a small farmyard, which has a magnificent collection of hens; they ignore me and continue to strut happily in the sunshine. Two dogs bound up to me. I used to be nervous about them, but they recognise me now and usually disregard my presence, preferring to sunbathe and sleep. Today, however, I am wearing a hat and sunglasses, and they cannot identify me, so they explode into noisy barking. I remove my hat and slide my glasses down my nose and say 'it's only me, don't worry', then, realising they only understand German, I calmly say '*Beruhige euch, alles klar*'. They stop immediately and stroll back to sit in the shade.

Returning home, I sit in the garden in silence, enjoying the shade of the evening and quietly sipping cold beer from a clear glass.

28

PATH

30ᵀᴴ May

It is yet another warm and pleasant day; 15°C rising to 24°C.
Once again I have a slight chest infection and tomorrow we are
leaving for Hungary, so I decide to put off my departure for a
few hours. Eventually, I set off at the very late hour of 3.30 pm.
Luckily, the few rain showers earlier this morning dimmed the
heat somewhat. It is a delight to walk in the lovely, late, cool
of the day. The sun shines only occasionally through dark,

glowering nimbus cumuli, which filters the light, making it gentle so that everything is bathed in a uniformly golden light.

The field directly below the Leonhardikirche was only recently sown with wheat, but it has grown so rapidly that it is already thigh height. A few stray electric blue cornflowers have encroached into the crop, their coroneted heads peeking majestically above the slender young pale green wheat. The whole of the bank along the path that looks up to the church has been mown, but where the marguerites are blooming the municipal gardeners have not cut even one down; their sensitivity impresses and gladdens me. They have left the small ones untouched; now they can reach maturity.

A woodpigeon is cooing in the near distance; for me, its call is the singular sound of summer. Although summer will not officially begin for another two weeks, today it certainly feels very summery.

The crickets are chirping, and I am keen to look at one closely, but every time I try to approach the noise stops suddenly and the crickets clam up. I would like to see at least one of the males make his 'singing' noise, rubbing his 'scraper' – a sharp ridge on his wing – against a series of 'files' on the other wing, but they are too clever for me. As soon as I pass beyond them, however, they immediately recommence their stridulating racket. I walk backwards and forwards, testing them out for a few moments. Every time the noise stops and then begins again, but I have no wish to alarm them. I watch a black redstart dismember a fly, his rusty-red tail flicking anxiously as he moves from railing to roof gutter; I don't think he likes me watching either.[85] Black redstarts are often too tame for their own good. I've seen cats in our garden getting too close, but thankfully this one seems more timid.

It is so very quiet that I can hear a cowbell far away, and the call of a crow, but little else. Before long I hear the stream trickling. The path through the orchard is very overgrown: I am wearing shorts, so I have to remove my rucksack and use it as a guard against the tall stinging nettles. I walk through purple meadow thistles,[86] pink clover,[87] interrupted by bright, glossy yellow buttercups, dark red campion,[88] a bright yellow patch of meadow pea,[89] and the ubiquitous, versatile dandelion. There is also a great quantity of poisonous cow parsley, which seems to grow further by the second. The little stream that flows into the river is all but invisible, bounded as it is by a five-hundred-yard strip of wild mint; the aroma is very strong and fills the air. By the stream edge, there is a long strip of beautiful, very tall, dark-green-leaved, purple-stemmed marsh woundwort.[90]

Marsh woundwort contains an essential oil that has antiseptic properties, and can be used to treat cramps, arthritis and joint pain. Monica Wilde, the forager and herbalist notes that Marsh Woundwort was in medieval times 'considered to be one of the most valuable herbs. Used directly on wounds as a poultice to encourage healing, as an ointment for gout and joint pain, and also used internally for cramp and vertigo as well as internal bleeding.'[91] In 1599 a Swiss visitor to the theatres in London, Thomas Platter, noted that the taverns and elsewhere (namely Shakespeare's theatre the Globe) sold tobacco made from a species of woundwort, the ground powder being lit in a small pipe and the air sucked into the mouth.[92] Once again I am excited to be able to see something growing in nature that I have only previously had an intellectual relationship with. I have never thought about the beauty and abundance of this plant before. I am tempted to tell Katie that she could make her own tobacco from it, but I think better of it because I may end up being involved in a cottage industry which I currently don't feel we have the time to indulge in.

Through this mass of wildflowers runs a very straight footpath. A group of hikers, two men and two women, all wearing Lycra shorts, pass by me, and although giggling at a private joke they pause momentarily to greet me pleasantly. They stride away, their eight walking sticks swinging in perfect unison. The straight, single-track footpath by the stream reminds me of Robert Frost's poem *The Road Not Taken*, and the famous opening stanza:

Two roads diverged in a yellow wood,
And sorry I could not travel both
And be one traveler, long I stood
And looked down one as far as I could
To where it bent in the undergrowth;[93]

Frost's poem always seems to me to keenly represent someone on the threshold of their young lives, at a moment when it is necessary to choose this path or that. The single track footpath I have just traversed, a vivid green one running through a lush meadow, is one that I have now trodden many times, and by the end of the project, I will have walked along it as many times as years that I have lived. I can, therefore, even though I am not on the threshold of my young life, look upon this path as representative of my new direction in life. I feel for the first time that the road I am now on is the right one and it looks, so far, as if it will be easy to follow. But like most people reaching the mid-point of their lives, if we are lucky enough to find ourselves happily travelling on a sure, straight path, we are painfully aware of the wrong turnings, dead ends, cul-de-sacs and dangerous motorways and highways that we have traversed.

Often, when we are in our 20s and 30s, we travel along the most treacherous roads, believing that we are making the right decisions. Sometimes we are coerced, or forced, by well-meaning parents, guardians or friends, and following their advice we end up travelling in a hopelessly wrong direction. But, even these badly-lit streets, dark alleyways and potholed roads lead us to a moment in time, right or wrong. It's a quest and a process. Eventually, we learn that there are not two diverging roads in a yellow wood, but finding the right path takes a lifetime of trial and error, and even then how long the path is and how long it will continue to be the right path we cannot know.

* * *

The whole landscape looks, more than ever today, managed and controlled – everywhere has been shorn, or new crops have been planted. Fortunately, the wild verges continue to provide a pleasing contrast to the manicured fields, abundant as they are with wildflowers. As I rise higher the wild lupins become the star players; they are tall and majestic in pink, purple, cerise and white, with a few pale yellow ones growing slightly apart from the others. I cannot stop marvelling at the beauty of the tall spiky blooms. The sky begins to brood as I soodle[94] along, the sky a mixture of dense steel-grey-turning-to-black cloud; a better backdrop for a stage of lupins could not be imagined. The sky also has patches of blue and the sun gallantly continues to shine strongly. I am so glad of it, because I am struggling to climb today, my heart races and I need to rest quite often. The cool shade of a small wooded area is more than welcome: I sit down on the fresh grass and watch as three cows laze in the shadows. One stands looking directly at me, a long wisp of cow parsley in her mouth. Her tongue curls round the tendrils and the whole is gone in an instant, but she never takes her eyes off me. I look deep into her eyes. She is so gentle and calm, a brown and white of the Fleckvieh breed, which is a popular one here.[95]

I take another short break and drink some water. It has taken me most of the day to reach the apple tree, so I see it much later than usual. It is a real delight to see it in the evening, and I am certainly rewarded. The tree stands in dappled light and in the midst of long, green-green grass, which sways gently and sounds calming. The base of the tree is surrounded by pink clover; the long, trefoil leaves are dark and lush and the yellow, taller and more elegant ranunculus buttercup that grows here shines out, while small wild nut trees shield the tree, their lime-green leaves catch the last rays of the sun. The tree moves into partial shadow and becomes backlit by a sinking sun; the hills in front of the tree are a purple-blue, the sky cerulean blue: it is a cliché of perfection. I look closely and see that it seems to have recovered remarkably well from the recent harsh and unseasonably late-season snow that threatened to destroy all the new buds in April. It will have apples, and I cannot wait to see them.

29

Fra Angelico

7ᵀᴴ June

It's a very pleasant 21°C, and tumbling cumulus clouds fill a sky of summer blue. It's very sunny too, but I am still suffering from the stomach flu; I haven't felt really well since returning from the UK in April. Although I had a bad night, I do feel a little better. Even if the walk takes me all day, I am determined to do it. As well as still being in recovery from my virus, I am also nervous about the fact that we have to return to Devon one more time.

We must completely empty Katie's cottage, and we shall have to cherry-pick, selecting only favourite and essential items to bring back to Austria. Having already done this with my belongings, I know how hard it will be. But we must be realistic: we have to release the equity from the house, mainly because the property in Austria needs essential work.

We cannot see out of the windows as the double glazing has 'blown' and there is a fug inside most of them; partly for environmental reasons, we hope to replace only the window glass and nothing else, but it is still a big and expensive undertaking. The heating system is noisy and inefficient, so it too must go. We would not be insured if it went up in flames, which certainly could happen. Essentially, the house hasn't undergone any real repairs since it was built forty years ago, so it must be done. The kitchen also needs work, but we will do our utmost to recycle and upcycle. We also feel that once we have cut our financial ties with the UK, we will be able to focus entirely on our new life in Austria: we will simply have to make a complete success of it.

* * *

The fields are very green and verdant, and I am struck by a stunning patch of marguerites, or as my parents always called them ox-eye daisies, their white and yellow faces turned up to the sun. I have never seen such a sight in nature, and I cannot really compute it, so I stand and admire it, also with my face turned up to the sun. Looking again I realise that it reminds me of the field of daisy-like flowers in Fra Angelico's *Annunciation* in Florence.

In the spring of 1993, I was studying the quattrocento art and the architecture of Italy, but I became very frustrated as I had to study some of the most beautiful paintings, sculptures and buildings only from books and photographs, so I booked leave from work and a flight to Pisa and travelled by bus to Florence. Within two days I had ticked off all the obvious places, including the trek up and around the inner walls of Brunelleschi's magnificent dome of the cathedral to admire the city of Florence from above, Ghiberti's *Gates of Paradise* at the Baptistery and the Massacio frescoes at Santa Maria Novella.

I didn't think I would have time for the Fra Angelico frescoes in the Convent of San Marco, but I found a free few hours and realised that I could manage to fit them in. I admit that I wasn't expecting to be completely bowled over, but it became so much more than a box-ticking exercise. As I entered and walked up the staircase to the cells where the friars slept, there was Fra Angelico's *Annunciation*, right there in situ in the corridor, where it has been since the late 1430s. It was so unexpected, so ordinarily placed, but viewing it from below made it look like Angel Gabriel had just flown in through the nearby window. The hairs stood up on the back of my neck, and while people came and went I still stood and stared.

There is something so delicate about a fresco, not only the pale, earth colours but the way its relationship with the building is so permanent, fragile and co-dependent: if the building moves, the fresco will crack. I looked closely at Angel Gabriel and his rainbow-coloured wings. Gabriel and Mary make eye contact, and echo each other with arms folded across their chests in mutual respect and supplication. I absorbed the main points of the scene and then my eye moved to the less dominant space which is always to the left in the Western art tradition, and there I saw a dark green field outside the loggia, studded with flowers. Fra Angelico adopted a usual trope here, the trope of a closed garden – a high fence separates the garden setting of the Annunciation from the cruel outside world. The fenced garden symbolises Mary's purity.[96]

Fra Angelico went to a great deal of trouble to give this area meaning and beauty: he painted not a few flowers but a field studded with daisy-like, marguerite-like flowers. If the biographer Giorgio Vasari is correct, Angelico was trained by the painter and miniaturist Lorenzo Monaco, one of the greatest artists of the Gothic tradition. Certainly, Fra Angelico shows in *The Annunciation* a concern for detail which affords his work a serene quality. As the Annunciation is supposed to have occurred in Nazareth on March 25th, and Nazareth means flower, the flowers also have a symbolic significance. I have had a fondness for fields of daisies ever since this trip to a small convent in Northern Florence.

* * *

The apple farmer and his young son are each in separate tractors and are working a large, sloping field which has views to the Koralpe. The son looks happier than his father. He is only just old enough to be doing this work. His curly blonde hair catches the light, and he already looks sunburnt from daily exposure to the early summer sunshine. Both father and son are dragging behind their tractors old-fashioned spring harrows, their flexible iron teeth making easy work of loosening the soil to prepare it for planting. I look intently at the apple tree to find some signs of life and after a few moments I see one very small green apple just beginning to form. I am ridiculously pleased to see it; after the heavy snowfall in late April, I feared that nothing would come this year. I feel lucky that I picked an early fruiting variety, as I will soon be rewarded with the sight of a tree full of yellow-green apples.

I pass more intense activity and see three large, new-looking green and yellow Krone tractors, dancing with agility around an immense field and mowing it efficiently but noisily. A small dachshund is darting between the tractors, occasionally stopping to admire a new blade of grass or savour a delicious new smell. One of the drivers steps out of his cab; he is wearing a Marlon Brando white vest (Brando in his later years, I think) and has a cigarette in the corner of his mouth. He opens the engine cover of his tractor and peers in, looking very worried, but when he sees me, he pulls in his stomach and shouts 'uh-ah' - the universal farmer's greeting, one that would be understood from Devon to Dubrovnik. I nod and smile at him in recognition.

It begins to rain gently; this part of the walk has a more substantial pathway, and the smell of rain on hot tarmac rises up. It's a pleasant petrichor aroma and instantly reminds me of my favourite hot summer in England, the summer of 1976. I enjoy the moment, but suddenly and without warning, I hear a low rumble of thunder, and it echoes around me, bouncing off the surrounding hills. I am still very high up, and I can see the storm approaching – a wall of rain sweeping in at a forty-degree angle is heading towards me, and there is no shelter anywhere nearby. I struggle to put on my portable raincoat, pulling the hood up just in time, because now I am in the middle of a hailstorm, and the hail is the size of ping-pong balls. I bury my head in my hands; the pathway is now a mass of ice.

The hail turns to sleeting rain, nearby trees are bending and swaying in the wind, and the sound of it whips around me; I try to move forward, try to see if there is a house, a church or even a shrine nearby, but there is nothing, and anyway I can't see much further than a few feet in front of me. A horn beeps behind me and I jump in alarm and turn to see a large, green four-wheel-drive vehicle coming out of the gloom and I recognise it as a forestry commission vehicle. It pulls over, and the man offers me a lift. I am very relieved to see him; I am completely soaked through. I hesitate for just a few seconds, wondering if I am wise to get into his car. I tell myself that it will be fine, but just as I am removing my rucksack I see coming out of the horizontal downpour another vehicle, and it is Katie. The wipers on our old Land Rover are working furiously, and I see her waving at me and flashing the lights. As soon as she heard the storm she had set out immediately to find me. I thank the man, signal to Katie that I have seen her and dripping wet I step into the warm car; steam rises from my clothes.

The rain eases off, and we enter a narrower track which is protected by tree canopies. I find an old blanket and attempt to dry my hair with it. Suddenly, Katie screeches to a halt and I all but bang my head on the windscreen. The car stalls. A female roe deer is standing in the middle of the stony bumpy lane staring at us, then in a single bound she leaps away and is gone. At home, I change into dry clothes, and we drink hot tea. I have never been so happy to be back, safe and above all, dry.

30
THISTLE

23RD JUNE

The heat recently has been blistering. I resolve to rise early today and walk. I tried to walk yesterday, but even at four o'clock the sun was still beating down and scorchingly hot. The sun is already shining at 8.15 when I set off, but it is a bearable temperature – a pleasant 21° C. For the first time, I wear shorts and a T-shirt.

I am very keen to get out as I have a new camera and I want to see the results. I also feel a great need to walk, because in the UK the madness that is the EU Referendum is being held today. I need to take my mind off this as I feel that it is an extraordinarily ridiculous, unnecessary and dangerous endeavour, entirely without logic. I was awake in the night worrying about the outcome. I believe above all that the European Union and the United Nations have been able to maintain peace in Europe, and this is no small feat; only those who have no direct experience of war could find it attractive. I am very fearful that peace is such a fragile thing and that if we stop talking to one another dissension and conflict could easily follow. It's a terrible worry, and I am angry at the Conservative Government in the UK for calling this referendum – it will lead to division and animosity, not only between the UK and Europe but between England, Ireland and Scotland. It will also tear families apart. When I awake tomorrow I will know the result, but I already have a bad feeling about it.

I take nothing with me to do, though, by way of distraction, I have to unshackle myself from feeling the need to walk while undertaking another task. I have increasingly begun to feel that being alone with myself, my thoughts and being immersed in the sounds, smells and sights of nature is the whole point. In fact, this seems blindingly apparent to me now; I am amazed that it has taken me so many weeks to understand this fully. I want to learn to live in the moment. I find that it's not as hard as I imagined it to be, but I know that it will take practice. It is easier today as there are so many wildflowers – purple violets and Canterbury bells,[97] blue and pink comfrey,[98] delicate, orange, brown and white painted lady butterflies[99] and large iridescent blue and green dragonflies are zig-zagging around madly. There is so much to admire that my appetite for distraction is fully sated. Everywhere

I can see and hear life pulsating and exploding around me, and the fields are a bright and beautiful verdant green.

In the wintertime, it is so lifeless; a still, pale, death-like beauty that is not easily detected. But now life and nature refuse to be ignored; it is lush and warm. The ferns have grown exponentially in the last few weeks and one thistle is nearly seven feet tall. The temperature is high today, so the crickets are very active, the cows are feeding, and their cowbells fill the air.

I pause for a drink of water from my water bottle. I see movement and a very large hare skitters up the road towards me, then suddenly halts and runs away. I hear an odd knocking sound coming from a nearby tree and see that it is coming from a black redstart. I often hear this sound when I am gardening, so now I can put a name to the noise.

The apple tree is in full splendour, full green leaves, young apples appearing, just transforming themselves from a tulip shape into perfect green round fruit. The white flowers of elderberry bushes weep beside the tree and a white horse stands nearby, but despite these wondrous distractions, it feels like a cold stone is lying in the pit of my stomach. I cannot believe that the Referendum was ever called, that so little information has been given out and that I have read so many racist and ignorant posts on Facebook in the past few weeks. I am very worried and despondent.

I walk away from the tree and trudge home. When I reach the footpath that runs parallel the road, I see lying in the dead centre of the roadway a fantastically twisted piece of metal, a knotted, flattened piece of barbed wire. It has a strange, savage beauty. I collect it as my found object for the day, but as soon as I touch it, I instantly feel that this is a nothing other than a metaphor for what the UK is doing to itself on this Referendum Day. I feel the hot metal in my hand, and immediately know that when the results come in tomorrow that the vote will go against my wishes and those of most of my friends. It is a catastrophe.

31

BEETLE

3ʳᵈ JULY

It's a misty and intermittently rainy morning, so while I wait for it to clear, I do some chores in the garden. The area around the high beds has been annoying me. The grass grows out from under the pallets that hold our make-do-and-mend high beds off the ground, so I fetch the gash tin of red paint that we bought for one euro from the cellar and in the shelter of the garage I slowly paint long pieces of wood, which we also inherited. The rain ceases, so I place down some weed stop and put the newly-painted pieces of wood against the base of the high beds and drill them into place, like skirting boards. Katie nips off to the local garden centre and fetches some cheap terracotta gravel, which is made from recycled bricks. The whole job takes about three hours and costs less than twenty euros in total. I am ridiculously pleased with myself.

I make myself ready and at 3.30 pm I make to leave, but as the weather is improving Katie decides to come along with me. My morning, filled as it was with gentle rain and the act of methodical painting, has made me feel calm and meditative, but Katie is her usual ebullient self. She immediately spots wild strawberries as we climb; more and more appear and we pick the tiny, scarlet red berries and eat them as we go. Katie is a much keener forager than I am; if there is free food to be had in the hedgerows, she feels compelled to collect it – and I mean all of it. As a child growing up in this area, the hills, mountains, fields and streams were all hers. This is certainly the way a child thinks, and she, her brother and her sister roamed outside in the long hot days of summer.

Katie reverts to her childhood days immediately we are out in the landscape. As the eldest child, she was allowed to go off alone; her favourite pastime was collecting beetles and making 'houses' for them in cardboard boxes. She stored these under her bed, much to her mother's disapproval. She became fascinated by both flora and fauna, and many of her ingenious clasps and hinges are based on the mechanics of nature, and especially from the close study of beetle anatomy. This is something she has only recently divulged to me; like most artists, she is quiet about her processes and influences. Katie's childhood in Austria was a happy one, with nature and the countryside playing a significant role in the feelings of freedom that she associates with her early years. This sense of liberty contrasted strongly with the strict nature of the Catholic school she attended, one that allowed only one hour of speaking a day. We both feel a freedom in nature that is almost impossible to feel in any other aspect of our lives.

We continue to eat rather too many of the small, intensely-flavoured wild strawberries. After consuming a countless number I realise that they taste oddly synthetic, but although they have a 'chemical' taste, I know that these are chemical free as they are far from farmland. In addition to the strawberries, wild gooseberries are growing abundantly, and the hazelnut trees are leafy and strong, but they are without fruit due to the continued period of heavy frost and the snowfall at the end of April – a snowfall that was utterly unexpected, and nothing like it has occurred for over fifteen years.

The crickets seem quiet today because the temperatures are too low. There is a direct correlation between the frequency of a cricket's chirp and outside temperature. The first person to note this was Margarette W. Brooks in 1881, when she published her work *The Influence of Temperature on the Chirp of the Cricket*. Annoyingly, it wasn't until a male scientist, Amos Dolbear, published an article in 1897 entitled *The Cricket as a Thermometer* that this idea was taken seriously. By counting the number of chirps in fifteen seconds and adding thirty-seven, it is possible to get a figure which equates roughly to the outside temperature in Fahrenheit.

As we rise the landscape becomes more open, and there is a little more sun. The ground is much warmer, and we do begin, at last, to hear the crickets tuning up as the temperature rises.

It is cloudy for most of the rest of the way, but just after seven o'clock we are heartened by a sudden burst of sunshine. At the highest point of the walk, we sit on our bench and eat shortbread and chocolate. Nearby, dozens of swifts and swallows fly over a huge dung heap, swooping low and into the field opposite. One swallow flies very close to us, skimming the gravel as he whizzes past our feet skilfully catching tiny insects and devouring them without missing a beat. I have never been so close to a swallow – instead of being just a forked dart shape in the sky it is a real textured feathered thing, all steely black and rufous tawny orange. I am in awe, but Katie sits swinging her legs, smoking roll-up cigarettes and pointing out every swallow and swift volubly, sometimes poking me in the ribs to make sure I am listening. I am attempting to write up my notes, and begin to laugh. It is undoubtedly a very different experience having Katie as a walking companion. I put away my notebook and enjoy having such joyous company on this beautiful day.

On the way back home, Katie decides that we should take a shortcut. In my experience shortcuts invariably fail to reduce the length of a walk, but despite this, I agree. We walk directly up a very steep hill instead of taking the gently meandering winding path. It's quite a hike, it's almost perpendicular and there is a sweet smell of pine sap filling the air which we enjoy, but unfortunately, the foresters have been out clearing pine trees and as we progress we find that the whole path is strewn with broken branches and huge bare tree trunks. We have to clamber over them, and it takes us twenty minutes of hard climbing to get to the top. We can see the path that we need to take, but it is completely blocked by even larger tree trunks. It is now late, and dusk is upon us, but we have no choice but to scale back down the hillside; this is even harder than the walk up, as we have no way to brake and have to charge from one tree trunk after another, bumping against them to stop ourselves from tumbling down the hillside. Luckily, I am only carrying my camera snuggly in its case. Katie, however, insists on bringing the bunch of wildflowers and vegetation she has collected on the way. Not content with having a handful of dandelions and spiky thistles, halfway down the hill she also finds a wine glass with a broken stem. She is very excited about this and insists on picking it up, asking me to take charge of it. When I consider my usual solitary and pensive walks, I have to admit that carrying broken glass while running vertically downhill is much more thrilling.

32
Hermaphroditism

15ᵀᴴ JULY

I have been desperate to walk all week, but we have had several
days and nights of thunder, lightning and heavy rain, followed
by the fear of hailstorms and possible landslides. The last days
have also been cold as well as stormy. Forty-five people are killed

yearly by lightning in Austria alone, so keen as I am to continue with my walks, I have been forced to remain safely inside. But today, I jump out of bed and immediately see that the weather is good enough for me to attempt the walk. My heart leaps a little at the thought. It's a pleasant 18.5° C, a little windy and the sun seems to be there, although it wants to hide periodically. I wait to see if it will improve even more.

* * *

A few months ago we decided to open our spare rooms up, as we have lots of space, and we like to have company occasionally. We have been quite successful, and so far we have found our Airbnb guests to be charming and friendly. We've shared our barbecues with our visitors and even taken single sojourners on trips and outings with us. Two friends who were travelling together from Holland even helped us to clean our car, which we found delightful, so later in the evening when it was still and hot we invited them to walk the few hundred yards to the nearby church. We walked in bright moonlight and hidden in a little basket we carried a small hip flask filled with schnapps and four tiny glasses. On arrival we sat on the church steps enjoying the cool of the evening and raised our glasses to toast the Man in the Moon.

Yesterday, however, I awoke to find one of our male guests happily sitting on the old sofa outside our bedroom window as I wandered around inside practically naked. So while I wait for the weather to improve, I busy myself by converting an old headboard shaped like a gothic ogee window into a privacy screen for our balcony, in order to separate our bedroom from the guest rooms. I go in search of materials and find a huge pot of burgundy paint in the cellar. I set about painting the panels and raiding my art supplies; I discover more old paint and cover the round corbels on the three summits with yellow-gold metallic paint. I am pleased with the final result.

Katie's daughter has come to stay with her two children, and after a lunch of fresh mushrooms on toast gathered by them from the nearby woods I feel that I cannot procrastinate any longer and at 2.45 pm I depart.

* * *

I decide not to hurry but to walk steadily and try to be as alert as possible to my surroundings. The first thing of note is once again the magnificent lime tree by the Leonhardikirche; it is in full flower and lit up by the sun. The lime tree has 'perfect' flowers; this does not refer to their beauty but to the flowers' bisexual qualities. Lime tree flowers are 'hermaphroditic'. Hermaphroditism is another topic that I find fascinating. One of the most beautiful and memorable things that I have seen on my many visits to the museums of Europe was the *Sleeping Hermaphroditus* at the National Museum in Rome, which is a mid-second century AD Roman copy in marble of an even more ancient Greek Bronze original, now lost. I remember approaching the recumbent figure, believing that I was looking at yet another representation of Venus. I was drawn to her pale marble skin and the delicate arch of her back. Her eyes were closed. either in sleep or in pleasure. Her hair was plaited into a bun to show the curve of her elegant neck. Resting her head on her forearm, she looked peaceful, restful and essentially like any other depiction of the Goddess, but as I passed around the figure, it became clear that this was not Venus at all – because in addition to her superbly crafted female attributes she also had male genitalia. The piece is so finely balanced and is a celebration of both the female and the male form.[100]

The Greeks and the Romans seemed to like such depictions, and this is not the only existing example. In both art and literature, there has long been a desire to explore this theme. In nature writing and botany the lime tree flower with its hermaphroditic ability is termed 'perfect'. For humans, gender fluidity and sexual identity is a battleground, and this seems strange to me. We seem to have lost the ability to embrace this topic with sanguinity.

For generations now in the Western world, most cultures have supported a strictly binary view of gender; irreversible drug treatments and surgical interventions are increasingly popular ways to 'fix' gender 'problems'. But what if binary opposition wasn't afforded so much significance? What if we tried harder to recognise that the sexuality and gender of many people, in fact perhaps most people, could be seen to be on a scale? Long before I clearly understood my own sexuality, I became fascinated by androgyny and the in-between space that it occupies. But this is not a conversation that the average person wants to have. It is yet another reason why I like walking, as it is not a gendered pastime. Perhaps I have to thank Dorothy Wordsworth and Mary Barker for this, for it was their ascent of England's tallest peak, Scafell Peak (standing at 3,200 feet) in the Lake District on 7th October 1818, unaccompanied by male escort, that changed so much for female walkers. Furthermore, Dorothy Wordsworth's extant description of the climb is among the earliest surviving accounts of this feat by a man or a woman. Mountaineering was an unusual activity at the time, and women walking by themselves were frowned upon. Today, thankfully, walking is seen as an acceptable pastime for both genders, and the more I walk, the more I take comfort in nature's ability to accept as ordinary and unremarkable the extraordinary and the remarkable. A hermaphroditic flower is of no consequence – it just is.

* * *

The hedgerows are full of the most amazing flora of all kinds. Mostly the farmers seem to leave roadside verges untouched, although the beautiful wild lupins have been mown down. At the side of the path, by the multi-coloured, wooden beehives, I see a bank of perhaps fifty elegant, tall yellow and orange verbascum.[101] Here they are growing wild, but the verbascum is part of the figwort family, and it is often grown in Austria more for its medicinal properties than for its beauty as the tall architectural plant so loved by garden designers. It can be used to make tea infusions or topical creams, for the treatment of disorders of the respiratory tract or the skin.

In amongst the verbascum, pale lilac Canterbury bells[102] are growing, and near the barbed wire fence delicate, pale blue five-petalled or meadow cranesbill[103] run riot, their spiky leaves seeming to cut into the surrounding long grass. I walk through a sea of what looks like lime-yellow green cow parsley, but although related to cow parsley I am fairly certain that I am looking at the more delicate blooms of sweet fennel. I wish I were brave enough to trust my ability to identify wildflowers with absolute certainty as I could easily harvest some fennel seeds, but I am not brave enough, knowing that many of the species of the Apiaceae family are toxic. There is a strong possibility that I could end up picking poisonous hemlock, water hemlock or fool's parsley. I definitely need a few more years in the field.

When I am asked to give one of my Shakespeare talks, Katie makes Tudor Jumble Biscuits, which she flavours with fennel seeds or anise, so it would be lovely to collect my own seeds. The recipe we use is from the sixteenth century, when anise was a luxury as it was imported from the Mediterranean or even Asia.

It wasn't cultivated widely until Shakespeare's lifetime in Europe, but here it is growing apparently wild and free for the taking.

I begin to feel a little cold, so I sip hot coffee from my flask, and a eat a fresh piece of Kärntner Reindling, a local speciality bread-like cake, which is made from a yeast dough which has been rolled in sugar, cinnamon, raisins and butter. It's rather like a drier version of an English lardy cake, but it has a distinctive hole at its centre. Kärntner Reindling is excellent fayre for the walker.

The crickets are less voluble today, quietened by the cooler temperatures. It's much easier to walk when the air is fresh and cool, but it is much less beautiful. There is much evidence of disruption from the recent storms; gullies by the side of the road are stony, and the soil has been washed away by the torrential rain of the last few days. The ravines, rivers and streams are full to bursting. The sides of the paths and narrow roads have collapsed, but I am impressed to see that emergency repairs have already taken place and I walk alongside red and white striped tape attached to metal poles to warn walkers and the occasional motorist that the track is not safe.

This reminder that the ground beneath our feet is never as secure as we think it is inevitably leads me to return to my worries about the recent referendum in the UK. Until a few days before it took place I was so sure that it would not result in the UK leaving, but now I feel like the ground has moved beneath my feet. After the shock announcement of the result I signed myself up for several twenty-four-hour newsfeed websites, scouring the internet for information, for answers, for an explanation, but I found none. I am not cheered by the appearance of the main instigators of the shabbily conducted 'Leave' campaign appearing on television looking pale and nervous – more defeated than victorious, and without any kind of plan.

Every day since the day of the Referendum I have signed at least five petitions asking the British Government to reverse the decision, but I know that it is futile. I feel bereaved, angry, sad, disillusioned and alienated. I have never been patriotic, and I actively avoid any kind of nationalism. But since I moved to Austria, I have been asked to articulate the things I love about the UK, and I have proudly defended and congratulated Britain: 'Britain is tolerant' and 'Britain celebrates diversity and difference.' But now, I feel as if I have been set adrift on an ocean of uncertainty with no map, no compass and in a leaky lifeboat. I no longer recognise my own country. I cannot bear to accept that racism is a cancer that is spreading almost unabated in Britain and beyond, and I am most concerned about the fragile peace that both the EU and the United Nations affords and fear that it may not hold in the future.

I cannot easily force my way out from beneath my fug of worry. Thankfully I see a small, yellow plastic bottle which has become half-filled with soil in the recent storms, and it looks so pathetic and forlorn that I collect it as my found object for the day. When I get home, it is past seven o'clock, and even though I am tired, I show my find to Katie. She realises that I am far from happy, so she takes the plastic bottle to her workshop and brings me back a pencil drawing, a design for a necklace made from the plastic bottle inspired by African tribal jewellery. I feel that this is the best use for an old, yellow discarded plastic bottle that I have ever encountered and know that I could never have imagined such an artful use for such an object. Despite this, I find it very hard to be positive, but I satisfy myself with Katie's act of loving kindness – her transmutation of base plastic to something useful and pretty is the only shred of positivity I can muster today.

33

POPPY

20ᵀᴴ JULY

It is already very warm when I begin at 8.45 am, and the temperature will rise to at least 25° C by mid-morning. It's hard to describe how beautiful the dewdrops look on the green, green grass, lit up by an already powerful sun. Mark Forsyth, who has an in-depth knowledge and fascination for the lost words of the English language, notes in his book *The Horologicon* that in Norfolk mornings such as this are sometimes referred to as cobweb mornings, 'when all the cobwebs are spangled with dew and gleaming in the misty hedgerows'.[104] The whole landscape is alive with these ghostly, dew-bediamonded labyrinths. As I continue I seem to have entered a museum of webs: open, vertical, horizontal, and three-dimensional, the latter lacing around and looped over dandelion seed heads or dripping off red-stalked weeds. These insect traps range from the perfectly circular to the shaggy and chaotic, low-lying or mid-height, clinging to the spurs of barbed wire. I take some photographs, but soon realise that photographing cobwebs is much more difficult than it seems, as the camera cannot focus on that which has so little substance. One large cobweb is draped across a thistle in bud. I snap one good image, and when I zoom in to look more closely I realise that every bud is encased in the tiniest of cobwebs nestling inside the thistle buds and these are covered in minuscule droplets of dew, but this was entirely invisible to the naked eye.

The beautiful cornflowers that I photographed only five days ago are completely gone, mown away. The crop field nearest to our house, which last year had a magnificent harvest of nine-foot high maize, will this year have wheat, as the farmers ring the changes to lessen the burden on the soil. This newly-sown wheat is just beginning to show signs of growth.

I have never seen the area by the river looking so eerily strange. An apple tree, which I have never even noticed before, stands, or rather lurks, in the middle of my field of vision; it looks like a painted silhouette. There is nothing behind it but blue-grey mist, and running in front of the tree the fence posts stand out like a row of blackened and broken teeth. The scene has a stark beauty, but the monochromatic film noir quality is unnerving; it feels like November, not July. But despite the mist, it soon becomes smoulderingly hot, and I need to stop at every bench to rest. By noon, I am sitting on the bench where I always stop for some refreshment, and I realise that it is still unusually quiet: the crickets are silent, the birds absent and the cows completely noiseless. Even the few wasps and flies that drift by are lackadaisical.

The sky is of a piercingly dark blue, but voluminous cumulus clouds lie in a ridge hovering over the distant mountains, a heat-haze rises up and partly obscures the horizon. A flash of red in the near distance catches my eye, and I approach it and see that a single poppy is flowering. I realise that I have never before seen any poppies on this walk. On a recent trip to Hungary we saw so many fields of red poppies that at first we mistook them for the bright red roofs of villages. Before we drove back home, we collected a mere handful of seeds from scrubland beside the road near Lake Balaton. Katie kept them and later carefully prepared a large bed and sowed the seeds. Our favourite part of the garden is now this sea of bright poppies, which flower day after day in endless drifts.

The poppy is my favourite flower, and it saddens me that it is so closely associated with war and conflict. The reasons are as much scientific as cultural. Poppies 'popped' up on battlefields because the seeds need light to grow, and can lie dormant in the soil for at least eighty years without blooming, but when the soil is disturbed they receive enough light to germinate, and they begin to bloom almost immediately. During the First World War acres of arable land were torn up by miles of trenches and scarred by bombs and artillery fire. The fighting was especially fierce in Ypres in Belgium, and the fields known as Flanders Fields became littered with poppies, and inevitably, seemingly overnight common or 'corn' poppies appeared. The association between conflict and the poppy was further cemented when, in 1915, a Canadian doctor, John McCrae, saw poppies growing abundantly near one of Flanders Fields' mass cemeteries and penned his infamous poem *In Flanders Fields*, which instantly became seminal. The poppy became a universal symbol of war and conflict, not merely because of its connection with Flanders but because it grows throughout the whole of Europe, the United States, Asia, and Africa.

I have conflicting emotions about the ubiquity of McCrae's poem. The stanza 'In Flanders fields the poppies blow, Between the crosses, row on row' has become so famous that it is has made it impossible to liberate the poppy from its association with carnage and death, and the wearing of poppies on Remembrance Day, 11th November, has become in recent years a politicised battleground: 'to wear or not to wear?' The extreme right has co-opted the poppy. Facebook ads posted by hate groups like 'Britain First' state, without any basis in fact, that 'Muslim scum' that don't support the poppy appeal should be 'sent home.' I find this profoundly worrying and deeply ironic, as it's precisely this kind of rhetoric that is known to have led to Hitler's ability to galvanise the poverty-stricken German people, unfairly crushed and punished after the First World War, against all and any the Nazis considered to be outsiders.

Remembrance for sacrifices made is vitally important, but as my father commented towards the end of his life, if perhaps Remembrance Day was renamed Remorseful Day it might alter the focus. For him, the parades, the uniforms and the medals, combined with Kipling's poetry and Elgar's powerful Nimrod, created a dangerous cocktail, so potent it can render those who take part unable to acknowledge the horrors of war. More problematically, it allows heads of state to make public displays of contrition which often serve to further their bellicose ambitions. And any politician wishing to stand apart from these displays is seen to be unpatriotic and even traitorous. In reality, the ordinary person does not create war and does not want war, but Remembrance Day anaesthetises and blinds us, reducing our ability to resist.

We grow poppies of every hue and colour in our garden, but we especially favour the white poppy. Taking our lead from the Peace Pledge Union, a pacifist campaigning organisation that began its life in 1934, we plant them in drifts and many people comment on them, but mostly to mention that they have never seen them before. The red poppy is so iconic, and so is its link to war. This is strange, as war is the ultimate destroyer, but paradoxically perhaps because it is such a vital force brimming and buzzing with activity, it is generally perceived to be exciting, as the hundreds of war films stand testament. Peace is more like the absence of something, so white poppies seem unnecessary because peace often seems simply to exist without the need for an external agency, so why do we need to campaign for it? Red poppies, on the other hand, stand for something and come loaded with meaning and make white poppies, which many people have never even seen, seem both literally and figuratively pale in comparison.

I stop to collect my thoughts; I always feel terribly sad and angry when I think about war and the loss of so much life. I force myself to breathe in the wonderful pine smell that surrounds me and admire a green and black striped dragonfly; as if to echo the dragonfly, a green and black stone lies nearby, and this becomes this week's found object. I strain to hear the clang of cowbells, and begin to feel a little better. I close my eyes and rest for a few minutes leaning against a large woodpile. I feel my heartbeat becoming more regular and I am enjoying the sunshine when, suddenly, two young bulls appear and make straight for me. I am terrified, so I duck behind the woodpile for protection. As quickly as the youngsters arrive, they stomp off. The farmer and owner of the apple tree arrives a moment later; he had obviously been leading the bulls, but they must have got away from him. He looks flushed and hot, and when his wife and son arrive a few moments later, they also look alarmed. It's only the third time I've seen the farmer, so I ask him in German how he is, and he replies 'erschöpft' which means exhausted. I nod in sympathy.

I walk a little behind them, and when I reach the tree I gesture to the farmer, asking if I can have one of the apples; he nods his approval. I am pleased because I so wanted to have one the last time that I walked here but did not like to help myself.

Many of the fields have been denuded of their crops; the fields have been ploughed or have been mown to perfection. Several others have become hastily-made temporary paddocks, and now pale golden horses gallop freely. The rough-hewn timber posts are draped with electric or even barbed wire in places. I have noticed, though, that horses are more valued than cows; barbed wire is always on the outside of the fences when used to encage horses, on the inside for other livestock. Another factor may be that cows like to rub against barbed wire and when they do the barbs are pushed further into the supporting posts, so the fence becomes stronger rather than falling over.

I am hot and tired, and have no water left. I was going to keep my treasured apple, but instead, I place it on a lichen-topped fence post photograph it and then sit on the bank and take a bite, it's sweet, delicious and fragrant. I don't think I have ever tasted a better apple in my life.

34

suspension

24ᵀᴴ JULY

It is six o'clock in the morning and it's already 15.5° C. It will rise to 30° C today. As it is Sunday, there is no one on the horizon, not even a farmer working. A half-moon sits in the middle of a pale limpid, blue sky. It would be near silent, but the internal combustion engine is almost ever present: only a few moments ago a man in black leathers but no helmet and riding a large motorbike throbbed past me, nodded, smiled broadly and turned back the way he had come. But as I climb, such noises too will diminish.

At the moment it feels cool, as the whole landscape is cloaked in a haze-fire of mist.[105] The huge meadow by the river presents me with a completely new and amazing sight: there are hundreds of lacy, gossamer cobwebs looping themselves from flower to flower, from leaf to leaf, as far as the eye can see. Most likely the builders of these fantastical silk towers are spiders of the family Theridiidae.[106] As I look around at this haphazard collection of almost invisible lines of silk I do not see them as cobwebs produced by spiders; to me they represent something else. My thoughts return to theatre and my endless fascination for the oddities and vagaries of live performance. When I was completing my MA in Shakespeare Studies, Coleridge was often mentioned for his three-word observation the 'suspension of disbelief,' a phrase so frequently quoted that it has become a mantra. Coleridge was talking about the need for a writer to imbue his or her tale with 'human interest and a semblance of truth' [so that] the reader can suspend judgement concerning the implausibility of the narrative.[107] But it is the reader who must have 'poetic faith.' To use his phrase 'the suspension of disbelief' in the context of a theatrical production seems to me to be a little more problematic. A lone reader communes with the writer on a personal level and can read and re-read passages at will, and the relationship is based on one mind connecting with another mind on an individual basis. It is much more difficult to ask the many members of a theatre audience to simultaneously suspend disbelief, and in my experience, this happens rarely. To use the field of looping, shimmering cobwebs as an analogy, when a production works the actors have managed to spin a web and cast their lines out to the audience; the more lines are caught the more the performance rings true and succeeds, the more the audience is captivated and the more they can suspend disbelief. It is possible to create a field of tangible energy that binds all within its embrace. Perhaps you have been in the audience when this has happened? Or more likely you have been to a matinee performance on a wet Wednesday afternoon when this most decidedly has not happened. In the theatre, when these silk lines are, metaphorically, caught by many hundreds of people, the performance becomes transcendental. It might be more helpful to suggest that actors are asking for the audience not to suspend disbelief, but to hold belief in suspension. Indeed, the Chorus in the opening prologue of *Henry V* urges the audience to 'Work, work your thoughts' and to:

> *Think when we talk of horses, that you see them*
> *Printing their proud hoofs i' the receiving earth;*
> *For 'tis your thoughts that now must deck our kings,*
> *Carry them here and there; jumping o'er times,*
> *Turning the accomplishment of many years*
> *Into an hour-glass:*[108]

Shakespeare could not put galloping horses on the stage at the Globe Theatre, so the Chorus urges the audience to imagine them.

In the several hundred plays that I have seen, I have witnessed only a very few such mystical moments. The most memorable was a production at Malvern Festival Theatre of *Uncle Vanya*. I still have the poster from the production. It was Monday 19th August 1996, the temperature, unusually for England, was a very hot 29.5° C, and it was probably much hotter in the auditorium itself. There had been some excitement and anticipation about this particular professional touring production directed by Bill Bryden being transferred from Chichester Theatre to Malvern before an extensive tour. The cast was a stellar one: Derek Jacobi, as the eponymous Uncle Vanya, Trevor Eve, Alec McCowen, Imogen Stubbs, Frances Barber and Peggy Mount. The theatre was full to capacity and tickets were almost impossible to get, but as I had not long since appeared in a production by Malvern Theatre Players of Peter Schaffer's *Amadeus* in the same theatre, I was able to cadge a day-of-performance ticket.

The house bell rang, and as we took our seats the air was thick with heat and anticipation. The stifling heat of the Russian summer, mentioned in the first few lines of the play, was replicated in the theatre, so as soon as Dr Astrov (Trevor Eve) said 'No, I don't drink vodka every day, and besides, it is too hot now,' a low rumble of laughter, the laughter of recognition, went around the auditorium. Trevor Eve had thrown out his first silky cobwebby line, and it had been caught by a great many of us. Very quickly the atmosphere became electric. The primary current of energy continued to be provided by Trevor Eve as Astrov and Imogen Stubbs, playing Yelena. The sexual tension between them grew in intensity, and each actor hit their marks and cues perfectly time after time. The web of connections built and increased until it felt like each and every member of the audience was holding their line of silk and willing it not to break. There was not a sound in the auditorium as the players maintained a unity of suspended belief in the performance. Derek Jacobi seemed to have caught connections from his fellow actors, and he spun out his lines adroitly. Taking a swig from his glass, he made his voice crack, as if he had been surprised by the strong and fiery nature of the liquor; I had never seen or heard anything like it before. There was a faint collective gasp from the audience, but Jacobi did not break the spell. It was a masterly moment.

Having had that experience I begged for a ticket for the following evening and returned, but the magic did not happen a second time, it was utterly mysterious.

Only on one occasion did a moment of magic happen that I was personally involved with. I once attended rehearsals for a production of *The Revengers' Tragedy* by Thomas Middleton, for which I had adapted a new script. As one, all the actors sitting in the auditorium awaiting their rehearsal slot suddenly stopped whispering, completing crosswords or reading, and lifted their heads. We were all witnessing the moment at which the actor playing Vindice had mastered his performance. The gossamer silk line from him to us was being held, and we all instinctively knew at that moment that the production would succeed. The director and I also knew that no more blocking or alteration of that scene were necessary.

* * *

I have been struggling for some weeks to come up with a way to describe the magic that can happen in a remarkable performance or rehearsal; that a field of cobwebs on a hot July day in Austria should help provide me with an answer is, I admit, as strange as it is fantastical. The entire walk was lost to me as I considered this idea and mulled it over. All I can recall is that the early morning mist, giving way to oppressive heat, the green fecundity of the landscape and the piercing blue sky all happened to me as if in a dream state.

35
Anniversary

31ST JULY

It is the first anniversary of my father's funeral today. I look at my diary entry for 31st July last year and the memory of that day, a day that I was so dreading, and it floods back into my mind. I was wrong to fear it so much; it was more bearable than I could ever have imagined. I recorded my immediate reaction to it at the time:

Imagine a perfect English summer's day. A large field newly mown for hay, the hay only partly gathered in so that it is quite thick underfoot. Imagine swifts and a parcel of linnets taking to flight. A buzzard drifting lazily and high in a blue, blue sky. Imagine a rickety, yet quaint hay cart being led by four men in smart suits along a close-cropped path to a single point in a vast empty meadow. Imagine about fifty people walking in the warm sunshine following the cart. Some are talking quietly in small groups, some walk alone. Some hide a few tears. Butterflies flutter by. This was the scene as we laid my father to rest. The wonderful Malvern Hills in the distance, a church spire far off in the landscape and hundreds of trees framing the field; such a perfect place of peace and contentment for anyone and especially suitable for an artist and ardent nature lover.

I cannot think of a better way to mark the day than by walking quietly and alone. My father invested in me a love of nature and I feel closer to him when I am in nature. I feel lighter and calmer today: all our fiscal ties with the UK are now cut, we neither of us own any property there (well, we no longer have properties that we lived in and believed that we owned, but in fact the bank was only ever going to be the winner). Of course, this lack of property in the UK may be a problem in the long term, but for now, it feels like a liberation. All my life I have been living under the misapprehension that mortgages, bills, debts, loans and responsibilities are status symbols and moreover, that one is obliged to be saddled with these things, that they are the mark of success. But I am enjoying my new-found feeling of freedom much more. In addition, my comedy about Shakespeare and the printing of the First Folio which I wrote some years ago has been accepted for publication. I feel happy, and frankly this is an emotion that I am completely unused to.

* * *

It is only ten o'clock, but it is already 20° C and will rise to 25.5° C; however there is a welcome breeze. I get organised, and within half an hour I'm ready to leave. As I round the first corner, I see that there are two small birds of prey flying very fast and high in the sky. It is not difficult to identify them; they are small and sleek. I can clearly see their orange-red plumage – two kestrels. They are in a fierce territorial battle right under the Leonhardikirche, the spire of which stands out vividly. A high-pitched screeching accompanies the battle throughout. Their orange-red bodies are clearly highlighted against a pale blue sky, which is streaked only with wispy white cirrus clouds and does not mar my view in any way. The more dominant bird breaks and flies away triumphantly, believing he has shaken off his adversary, but a few moments later the second kestrel returns to fight again, and I witness a duel worthy of the so-called 'Knights of the Sky' in the First World War. Then there is more screeching, and suddenly they are gone. If I had left home a moment later, I would have missed them.

Aside from battling birds of prey, it is a very quiet and peaceful Sunday. New-born calves are sunbathing happily. A rich aroma of pine sap fills the air as in the field by the river a great many large conifers have been felled, and a massive wood pile has been created. I am glad that I did not see this happening, as I hate seeing trees being felled.

Just before I reach my refreshment bench the temperature becomes almost unbearably hot. It is somewhere in the region of 27° C in the shade, but I am walking in full sun; I have never walked in such high temperatures. I spy a little mountain stream and soak my hands in it, taking the cold water and dripping it onto my arms. It feels wonderfully refreshing. Several swifts fly past me at close range as I crouch down to reach the stream. Luckily, the sun goes behind a cloud for a short while, and I enjoy a few moments of relief from the heat. I watch a sparrow take a dust bath in a patch of dry earth by a farmyard entrance, and I see some smoke from a bonfire rising. I take out my notebook and write:

One hundred and twenty swifts swish, perch, feed and turn, flash and burn. Catching supper on the wing, chase and spin, dive and grin – bubble-blowing cries of summer.
While the good-old, boring-old, wonderful-old sparrow
Simply takes a dust bath in the soil.
Air meets earth.
Bonfire blazes;
Hot rain arrives ere long.

I leave the birds to their labours and reach the wooded part of the walk and, as I have been trained to do by Katie, I search for edible fungi. I see little patches of mustard yellow chanterelles (here known as Eierschwammerl, as they resemble scrambled eggs – Eier means egg) and I fill a small bag with them. As I clamber back down the bank, I notice the first blackberries growing. They are at this stage very small and green, but this is evidence that autumn will soon be upon us and I must enjoy the last few weeks of summer as much as I can.

I like to time my arrival back home for about 4.30 pm, because that way I can legitimately relax and enjoy the rest of the day, it being, thankfully, too late to begin any real work in the garden or in my study. I sit in our little pavilion with a glass of wine from the vineyards of nearby Burgenland, and admire the view. I think of my father. As I look out on pine-clad hills and a stretch of verdantly green grass, I think of his last resting place and know that we are at least sharing the same blue sky.

36
SHORN

5ᵀᴴ AUGUST

It's a little cooler today, expected to rise to a maximum of 22°C. I set out fairly early at 10.20, as storms are expected this afternoon. Thick dark grey clouds are relieved by only a few patches of blue, but there is sunshine too. The high, golden wheat fields that I photographed in July must be nearly ready to crop. I know that the time for harvesting must soon be approaching because ripe seed heads droop towards the ground and many of them are so heavy that they are kissing the soil. In comparison, the new crop of green wheat in the adjacent field is only a few inches tall. Their erect stems stand up proudly, and so the process begins again. The twenty horseradish plants growing wild outside on the verge as I pass out into open countryside have also gone.

In every field there is a farmer on a tractor harvesting, and the crows circle, knowing full well that today they will find a ready meal. There is a reek of silage fertiliser coming from the fields. The vast field by the stream, which throughout July was a fecund multiplicity of wildflowers, has been shorn and now has a 'number one' haircut. The field is now a closely-cropped swathe of velvet green, as tidy as any military parade ground. I cannot help feeling taken aback by this. Where Katie and I recently collected wild mint from the bank by the little stream, not a single flower remains. But they have laid their seeds, and they will return next year.

The huge house-sized woodpile that I saw last week is represented by nothingness; it too has gone to be turned into product. Nearby, I watch as a red and yellow machine, inscribed with the words 'Woody to Go' (in English) trundles along noisily, completely and effortlessly eating tree trunks as it goes; it denudes long, narrow trunks of pine of their branches, and spews out from the back peeled, creamy white logs with blistered, copper-red knots which look like fresh wounds. It's a painful sight to see. In the next field a large lime-green combine harvester is trundling along methodically, its drone irritating, yet so regular that it seems comforting. There are women in the fields; they are dressed only in shorts and sleeveless tops. It is their job to rake the fresh green hay or heave large obstacles, sticks and the like away from the machinery. The women seem to have to undertake the more laborious tasks, I notice. The sun is hot, and the work is both tedious and difficult. I cheer inwardly when I see that in the distance there is one female tractor driver, a rare occurrence; it is the men who usually get the shaded seat in some kind of machine and the women who labour on foot as they have done for a millennium.

The hedgerows on the way to Schiefling are bare and cut back. As I rise higher, I see that here the wildflowers have been deliberately saved from cutting; my heart lifts at the thought. Growing in the cool of the pine wood is a stunning example of a wild angelica.[109] It towers above me. I have never seen anything like this healthy, large and strikingly beautiful specimen. It has little balls of white flowers that branch out from a central umbrella like little lollipops. When I moved to a small flat near Stratford-upon-Avon so that I could finish my Shakespeare studies, I inherited a garden and a small crop of angelica, but the soil was poor and it never grew well. My childhood was somewhat marred by a delicacy known as candied angelica. In the 1970s this was served as a decoration on puddings and seen as a luxury - a sophisticated delight. As it tastes a bit like celery, even boiling it in sugar does not turn it into candy, so I learnt to avoid it. In Finland, much more sensibly, it is treated like a vegetable and the stems are eaten raw. The leaves can be used as a fragrant herb in salads and soups. As is usual, in Austria it is yet another wild flower that is used for medicinal purposes: the root ground to make a tea for the treatment of the gastrointestinal tract disorders, fevers, infections, and respiratory problems.

I am quietly admiring and photographing the wild angelica when I feel a presence. I turn my head slightly and see two small fallow deer calmly grazing very close by. I watch them for a short time, holding my breath and not daring to move, but they soon become nervous, and in a few moments they leap away, and the thick wood devours them. More wondrous nature appears in the form of a buzzard which slowly circles overhead.[110] I long for a really good pair of binoculars, but like my ancestors I make do with my good eyesight, feeble as it is by a bird's standards. I climb a little higher and see cows, their bells jingling a little. A small calf lying nestled in among them is surrounded by wildflowers; they all look very hot, and I wonder that they don't seek the shade of the fir trees.

There is a reek of manure in the fields, which becomes intensely sweet and pungent as I climb. I too am hot, so I bathe my hands in the mountain stream. At my favourite bench, I spot a single solitary swift, which flies low: low-flying swifts signal a drop in atmospheric pressure and presage rain. A welcome breeze whips up, and knowing that a storm will surely come, I quicken my pace. As I cross the old moss-covered stone bridge I can hear the brook babbling and crashing. A black ewe and her baby lamb skip away, the latter bleeping quietly, and scamper into their small roughly-made wooden and bark shelter, which sags under the weight of a corrugated iron roof. I continue down the wooded, winding lane, and note with sadness that ten immense fir trees have been felled. There is a sickly and overpowering smell of pine sap, and the debris of the carnage is spread around everywhere.

I return home just in time. The storm begins almost immediately, and the rain comes down in torrents. I am warm, relaxed and sleepy, but I am a little traumatised to see that so many of the wildflowers have been uprooted, and also think of the ten tall trees that now lie felled. I know that in truth the landscape looks as it does because it is managed; it has to create an income for the farmers. This is capitalism at work, and capitalism is brutal. But I know that there are ways to work more closely with nature, by employing more ecological methodologies, ones that are less brutal, and this is happening in Germany and beyond. I have to hope that more ways to consider long-term goals and chose preservation rather than destruction are being considered.

37

sunflowers

14ᵀᴴ AUGUST

It is hot, 24°C, very sunny and likely to become hotter. It is so, so quiet. A typically peaceful Sunday in Austria: not even lawn mowing is allowed on this day. All is still, and it is a stunningly beautiful day. The air is filled with the sound of buzzing bees, and high in the distant sky a wake of buzzards circle, occasionally screeching to one another. There is a rasping sound as a gentle breeze rustles the trees. Even the smaller birds, usually so vocal, are quiet. An old but pristine vintage tractor painted turquoise blue stands outside the veterinary practice, the engine ticking as it cools. From the garage, the sound of someone quietly practising the accordion fills the air. The light is dappled in the glade approaching the first crop field; the stream is just a gentle trickle, and the bells of the church dedicated to Saint Leonhard ring out: a deeply sonorous, solemn sound marking the midday hour. So begins my thirtieth walk.

The peace is shattered by a gaggle of farmers; every farmer is wearing a traditional Carinthian brown jacket with green detailing and a felt hat. They are driving a stream of vintage tractors, green, red and bright blue, along the main B78 road. I wave, and they wave cheerily back as I raise my camera to photograph them. I have noticed that during the period when I was using a mobile phone to record my life here, subjects rarely responded to me, so quickly have we all become conditioned to think that someone raising a phone to snap an image is only of interest to the photographer. But now, when I raise my half-decent camera, I find that my subjects pose, wave and immediately understand that I want a photograph of them with their prize possession. The narrative of the image includes them in the story; we take pictures with our phones because we want to tell our personal stories, but a photographer with a camera is likely to be documenting something bigger than themselves. It has made it easier for me, for my subjects know that I am interested in documenting them and that I wish to be inclusive and focus on them as individuals.

The somewhat scruffy woodpile by the river has gone. It was lopsided, with a slightly sagging black felt roof; now there is just an indentation on the earth where it once stood. I used to like to sit on the uncomfortable homemade bench and lean against the seasoned wood. I look for a moment at what was so recently a lustrous yellow cornfield; it too has been reduced to stubble. I feel a little sad about the loss of these wondrous sights, but the multi-coloured beehives that separate me from the rusty barbed wire fence are cheery, and I can hear that the bees are alive and thumping with life.

Out of the corner of my eye, I see an elderly woman calling her dog. I turn to look, and I see not only her lilac shirt shining through the hedgerow but a vast field full of towering yellow sunflowers, framed against a vivid blue sky. Perhaps a thousand blooms reach high into the air, tall, elegant, magnificent. Even though they are hidden behind a scrub of alder – or an aller-grove[111] as they call it on Exmoor – I cannot imagine how I have missed them before. Jumping up, I skip down the path, like a child, past the broken gate and into the field. I have never been so close to a field of sunflowers before, and they tower above me; I feel like the small child in Claude Monet's painting *The Artist's Garden at Vétheuil*, dwarfed by their immensity and overwhelmed by them.[112] Monet cultivated a garden in Vétheuil and in this work he depicts a honey-coloured path running through the centre of the painting; tall nodding sunflowers flank the path. The dominant complementary colours – the vivid blue of the sky and the yellow-orange sunflowers – are joyful and vibrant. It's clear that Monet painted this work quickly, dabbing the paint onto the canvas; this creates a sense of movement, and the flowers seem to be stirring in the warmth of a welcome summer breeze.

Crates and blankets are strewn around, abandoned by the sunflower pickers, who must have gone to shelter from the heat of the day. I think of Van Gogh and how the sunflower paintings he created for Gaugin were so full of hope and love, and my spirits are immediately lifted. Not more than a few hundred yards from the field of yellow, I encounter a new and enormous woodpile – it stands as high as any house in the area. A zipper of redstarts is pecking at the hundred insects that the newly-cut wood is host to.[113] I am in awe thinking that a short while ago these birds were in Africa and they are here now seeking food and the less intense heat of Europe.

I am very hot as I begin my ascent, and rest a while in the shade of a high maize crop. I have never really appreciated the frothy strands that radiate out from the end of a sweetcorn cob; on one cob it is golden yellow, on another nearby it is candyfloss pink. I have never paid this much attention, but I have since discovered much more about these fronds, which are correctly known as 'corn silk'. The corn silk grows out of the ear and is the female part of a corn plant, and the tassel growing out the top of the corn stalk is the male part. The corn silk is the stigma and style of the female part of the corn. The stigma is the sticky end of the silk and pollen attaches to this part. The style is the tube from the stigma to the ovary. The corn kernels are embryos which form on the cob. Every ovary has its strand of corn silk, and pollen forms in the anther on the corn tassel. As the pollen matures, it is released and carried by the wind to the female stigmas of nearby corn plants. The pollen then travels down the style and fertilises the ovary, which develops into a kernel of corn at the other end of that strand of corn silk. Corn silk is a natural source of vitamin K and potassium, renowned for treating bladder & kidney infections. When I discovered this we immediately went and bought some fresh organic sweetcorn and made corn silk tea by adding boiling water to the yellow silk; we allowed it to steep for a short while, added some local organic honey and drank it, finding that it tasted a little like popcorn.

* * *

After I have been admiring the corn silk intently and for probably too long, a welcome breeze beckons me out from my shady forest of maize. The gentle wind catches the silvery green undersides of the leaves on distant trees, reminding me that I still have a long way to go. As I step out from the shade, I realise that the sun is shining even more brightly and the day becomes increasingly sweltering. I climb further and further, the lovely cool breeze disappears and I long to rest for a few moments, but before I have time to think about it much more I hear a cacophony of sound from what seems like a hundred cowbells, although I cannot see any cows. As I round the bend, I see just three rather small sandy-coloured cows quietly grazing and swishing their tales. I'm not sure how this trio managed to make so much noise, but I am very relieved not to have met a hundred-fold herd.

I spy my bench in the near distance, and when I reach it, I plonk myself down on it heavily. I am dressed in only a short-sleeved vest and shorts. I look at my brown legs and muse generally on my current state of health. My old, too-regular stomach aches and stress headaches have mostly gone. My walks and my new life have caused my health to improve greatly. I am also more content, and my head races less. Most happily, I don't feel the need to analyse my health, my worries and my situation all the time, just at odd moments such as this, and then in a positive light. I realise that perhaps I have made some progress and my quest is now taking on the properties of a pilgrimage.

38
SPINDLE

20ᵀᴴ AUGUST

I wait until it is cooler and finally leave at 2.45. It is over 21°C and very hot and sunny. Luckily there is a slight breeze. It is utterly quiet, save for the very distant tolling of cowbells. As I approach the river by the meadow today, close to the abundant wheatfield, I hear a flutter of a blackbird's wings in the undergrowth, and its typical click, click, click alarm call. I am reminded of my last garden in Devon, where under the laurel bushes at the edge of my small plot many blackbirds hopped and scampered. I have a deep relationship with this bird, although until I was in my twenties and went on a short holiday to the Lower Normandy region of France, I did not know that the blackbird resided anywhere but the British Isles. I was visiting the Renaissance Château d'Ô, a fairy-tale castle built in the centre of a lake, and on the approach to the entrance I heard the song of a male blackbird. I was amazed and a bit upset: I think this was a ridiculous rearing up in me of a kind of possessive nationalism – 'don't the British have sole rights on the blackbird?' It was an odd moment and I remember it very well. I even remember recalling to mind the poem *Adlestrop* by Edward Thomas,

And for that minute a Blackbird sang
Close by, and round him, mistier
Farther and farther, all the birds
Of Oxfordshire and Gloucestershire.

Thomas here identifies all the birds he can hear with an essential Englishness that they do not possess. But of course, birds do not recognise borders, need no passport or documentation and to them, the natural environment is a suitable home wherever that may be, but it is typical of humans to want to possess even something as free as a bird. That said, the common blackbird is – alongside the robin – the best-loved British bird. Perhaps this is partly because they are the most numerous breeding birds in the British Isles, with a population of around six million pairs. Both the female and the male are relatively large at 9-11 inches, weighing 2-4 ounces. The adult male has a glossy, black plumage, with a superb gold-yellow beak and co-ordinating gold-yellow eye-ring. The adult female is sooty-brown with a dull yellowish-brownish bill, a brownish-white throat and some delicate mottling on the breast. They are easily encountered, often scampering in the undergrowth or flying low in front of people and cars. Even an inexperienced birdwatcher has a fair chance of seeing and recognising a blackbird.

Their song is wonderful and melodious; there is no more beautiful a sound than the song of the blackbird. They often start to sing at the end of January or early February and the song period continues well into the summer. The best time to appreciate it is in the warmth of late afternoon in May or June, or after it has rained, because when the air is saturated with moisture, the sound waves travel even more clearly and resonantly. The male blackbird becomes more adept at singing as he ages, and a blackbird can live to be twenty years old, so has plenty of time to perfect his craft. Older males attract a mate more easily because their song is more refined: the female analyses it carefully to assess the male's maturity and fecundity.

When I made my blackbird sighting in France, I must have been watching a young male blackbird in his first year of courtship, because his song was scratchy and not very tuneful. He trilled and fluffed his way through a few notes, then stopped, like a young boy learning to play a musical instrument, who, frustrated with his progress, sighs and pauses to summon up the will to continue. This bird persevered, and I carried on watching one of the most charming things I have ever witnessed. It was a defining moment for me too, as since then I have always looked for the blackbird wherever I have travelled. Most recently, in the Giardini Public Park in Venice, at the end of an exhausting day of art tourism, hearing a blackbird singing loudly and clearly came as a blissful moment of calm. Sitting on that wooden bench in the park and letting my mind drift is as memorable to me now as recalling the Bridge of Sighs or standing in St Mark's Square and soaking in the beauty of the architecture.

I no longer think of the blackbird as resident only in the

British Isles and as a British bird, partly because I am no longer a British bird myself. The European population is estimated at between thirty-eight to fifty-five million pairs. The only European country with no breeding blackbirds is Iceland, but even here small numbers sometimes appear in winter. Even when the number of resident blackbirds is comparatively low it may still be considered to be of great importance; for example, it is the national bird of Sweden, even though the breeding population there is only one to two million pairs. Many of the birds in the British Isles are joined in winter by large numbers of migrants from Europe, mainly Scandinavia, the Baltic States, Russia and Germany. Even the quintessentially British song *Blackbird*, written by Paul McCartney and included by the Beatles on their 1968 double album *The White Album*, was inspired by the German composer Johann Sebastian Bach. Bach's well-known lute piece the Bourrée in E Minor was the basis for McCartney's guitar accompaniment to the song. The more I travel, the more I realise that we are all connected by so many things, and that nature is the one true uniting factor.

* * *

The meadow by the stream was cut back savagely a few weeks ago, but I see that it is already showing signs of regeneration. A small clump of wild mint with pointy sage green leaves grows abundantly; it has small, lilac, buddleia-like blooms. I steal a bit and eat it; it is deliciously spearminty and refreshing. Buttercups and clover are again becoming plentiful, and I am excited to catch a glimpse of a clouded yellow butterfly. Both the male and the female have a large orangey-yellow spot on the upper-side of their hindwings and a single, black spot on their forewings.[114] The one I see is a male; the male has a bolder yellow centre and a more striking black border than the female. He is collecting nectar from a wild red clover flower; I am so relieved that the meadow is providing this sustenance.[115] I am, like many people, deeply concerned by the use of chemicals and pesticides in farming, but I have seen little evidence of spraying in Carinthia. I think, or at least I hope, that there is a respect for nature here, which has meant that the worst excesses of industrial farming methods have been avoided. For example, I note as I pass a large farm,that at their gate a small crop of wild white Canterbury bells are growing in a most inconvenient place by the entrance gate, but they have not been sprayed or removed; instead they are lovingly and neatly tied into place, and I sometimes see a trickle of water that indicates that they have been watered recently.

During the months when I spoke to my father about his life in Austria, he told me a great deal more about his work as a commercial artist working in advertising. He recalled that in the 1950s when he worked for Crawford's Advertising Agency, he was one of the principal artists employed on projects to market and sell the new pesticides and weed killers that were developed both during the war and post-war period. As a passionate nature lover he remembered enquiring about the possible problems of contamination, but he was told, as everyone was, that this was not a problem and that he should not worry.

When on one occasion my father broke down and became tearful, I, of course, immediately gave up this line of enquiry, as I realised that he still felt very guilty about his involvement, although he was still very young and the full extent of chemical contamination was not known at the time and is still disputed now.

After what was to be our final conversation on the matter, my father gave me his Penguin copy of Rachel Carson's book *Silent Spring*. Carson's book, published on 27th September 1962, caused a sensation, as she was one of the first commentators to document the detrimental effects on the environment of the over-use of pesticides. She stated: 'During the mid-1940s over two hundred basic chemicals were created for use in killing insects, weeds, rodents... with the power to kill every insect 'good' and 'bad', to still the song of birds and the leaping fish in the streams, to coat the leaves with a deadly film, and to linger on in the soil – all though the intended target may only be a few weeds or insects.'[116]

This was an endemic problem in the immediate post-war period, and the widespread use of pesticides was not confined to industrial means of production. I have a copy of *A Gardener's Diary*, published in 1953 and written by the Principal of the Horticultural Training Centre, Dr Shewell-Cooper. The advice that he gives even the ordinary, everyday gardener is to be attentive and to be constantly spraying, as if every insect was a deadly menace in dire need of eradication. According to Shewell-Cooper, in May apple trees must be dealt with by applying a 'post-blossom spraying for Scab, Red Spider, Sawfly... with lime-sulphur and liquid nicotine.'[117] Liquid nicotine is highly toxic and was finally banned by the European Union in 2009.[118] We have several apple trees here in our garden, and I cannot imagine that as a matter of course we would automatically spray our trees without any evidence of infestation, and in this respect, I don't believe that we are alone. There is now at least more awareness of the harm that these chemicals do to insect and bird-life, but the battle with large companies like Monsanto continues, and with increasing reports that these chemicals cause cancer it has gone beyond the point where we can simply shrug off these issues.

* * *

On three separate occasions I see small cabbage white butterflies;

they especially like to fly in warm weather, flying very high, and often there are three flying together in a dancing triple-tiered formation. Nothing could be more evocative of high summer than this.[119] By the river my eye catches the reddish-pinky glow of the berries of the large-leaved spindle.[120] The shape of the berries is most unusual, with four lobes, each lobe divided into two. I immediately think of Raphael's sombre *Portrait of a Cardinal*, circa 1510, which hangs in the Museo del Prado in Madrid. The red ecclesiastical hat that the Cardinal wears is exactly the same shape as these berries. I collect a few examples in the hope that the gorgeous shape or the vivid colour will inspire Katie to make a piece of jewellery, although I have discovered that it is often something simple, ordinary and plain that leads to the creation of a finished piece.[121]

High summer it may be, but there are already signs of autumn: the odd reddish stalk and yellowing leaf, flowers turning to seed, the first appearance of pine cones on the conifers. The sunflower field is nearly all harvested now. The large flower heads which were so fresh and magnificent a short while ago are already looking droopy and bedraggled. But the azure blue sky and white cumulus clouds, hugging the Koralpe like iron filings hugging a magnet, still denote a summer's day, and I am in no rush to see the summer end. I am determined to think summery thoughts. I usually take little notice of displays of mass-produced bedding plants, but the quaint building that is used to store the beer barrels adjacent to the inn in Schiefling is bathed in sunlight, and outside the display of petunias and geraniums is so attractively conceived, planted into hollowed-out tree trunks, that I have to admire them. Seeing so many colourful blooms makes me think that, perhaps, after all, the summer will roll on and on.

My apple tree is looking completely resplendent today; it may never look better. The acid lime-green fruit glow like peridot jewels. One apple has recently fallen and is lying in my path. As I had not picked it, I feel no guilt in collecting it. It is past 6 pm, and I am hungry. It tastes very good indeed: a lovely taste, as sweet as any candy. A faint chorus of chirruping crickets encourages me on my weary way back home. I return home tired but contented.

39
DEW

In the very early hours of the morning I am awaken by very loud gunshots, but after a while they subside and no emergency service sirens sound, so I drift back to sleep. At 7.30 am it is once again hushed and still. We have guests staying here, so I sneak downstairs, grab a few fresh strawberries and pluck two bright red cherry tomatoes from the large terracotta pot outside the kitchen window as I leave. It's a little before eight o'clock, but it is already 12.5° C, and the forecast is for 25° or more. It is sunny, but a mist obscures the lower ground so that the hills seem to float in the pink-tinged light of a perfect early summer morning.

As I approach the stream, rolling clouds of rising mist billow and increase. The sun is low in the sky and casts topaz rays which fracture as they pass through the rich canopies of trees. Where the sun has warmed the ground the mist rises like steam from the grass. Everything is coated in a thick dew which casts a white pall on the verdantly green grass. Three placid cows, one wearing a small cowbell with a high-pitched clang, graze calmly in the deep shadow of the wood. Lemon-yellow and mauve-purple nettle flowers nod lazily in the cool morning sun. I have always been nervous of nettles; when I was five or six years old I was walking along a low stone wall, lost my balance and fell into a patch of them, and it was very painful. I skirt around these carefully. Low-lying dense gossamer spider webs lace and thread around the leaves in triangular formations; I have never seen cobwebs look so beautiful.

Somewhat incongruously, I pass two very smart young men in dark suits looking very serious. A few houses down, two young women in pink satin dresses stand by as their menfolk, also in suits and pastel coloured ties, manoeuvre their cars. I infer from this that someone who lives on this road is getting married. Perhaps the two serious young men are the bridegroom and best man? But they looked so stern; I had at first thought that they might be going to a funeral. The two women dressed in peach allay that thought. Neither of them catches my eye, so I leave them to their duties.

I realise now that the early morning gunshots I heard were the Böllerschießen (cannon shooting). On the day of a wedding, in an event organised by local bachelors, shots are fired from a small cannon to 'shoot the bride out of bed.' These loud noises supposedly drive evil spirits away. It is essentially a more pleasant variation on the medieval Charivari custom which was once widespread in the whole of Catholic Europe. A woman who was too obviously intelligent, witty, or outspoken was seen to be in need of circumscribing, because a shrewish, scolding wife implies that the husband cannot control his household.

In Britain during the medieval period, Charivari was a community event commonly referred to as 'rough music'; people of the town gathered in the streets clanging pots and pans together to make a discordant sound. This 'rough music' would be directed towards the 'scold or shrew', who was sometimes placed on a mule facing backwards to make it clear that her behaviour was unacceptable because it flouted gender expectations. In rural areas, this custom continued into the Tudor period. Shakespeare incorporates the idea into both his early comedy *The Taming of the Shrew* and to a lesser degree in his later and much less problematic *Much Ado About Nothing*.

Intellectually, the Böllerschießen custom makes me feel a little uncomfortable, but as I have now met quite a few Austrian wives I don't think there is much danger of any of them being put onto a mule facing backwards any time soon, and the thought of clanging expensive pans together is definitely seen as anathema.

* * *

The dewy fields are dazzling with a million be-diamonded dewdrops shining in the light, and there are many colours to admire: the once bright green trees are beginning to turn russet-brown, claret-red and plum-yellow in places. I rest for a while and find that the coffee that I made quickly and packed hurriedly has leaked: that was the comforting warmth I felt on my back not long after my walk began. I drink what is left and admire a slow-moving cargo train, its red engine pulling twenty carriages of timber, its whistle blowing as it nears the railway crossing. It's strange, but a series of lorries filled with lumber on a motorway could never look so attractive or evoke such a warm feeling, I suppose there is a romance associated with trains which will perhaps never completely diminish.

The early morning quiet of this Saturday morning gives way to harvesting and haymaking: almost the whole acreage of the open fields is being worked. As is usual here, the men sit in their very splendid tractors in some comfort, although I admit it must be hot and noisy work, whilst their long-suffering wives and daughters help by raking the grass into even tidier and even more beautiful neat furrowed lines. Arduous work indeed, but it is essential to ensure that the grass dries, or otherwise it will rot. When it is dry, it then has to be turned, and finally it will be gathered in.

I leave the workers to their industry and begin to anticipate the rows of birch and the bank filled with lupins. I am not disappointed; the spiky blooms climb up the incline in serried rows of pink, mauve white and occasionally yellow and I mentally give them a Chelsea Flower Show Gold Medal. There are also fresh, new white-petalled marguerites with their bright yellow centres enjoying a second flowering.

A small dwelling clinging to the hillside now sports an array of apexed solar panels. Because the property is built into the hill the five tiny fawn-coloured goats that continually prance around bleating are eye level with the new panels; today they seem to be almost manic, and less than impressed by their owners' sudden fit of environmental awareness. When they see me, they clamber down the hill bleating furiously, as if in complaint, or more likely they think I have food for them, but sadly I have nothing to offer them. Two huge cows lying very still on lower ground very near me shake their heads at me as if to say 'goats, tut, what can you do?' I nod back to them as the owner of the house comes out and I point at the panels and raise my thumbs in congratulation. He waves and smiles removing his hat to thank me, and I smile too as I stroll off in the direction of home.

* * *

It's strange but I have never stopped to study the apple tree before; I think I was not attuned enough to my surroundings in the beginning or it was too cold to stand for too long. I stand and drink it in for some time. It stands apart from the other eight or so apple trees in the orchard, which disappear down the hillside and are randomly placed. The tree that I chose, or rather the tree that chose me, is nearest to the farmhouse and outbuildings and in this way guards the entrance to the property. It is erect and straight, it carries its hundred years well, still looking fresh and supple, at least from a distance. Up close it is easier to see that the branches are laced with green lichen and moss, especially on the north-facing side. From the main trunk four large branches divide, two sturdy and two thinner. The two thicker ones divide each into yet another branch. A long branch hangs down on the right and is only a yard from the ground. The whole of the area around the tree is studded with small green apples, so that most of its abundance lies fallen and rotting on the slope on which the tree stands, with its magnificent views over the valley; once its crop would have been more keenly appreciated. The tree has a pleasing shape: with one branch reaching high into the sky and towards the Koralpe and Karawanken and on the opposite side the low branch reaches towards my home town of Bad Sankt Leonhard. It embraces all that it surrounds.

* * *

A buzzard circles high, slow and calm; swifts fly low but hurry, hurry - they are always so urgent and frantic. The buzzard soothes me, but the swifts urge me on. They represent my divided self, forever struggling between contemplation and action. I want to sit and admire the view, draw the day out, sleep under the stars even, but like all of us, I have things I must do and things I need to do. Feeling rather hot and tired and not knowing whether to dawdle or hurry, I walk at a moderate pace instead and return home at 1.30 pm in time for a bite of lunch.

Katie has plans for us: there are two workers in the meadow next to our house and as one scythes the high bank the other works a huge machine which looks exactly like an electric shaver. They are brothers and always work together. We call them over and offer them homemade elderberry syrup with sparkling water from the local Preblau spring. When they take their hats off, they both have new home-made haircuts. I point to the large machine and ask them if they used the machine to cut their hair. They laugh good-naturedly, shaking their heads in unison. Before they leave, Katie asks them if they have time to mow our near vertical bank of weeds. They agree to do it immediately, so we all set to, and after a gruelling, hot three hours we have a shaved area in which we can plant pumpkins and squashes ready for autumn picking. Before the brothers leave, they take a shine to a small dining table and four chairs which are lurking in our garage. We are only too glad to give them away; they are delighted and pack them onto their trailer with their gardening tools, and trundle off waving and smiling.

40

BIrTH

2ᴺᴰ SepTemBer

One of my greatest friends, Tali, is here visiting us from Jerusalem. We have known each other for over twenty years, having first met when studying at the Shakespeare Institute. I am not completely convinced that she wants to do the walk, so I don't mention anything about it until after breakfast, which we enjoy in the warmth of the September sun. Breakfast becomes quite a long and drawn-out process as we make a tour around the garden, picking herbs and fresh tomatoes before we begin. I offer my friend details about the pedigree of all our vegetables, and perhaps I am too enthusiastic, not to say boring, because smiling cheekily she leans over dramatically, selects a lovely little orange tomato, winks at me and says 'Amelia, is it okay if I eat Moses?'

I collapse into laughter, because to me, Moses is a character with a long beard, wearing flowing gowns and gallivanting around on mountaintops while holding slabs of stone, but she explains that actually it's a very common name in Israel (of course) and so my interpretation of her joke is much funnier than she intended. I realise how glad I am that she has come to visit and how much I have missed her good-natured teasing. I persuade her to join me and at least attempt some of the walk.

We leave together just after midday, and thankfully it is a cool and perfect 20.5° C. There are black, ominous clouds hanging over us, but they sit only on the distant hills, so I am not unduly worried. As we progress the sun shines, but it is still a pleasant temperature, and there is a slight breeze, excellent weather for walking. As we approach Mauterndorf we are talking away happily when suddenly out of the corner of my eye I see a cow's rear end arching up, her tail flying like a kite in the air. I touch my friend's arm; we stop dead in our tracks. A calf slithers out from the mother, and then the placenta. The calf takes her first breath, staggers to her feet, and on shaky legs walks a few steps. Right on cue, the bell from the church in Schiefling strikes one. The umbilical cord, a little red string, is still hanging delicately from the mother, quivering gently. The baby calf, just seconds old, is unconcerned, and and after only a few attempts she begins to suckle from the teat. We watch for a few moments as the mother licks her calf. It is a magical moment, but it is so astounding that we are speechless. If we had left a few minutes later we would have missed it. With perfect comedy timing my friend waits a beat, and as mother and baby amble over to join the rest of the herd, she provides a commentary:

'So, Mary, what ya gonna do this afternoon?

'Nothing. Just had a baby, so I'll probably just go get my hair done, do my nails, nothing special.'

I am glad of the light relief. Had I been on my own I would have found the whole experience too overwhelming and been tempted to over-sentimentalise it.

We walk slowly and steadily up the hill towards Schiefling; it's quite a climb. Two cyclists pass us at high speed, and the first, his shirt flapping, shouts 'Hallo!' The second, in slick Lycra, merely passes us with his head down, looking terrified – he seems to be focusing on staying upright and keeping up with his cool friend. After a short pause, five female cyclists file past, also at speed, but the odd squeaky sound indicates that, unlike their male counterparts, they are occasionally applying their brakes on the very steep descent to the main road. I don't blame them – I would do the same.

We aim for the church and rest on the bench, with our backs leaning on the stone wall of the graveyard. We sip our water in companionable silence. The proximity of the graves and a prominent war memorial provoke a more serious tone and we begin to talk about our family histories. In the twenty or more years of our friendship, I have never felt that I could ask my friend about her religion or her family's Second World War experiences. I have always wanted to know, but I was afraid to ask. I am aware of the taboo of talking about religion, politics or war with friends, it is seen as tantamount to madness, but why is this so? Aren't these three of the most important subjects that we can face, and perhaps ought to face? I know that I can learn from her life experiences, because the life she lives in Israel forces her to face realities, realities which I, hopefully, will never have to face. She has to live in a world riven by religious divisions and tensions. She has an excellent aptitude for finding the right phrase, and when I ask her about her religious views she answers me directly, telling me that she is a 'dedicated atheist.' I think that this is an elegant axiom which tactfully makes her position abundantly clear. I cannot help but agree, for as much as I may want to believe in a spiritual entity and I certainly 'pray' for the day when we stop killing each other and look after each other instead, I see organised religion as part of the problem. If the practising of faiths were peaceable and inclusive, it would most likely be a force for good, but this seems increasingly unachievable, nor, it seems, is it the desired objective.

Having taken on the topic of religion I feel that perhaps I can ask her about her family. She opens up and tells me more than she ever has. I am very relieved to hear that her family had moved to Israel some four generations before the terrible events of the bloodiest century in history. She continues, going on to explain that living in Jerusalem is painful for her, because of the continuing problems surrounding the Israeli-Palestinian conflict. Of course she has considered leaving, but it is not an easy decision to make. I know that she does good work in the university encouraging discussions about politics and religion and facilitating discussions between groups that are currently thoroughly alienated from one another. Although she feels she is not doing enough, I think her work is of vital importance, and I tell her this.

We step into the small churchyard, and she comments on the immaculate graves which are impeccable and completely weed free. In this respect, the graveyards in Austria are very unlike those in Britain, where gravestones are left to tumble down; the lichen-encrusted tombstones are considered to be romantic and picturesque, and I can see the charm of this. But here death is much more sanitised and is dealt with in a more matter-of-fact way. In essence, graveyards are treated no differently from the streets and houses, which are also invariably impeccably clean. We admire the orderliness of the graves and conclude that order, especially in death, in some ways is a way of refuting and controlling it, and also a way of accepting it: it's just another stage in our lives. In many cases, the most pristine tombstones are those where early deaths occurred: people dying in early adulthood, or worse, as children. Perhaps this helps with the pain of loss. We take a moment to reflect that only a short while before we witnessed a new birth, and now here we are staring at the inevitable finiteness of life.

We enter through the open door and into the small, jewel-like church to admire the beautiful, splendid altar, the silver and gold-leafed wooden statues, the carved pulpit, topped with three-dimensional golden clouds, and the chubby cherubs. We discuss the evident artistry, but as 'dedicated atheists', we feel little.

Once again, as on the occasion of my walk with my sister and niece, a long period of time spent in nature has facilitated a mood of sharing and allowed for discussion. We move on to the next stage, which is another short but tough climb; I warn my friend that it may raise her heartbeat considerably, and she clutches her chest in mock alarm.

After about twenty minutes of walking, she decides that instead of marching on we ought to sit down and look at the mountains for a while. I rarely, if ever, do this, but I think it is a splendid idea. Wildflowers and long grass surround us; the time passes happily but too quickly. Eventually we saunter on, occasionally pausing to admire the incredible fecundity of nature as we pass. Nestled under a small copse of pine trees, I spot my first ever silver thistle; they only begin to flower in late August and are native here, so I am unlikely to have ever seen one before.[122]

It is another member of the extraordinarily varied Asteraceae (daisy) family. It's a stunning specimen, so low-growing that I have to bend down to admire the silver disc of the flower. It's exactly like a tiny bleached-out sunflower head: silver alchemy at work. The centre is filled with pollen, and to protect this precious cargo, it can even close up in wet weather. It is known as the dwarf silver thistle, but is also sometimes referred to as the Charlemagne thistle, after the medieval emperor who ruled much of Western Europe from 768 to 814. When plague decimated his army, Charlemagne prayed for delivery from the pestilence, after which he dreamt that an angel instructed him to shoot an arrow into the air: where it struck the ground he would find a medicinal herb that would provide the cure he sought. The rhizome of the plant does, in fact, contain essential oils which hold antibacterial properties. I am excited about this find as I know that Katie will be very drawn to its delicate silver-like appearance.

We have been walking for four hours already, and it is late, so even though we have not completed the walk I call Katie. She is out mushroom hunting, so she arrives within minutes and collects my friend, and they drive away waving and laughing at some joke unknown to me.

I continue on alone, and when I return home there is yet more evidence of merriment. Katie is cooking, and my friend is admiring her skills from the comfort of the kitchen stool. We all drink local beer, from the brewery in the nearby town of Villach, and eat Katie's recently gathered mushrooms in a goulash with homemade bread dumplings. We wash this down with a wine we have never tried before, a Rösler Barrique made locally in Feldkirchen only an hour's drive from us. Exhausted by so much walking, talking and laughing I am by midnight so tired that I cannot keep awake any longer, so I retire to bed and instantly fall into a deep and dreamless sleep.

41

HEAT

24TH SEPTEMBER

A great deal has happened since I completed my last walk on 2 September. I have been at a residential school in Somerset, four glorious days teaching Shakespeare and accompanying my group to the Royal Shakespeare Theatres in Stratford-upon-Avon. I am delighted to have got some paid work. But I am very much in need of my day of walking and contemplation.

It is a beautiful September day, already a warm 22.5° C, and sunny. Billowing white cumulus clouds enhance a pale blue sky, and I know that the temperature can only rise. The bank by the stream has been mown, the long grasses and wildflowers left strewn on the ground as if in preparation for a simple country wedding. The path is cobbled with little greeny-yellow apples, in various stages of decomposition. In winter this area is thick with ice and dangerous to traverse, and in autumn the apples make it pretty treacherous underfoot too. No fewer than six blackbirds alight as I pass, two feeding on the apples, the others flying up from the undergrowth; their alarm calls are urgent and bad-tempered. I hear a tractor, and then see its vivid lime-green and red panels as it approaches. I'm a little disappointed to see that the farmer is collecting the strewn grass – no wedding after all?

The path continues to the river and is awake with vibrant colour, lush green grass, tall purple thistles, a long row of apple trees, leaves of yellow and green, apples of red. The maize field which was so high, fertile and impressive in August is now a field of yellow stubble, and thirty or more jackdaws feed voraciously on what goodness there is left. The strong aroma of silage fills the air.

Out of the corner of my eye, I see something moving to my left and notice that a heap of maize and hay has attracted an ant colony. I watch in utter fascination at the throbbing mass. I see ant eggs being hoisted, lifted buried, even dragged into place – their frenetic activity is astounding. I watch for quite a while. I no longer hurry on these walks, I listen to everything around me, look, stoop to peer at things on the ground, or to raise my eyes to see what is above me. Today I have brought nothing with me other than a bottle of water, no snacks, no books, no podcasts, and my phone is firmly zipped up in my pocket. I've learnt to be at one with nature and to listen to the quiet sounds around me. It's taken me nearly eight months to wean myself from distraction and to stop timing my walks and trying to beat my own record. I sit at my bench, sipping from my water, while a black redstart's click-clicking keeps me company. I gaze at the two rows of yellowing maize, all that's left of last months' sea of corn.

Many fields are showing signs of new wildflower growth, with thistles, clover and dandelions most prominent. More electric fencing has appeared to provide areas for grazing herds of cows; the calves are getting larger and stronger now. A few gusts of wind bring flurries of leaves down, but this is the only real sign of autumn that I have seen so far this year. A cabbage white butterfly skitters along beside me, another appears and shadows the first, and they lead me to another rest stop. A small bronze-winged damselfly or dragonfly alights on the electric fence opposite, thankfully unaffected by the electric current. I round the corner to turn towards Mauterndorf and see that the lovely birch tree now has crimson-orange leaves. A gentle rustling in the breeze and a trickle from the small stream is punctuated by the bellowing of a cow in the distance.

At Schiefling I sit on the bench in the village square, which I have never done before, but I need to rest. After a few moments a small blue car pulling a trailer roars past, and on the trailer, a man sits astride a motorbike. He is in his fifties, and his flowing locks fly out behind him in the wind. The driver of the little bright blue car, a woman in her thirties, perhaps his daughter, begins to hoot with laughter as I lift my camera to take a shot. She waves and smiles, while the man looks fixedly ahead. It is a most bizarre and dreamlike sight.

The day becomes more and more stunningly beautiful as it becomes ever hotter. The pull up to the apple tree is killing today; it is sweltering, and I can feel my heart beating in my chest. I slow down, and as I rise higher to well over 3280 feet it becomes cooler and more and more peaceful, and as it does so I become calmer and calmer. I hear only the sound of high-pitched bells made by grazing cows.

The apple tree has not a single apple on it now. I hope the farmer has harvested the crop to useful purpose. I am still hot and thirsty, so I scrump a delicious red apple from an adjacent tree and eat it, enjoying the sweet, refreshing juice. I can see the apple farmer, his son and another worker nearby manoeuvring large farm machines expertly, synchronising the harvesting of one huge unbounded field. The son waves and smiles, but the older men are concentrating fully on the work in hand.

I stand in the shade of the tree and gaze out over the view. I watch as in the far distance two tractors work the land in the heat of the afternoon, passing each other like two swimmers completing laps in a pool, each aware of the other without the need of communication. I sit and enjoy the quiet resting against the tree, after a few moments I realise that I am not alone; just to my side a cow is grazing quietly. She is backlit by the late afternoon sun; I have never seen a cow anywhere near the tree before and rarely been so close to one, and she is so quiet and gentle. I try not to disturb her and take just one photograph. When I rise and stoop to pick up my rucksack and turn to leave, I look back, but she has already disappeared and is nowhere in sight.

42
Erntedankfest

1ˢᵀ october

As part of my growing appreciation and understanding of the local area, I like to learn more about the local customs here, so a few days ago Katie took me to the Erntedankefest (Harvest Festival) in the nearby town of Reichenfels. We awoke to the most glorious autumn day of full sunshine and blue skies, and the drive there was filled with golden-leafed trees nestled among dark green conifers. When we arrived, we heard the bells of the Parish Church of Saint James. The church, white and pristine, looks much younger than its years, with a splendid onion dome of verdigris copper. Behind the church stands a wall of a thousand thousand spiky pine trees which completely cover the Sommerau hills, forming the most glorious backdrop. We saw people gathering for the service. Nearly all the women were dressed in traditional Austrian Trachten: Dirndl dresses, and the men in their best Lederhosen. Some of the younger men were wearing white sunglasses, their socks artfully arranged and falling down. Without exception they were all staring at their phones intensely – an age-old scene transformed into a contemporary one.

The church was packed to capacity, and many people were standing, as there was nowhere left to sit, but everyone was very welcoming, and the mood was one of acceptance and friendship. From high up in the gallery, a small choir was singing (in German) *We Plough the Fields and Scatter*, and this transported me back to my own Sunday school days in Malvern. I later discovered that *We Plough the Fields and Scatter* is not an English hymn at all, as I always imagined it to be, but is of German origin ('Wir pflügen und wir streuen'). The words were written in 1782 by Matthias Claudius, and it was set to music in 1800 by Johann Schulz. It did not become popular in England until 1861, when it was translated into English by Jane Montgomery Campbell. Again, I discover that something I think of as quintessentially English has its roots buried deeply in Germanic culture; we are united by so much more than I ever imagined.

* * *

It's the first day of October, and I am quietly humming 'Wir pflügen und wir streuen' and musing on our visit to Reichenfels. I am determined to walk today, but I am having a little rest because we rose very early this morning to clear out the attic in readiness for the loft insulation which will be laid next week. We found buckets of builders' rubble, which we removed, and in the corner of the attic, all very neatly packed in boxes, we found lying unloved all the old accounts going back to 1966 from the Schwefelheilbad, the healing Spa that Katie's family once owned and ran in Bad Sankt Leonhard. I study the precisely-entered columns of numbers, and coming across a yellowing leaflet I imagine the series of treatment rooms each holding a patient sitting in a large bath filled with the curative waters and the doctor popping in to discuss other treatments. I also imagine Katie's mother cooking lunches in the large kitchen, and the outside patio area, under a balcony pretty with trailing red geraniums filled, not only with guests and patients soaking up the sun's rays but Katie's Viennese grandmother, who stayed at the Schwefelheilbad from May to September with a group of her girlfriends. I also find a photograph of four-year-old Katie outside the Schwefelheilbad, which makes it seem newly alive to me.

When I leave the house at 1.25 pm it is partly cloudy, but the sun has appeared on and off all morning, and a relatively stiff breeze accompanies me. At 17° C, it is very pleasant and feels surprisingly warm. The local newspaper recently reported that Carinthia had had the warmest September for two hundred years. Although it is 1ˢᵗ October there is no sign of snow on the distant Koralpe and I could easily be wearing shorts. I remove my light jacket almost immediately, as I am far too warm. I am completing the walk in the opposite direction today, walking up to the Leonhardikirche first, this way I can appreciate things from a different perspective. The lime tree is a tapestry of beautiful lime and lemon colours. There are tiny little sunflowers, just a few inches high, growing out of the very high retaining wall around the Leonhardikirche, the roots grabbing hold in between the stones. Life is keen to get a foothold even when it seems futile. They cannot possibly survive here.

After a short time, I notice that a yellow van has passed me twice already, but I think nothing of it. I have a special treat today, as it is still warm and soon I know that it will be too cold to stop to enjoy the beauty: a flask of strong coffee and some dark chocolate. I sit on a sunlit bank for a few minutes to admire a sea of bright yellow, wild arnica, their petals shaggy and unkempt, contrasting with the slender, delicate, glossy yellow buttercup blooms. The whole area around me is filled with yellow, and right on cue the yellow van returns. A tall, lean man with greying hair leans out of his window and asks me if I would like a lift. I explain in my halting German that I am on a hike and refuse politely. He shrugs as if to imply that walking is a monumental waste of time and energy, and drives off.

I pack away my flask, and as I rise I notice that a part of the bank previously wholly covered in pine trees has been savagely felled, and broken stumps and torn branches lie in disarray all around waiting to be cleared. Walking regularly across the same terrain is a way to appreciate the sober fact that the scenery is an intrinsic part of the economy here and the woods, beautiful as they, are not here only to be admired; they are planted for commercial reasons. I am becoming less and less enamoured with capitalism and neoliberalism, but fear that no good and feasible alternative will be found in my lifetime.

I climb higher, and the breeze becomes a gust. Suddenly I am walking in a hail of autumn leaves which revolve around me, falling like a shower of golden rain. As quickly as it arrives the wind dies down, but I enjoyed the few magical moments in the eye of the leaf storm while it lasted.

The yellow van once more looms into view. This time the man jumps out of his van and says to me, quite without ceremony,

'Ich bin Deutscher. Ich bin geschieden.' (I am German. I am divorced.) I do like a man who comes straight to the point. He opens the door of his van, hops in, tripping slightly on the step as he does so, but recovering quickly, he flips open his glove box nimbly with one hand. From this he produces a bottle of white wine, proffering it to me at an angle across his palm as if he's a waiter in a top restaurant; pretty impressive in the circumstances. It's a bit early in the day for me, so I politely decline. He pops the bottle back into the glove box in a single motion, realising that despite his obvious charm he is not going to succeed, and jumps back into the driving seat. Waving, smiling and pausing only to wink, he drives off. I would have happily taken the wine for later, but I don't think that was on offer.

On the way to my apple tree, I pass an orchard. All the apple trees are weighed down with bright red or green fruit, and people are out with long ladders harvesting the delicious orbs of autumn goodness. They scale ladders adeptly, and the cows have moved in, probably hoping for a few juicy apples. All of them are wearing a cowbell, each of a different sound and pitch. It's a beautifully musical sound, but I am surprised at how loud their bells are at close range.

I finally reach the apple tree at 3.45 pm. The wind whips up, and the temperature begins to fall. I take my photographs quickly, and as I round the corner, I see the farmer who owns the land with his wife and daughter herding their cows, each of which has a small calf. Apart from the bright yellow glow of the farmer's T-shirt and the bright orange bucket he is carrying, this is a sight that has not changed for centuries, but one that I have rarely seen. I stand to one side to take a few discreet photographs and we all exchange pleasantries. I can see that they recognise me, but they look surprised to see me walking here once again.

Nearby, the birch trees have the kiss of a gold Klimt painting.

In the far distance, the Karawanken Mountains are backlit by a golden light, but they are shrouded in too much haze to see well. It is still warm enough to hear the crickets, which add music to the scene, but otherwise it is still and quiet. Until, that is, a large black Labrador, heavily muzzled and out walking with his owner, lollops over to me in a very friendly manner. When he arrives he pauses, looks at me quizzically and promptly sneezes. I politely say 'Gesundheit', which the dog owner hears and thinks is very funny. They both amble off, the man waving and laughing as he departs. Once again humour has saved me from the embarrassment of not yet being able to hold a full conversation in German.

As I begin my descent from Schiefling, I hear the church bells chiming five o'clock, and I am hungry. As I pass through a wooded area, I see a perfect parasol mushroom, our supper. I pick it carefully using my pocket knife, so as not to disturb the fine network or mycelium under the soil through which the fungus absorbs nutrients from its environment.

There is little to see as I follow the track towards home, not even maize fields; how bare and brown it all seems.

I arrive home, and Katie cooks my foraged mushroom, dipping it in a beaten egg and frying it lightly. We eat this with fresh, dark rye bread and in celebration of my fungus find, we open a bottle of Austrian sparkling wine.

43

BETWEEN

9ᵀᴴ OCTOBER

We have been overwhelmingly busy, mainly because the person we contracted to prepare our kitchen ready for our new major refit cancelled at the very last minute. We set to immediately and took out the old sage green cupboards, placed them outside on the patio out of harm's way and painted the kitchen and the old room which we used as a larder, finishing the job in two days. I had forgotten how much I disliked painting ceilings, but after I had completed the task, I felt pleased with my labours.

We called a local carpenter who arrived almost immediately, and keen to re-use as much as we can, together we re-erected the forty-year-old kitchen in what was the untidy larder, turning it into a serviceable utility room. For four days we managed with only makeshift cooking facilities, but quite enjoyed making do.

On the appointed day two lovely guys arrived, one Croatian and one Hungarian, to fit our new kitchen. They worked so hard and so skilfully, and we laughed together when we couldn't understand each other. Such a mix of talents and languages in one room; it further endorsed my sense that living in the middle of Central Europe is not only an experience but often brings unexpected joys.

Three days after the kitchen was finished, a new boiler, solar panels and loft insulation were installed. My German lessons have begun in earnest, and the homework takes me a long time to complete, as I am by no stretch of the imagination a natural linguist. So finding time to fit the walk into my life is becoming increasingly difficult. It's hard not to feel selfish about it, but the walk has become so crucially important to me that I am determined to continue with it.

* * *

On the 9th of October, I awake to find that it is a cold sunny day and the blue sky is streaked with delicate cirrus clouds. It is only 3° C, but it will rise to a respectable 8°. I am surprised to realise that when autumn arrives here, it comes very quickly, and the early mornings are much colder than the much more temperate climate of Devon. I rise early to complete a few little extra jobs in the morning and sneak away at 12.30 pm. For the first time since March, I have to wear thermal clothes under my lightweight jacket, but there is an in-between feeling. It is neither cold nor warm, sunny nor cloudy; it does not feel like autumn has quite arrived, but it does feel as if the summer is all but over.

It's heartening to see that the fields are still a very vivid green and will remain so until the hard frosts begin. Cows still dot the landscape, and I hope that they really are as happy and contented as they seem; their calves are almost fully grown, and they certainly look healthy. Unusually, a lone black horse, large and impressive, stands in the highest field - I can see it clearly from my low vantage point by the river. I hope that when I pass by the same field in several hours on my way back that the black stallion will still be there and I can admire him at close range.

The river is shallow; I can see every stone in the river bed. The large flat, smooth stones are pale and dry, as there is only a trickle of water lying in shallow pools here and there. A weir manages this part of the river, so it may not be entirely due to lack of rain, but I am sure that this is a factor. The crop of once magnificent sunflowers has been reduced to a few limp specimens, which look very sad, but the seeds are a vital source of sustenance for birds. I allow myself to sit quietly and rather painfully on the ground by an abandoned old gate. I see several great tits flit quickly to the enormous drooping sunflower heads, and try to will into existence a rarer bird, so that I can make a new sighting. I lift my binoculars for the tenth time, and by a miracle, as I look through them, I see a bird with white cheeks, a black head and pale brown wings. It's a marsh tit or perhaps a willow tit (even expert ornithologists cannot tell these birds apart). But as his neck is stocky, and because I am by the river, I am reasonably sure that today I have identified my first ever marsh tit.[123] I am excited, but as there are at least 6,000 species of the passerine birds to which the marsh and willow tit belong I have many more bird sightings to enjoy.

I have a long way to go, my leg has gone to sleep, and I am

suddenly very cold. I drink my coffee and eat a few squares of chocolate, but rather than reviving me this makes me feel drowsy. I shuffle along, feeling a little sad that the warm hot days are over for this year. Last week everywhere I looked I saw activity and industry, the farmers keen to gather in the last of the harvest. Today, the landscape has been transformed into a patchwork of brown and green, and many of the fields, having held maize crops, sport regular lines of gold stubble. There are still some signs of life: a large bumble bee with the brightest yellow and the darkest black stripes I have ever seen alights on my orange jacket, possibly confusing me with a pollen-filled flower. But the few drowsy wasps that buzz around me seem to lack enthusiasm.

In sparse patches, my new good friend the dandelion is still growing. A beautiful purple lupin is flowering on the bank as I pull up towards a rest stop, and a few bright white and yellow marguerites spill onto the path. I can hear cowbells tolling quietly, and a few gnats fly lazily. A sleek, well-groomed cock blackbird sits on the crossed hatched fence with his tail up, looking very pleased with himself.

I so want to see some autumn colour and dazzling red autumn leaves, and I am in luck. The vinegar trees are glorious, as well as having orange-red autumn leaves; the female trees also have dark burgundy red flowers, which resemble a tail, a candle or a bottle cleaning brush. This is called the staghorn sumac, or the rhus. I stroke one of the red flowers; they look and feel somewhat like fuzzy velvet. The vinegar tree is a relative newcomer to Europe, having arrived only in the 17th Century from its native North America.[124] The sumac part of the name derives from Arabic. The dried and powdered fruits of the red rhus are used as a spice – also called sumac – in Middle Eastern cuisine, to add a tangy, lemony flavour to dishes.

The sycamore, rowan and birch are beginning to turn yellow and red and the low-lying bracken is preparing to rust, but most of the other trees have yet to change. The Koralpe has a good layer of snow on its peak, the first I have seen for many months now. The sun breaks through the clouds and warms me, giving me some energy to tackle the climb up to Schiefling. It is as hard as ever, but I soon become warm enough to take my jacket off. The small road by Schiefling church is buzzing with activity: a church service is just finishing and the local bandsmen and women, dressed in smart navy jackets with red epaulettes, are pouring into the old wooden inn which is opposite the church. They are carrying instruments, chatting noisily and laughing. This is the reason for it being a Bank Holiday today: it marks the Carinthian Plebiscite of 10th October 1920. After the First World War, much of the border regions of the Carinthian area were predominantly populated by Slovenes. To determine the final southern border between the Republic of Austria and the newly formed Kingdom of Serbs, Croats and Slovenes (which later became Yugoslavia), it was decided to ask the inhabitants to take part in a plebiscite. 59% of Austrians voted to stay with Austria and 41% to stay with the Slovenes.[125]

The day is still marked annually across the whole region, and most towns have a road named after the event; if ever I want to get to the centre of any Austrian town and I don't have the full address, I enter '10 OktoberStraße' into the Sat Nav, and it rarely fails to get me to the central precinct.

At my final rest stop before the apple tree, it suddenly becomes much colder, and dense cumulonimbus clouds begin to appear. I worry that I will be caught in a rainstorm, but the sun shines down on me, and as I walk through the wooded area I am offered a corridor of dappled light to admire. The farmer and his son have completed two of their three farm doors now, but there is still much work for them to complete on their farmhouse, which they are building themselves. However, every time I pass by a little more work has been done: some rendering on the outside over the bare bricks or breeze blocks, or a balcony installed. All the repairs and building work has to be undertaken between farm duties. Their working day must be a very long one, and I feel for them.

44

Autumn

ᐦ

16ᵀᴴ October

It is foggy and misty in the morning, but the light is suffused with a glow, so the sun must be up there. However, it is currently only 8° C. There is also a chill to the breeze. I cannot help feeling a little melancholy as I can see and feel that summer is beginning to slip neatly into autumn and the long days of summertime will soon be over. I do not feel motivated to start the walk until

1.30 pm when thankfully, as the weather forecast promised, the temperature reaches a hot and sunny 20° C.

After about an hour I pass through a farmyard which is on a public footpath. In all the time I have walked through it I have never met anyone. As it has become a gloriously sunny October day, the farm owners are sitting outside with friends and family. A tall, slender man in a long blue overall and a little black cap is roasting chestnuts over a brazier; he expertly grips a huge cast iron pan with a long handle. I have noticed that the Austrians are very good at both wearing the correct outfit for the right occasion and using the right tool for the job. Everyone is seated on a long trestle table in the hot sunshine, drinking beer or homemade lemonade. Immediately that they see me, they offer me chestnuts hot from the pan. They question me, and in my broken German, I manage to explain that I am not on holiday but live in the local town; this is met with astonishment. They gesture to me, inviting me to sit with them and shifting along the bench to make room for me. One of the party notices my camera and offers to take a group photograph of all of us. I am impressed with their generosity and friendliness. After a short time, I make my excuses and gather up my belongings. They force hot chestnuts into my accepting hands, and as I leave they wave and shout their goodbyes.

I saunter along happily and slow down even more as I approach the curve in the path that affords a view of an old, gnarled copse of deciduous trees, including oak, chestnut and beech. But to my dismay, I discover that the whole grove has been felled and torn down. I stand in amazement looking at the carnage. Immediately I think of Paul Nash's painting *We are Making a New World* (1918),[126] a savage oil painting filled with torn, ripped tree stumps and clumpy clods of exploded soil as if seen moments after a bombardment. Nash's ironic title beautifully mocks the pointless ambitions of war; the pale, colourless sun is rising on a new day, but it shines on a world that heralds nothing other than more slaughter and desolation.

I am so saddened by what I am seeing. Every week, as I have turned the bend of the path, I have had the image of Thomas Gainsborough's view of a landscape in my mind.[127]

Gainsborough, although a portrait artist by profession, was in his heart a landscape painter. I have always idly mused on his unfulfilled desire to give up the constant pressures of his day job as a portrait artist to take up his 'Viol da Gamba and walk off to some sweet village' to paint 'landskips and enjoy the fag end of life in quietness and ease.'[128] His trees are always in perpetual motion: he never defined a leaf, but instead painted a froth of blurred, softened, melting umbers, greens, and yellows. His paintings are mystical and mysterious. I hold Gainsborough's idea of trees in my mind and compare it to the reality in front of me now – a scene of desolation.

I can remember so clearly how in that first walk in July 2014 I admired the sea of swaying light green as the wind turned the leaves inside out to reveal the paler, more delicate undersides. I enjoyed hearing the bending of the branches, bowing as if obeying the baton of an invisible conductor. Over the weeks and months I had sheltered from the sun here, leant against the knotty bark of the trees, sometimes tracing the grooves with my fingers. I avoided trampling tiny seedlings or stopped to look at the different grass varieties and seed heads. I once stumbled into the wood to spy the distant horizon of the spire of Schiefling church through a lattice of branches and leaves. I always listened out for bird song here too. Perhaps I was one of the last people to photograph the sun streaming through the slatted canopy, looking high up into the branches feeling safe in the knowledge that these gentle giants would outlive me. I feel forlorn, because ancient broadleaf trees are rare here and I am shocked to see them felled so brutally.

The pine forests that grow here in Austria are planted for commercial reasons, and in sequence, sections of the forest are regularly felled. But at least replanting is continuous. I take comfort in the fact that this is probably a one-off occurrence and has most likely happened because of a recent change of ownership.

I force myself to put away any thoughts of despair and sadness and move on, looking to the beauty of nature for solace. Buttercups, dandelions and clover are all flowering still, and wild horseradish is very abundant. A few days ago there was snow on the high ground, and the Koralpe looks impressive; I will never tire of seeing a snowy mountain peak. The fields are beautifully ploughed, and I think that despite the problematic and complex ethical issues surrounding farming, I cannot deny the evident artistry of the farmers in their work; it is everywhere so apparent, and links all farmers in a great family of artists whose huge canvasses are the fields and hills.

I become very hot as I climb, and eat the sweetest wild strawberries which, despite their small size, refresh me. It begins to seem less like autumn: bumble bees buzz past me and I hear crickets. Cows are lying down sunbathing, and the sky is the blue of a summer day. But as soon as I get into the woods, dappled light shines through golden yellow birch trees, and there is autumn again, I can smell it in the air. Everywhere I look I see cloud-like formations of fungi growing, and a host of tall red fly agaric toadstools shine out. In the distance as I descend, misty fir trees stand in staccato silhouette and the whole scene has become one of fairytale wonder.

I realise that I am fortunate and that this has been one of the most enjoyable walks of the year. It has been a stunning day, and the sun never stopped shining with beautiful delicate light falling through golden leaves.

45

APPLES

23ʳᴰ OCTOBER

I leave after lunch. It is pleasant 10° C, a gorgeous sunny day. I have sun cream on, as the sun felt hot when it shone through the windows this morning. A band of dense white fog obscures the crown of the Koralpe, and the lush bright green of the fields is lit by the sun's rays shining through white clouds. Yellow, gold, amber and red trees nestle amongst dark green pine trees which are studded with large orange-brown pine cones.

Showers of golden leaves are falling on me from twenty birch trees, carpeting the ground in a layer of gold leaf. The sound is of gentle wind and rustling leaves. Clouds hang low to the southwest, obscuring the fir trees, but above this is an azure sky. I look up and watch a bird of prey circling slowly above me; all wild things are free, but birds have that coveted ability to fly too. I am standing near the edge of a commanding view and high enough to imagine that I too am flying. I close my eyes, and for a fleeting moment I feel, perhaps for the first time in my life, unfettered, weightless and unburdened. Back down on earth I smile from ear to ear and sip a little of my whisky-laced coffee – it is hot, sweet and delicious.

It soon becomes cooler and I need my gloves, so I ferret them out and as I pause I watch three great tits dipping, diving, calling and feeding in a wild hazelnut tree which has only fragments of green-gold leaves on it now. A woodpecker chuckles away in the pine trees higher up. I have a new guest to introduce myself to: a lovely caramel and cream mare. She whinnies and poses for a photograph, then carries on grazing, her pale mane backlit by the sun. Pink clover flowers and a few yellow buttercups still cover much of the wilder areas, but not much else is around to attract the eye: the fields are now mostly composed of ploughed earth, beautiful regular stripes cut into the soil, straight and true; the result of adroit ploughing skills.

High up above the field that is a vast, lush meadow in summer, there is a large irregular patch of dead grass, so unlike all the ground that surrounds it that I suspect it may have been caused by chemical spraying. But no crops are in this field, sometimes horses graze or deer feed in the vast area, so I cannot understand what has happened to cause this. The more evidence I see of spraying of any kind, the more I support organic farmers and their methods. Even though Austria is one of the highest producers of organic produce in the EU, currently running, according to the Austrian Parliament, at 21.2% of the total output, this still means that nearly 80% is not organic. I find this increasingly alarming. I am increasingly sure that, despite the many hours of hard work that it takes to grow enough fruit and vegetables to feed us year round, we have struck gold by inheriting a large garden with fertile, chemical-free soil.

The stream by the weir is much calmer. The waters have subsided, the sun glints off the surface, and the wet rocks now protrude above the water line. The maize crop by my first bench rest stop has completely gone – I watched only last month as several rows were gobbled up and eradicated – and now the other rows have been harvested. I did not realise before that maize fields are only reaped when the crop is needed and in small quantities. Now all that remains is corn stubble, which glistens brightly in the sun against the rich dark brown of the soil.

I note that where once stood the copse that I loved so much, eight or so cows lie sunbathing: cows, I suppose, are more lucrative than an old deciduous wood. Two jet black crows alight from the scrub as I climb up to Schiefling, fleeing some unseen evil foe or predator. I can hear their complaining long after I have passed by, as they squawk and moan for several minutes afterwards. The sky is now striated with cirrus curls, and the sun has a corona of light around it - it is very bright, and I could not manage without my sunglasses. I am warm again and have to remove some layers.

I pass the first of two hotels in the small hamlet. One has been closed for several years but has now reopened, and a large consignment of beer, wine and spirits is being delivered. A blackboard outside lists the simple menu. I was always sad to see it empty, so I am pleased to see it freshly painted and imagine it full of people happily enjoying the ambience inside. I can hear some chatter rising up from within, and am tempted to go in, but I must continue on my way.

The other hotel now houses refugees fleeing the horrors of war in the Middle East, mainly from Syria. Just this morning before I left I watched a short piece on the Austrian news: the United States is currently bombing Syria, Iraq, Yemen, Afghanistan, Pakistan, Libya and Somalia. Trillions of dollars wasted and millions of lives lost. Congress approval is not even needed for these bombing attacks. I cannot stop thinking about how terrible this is, and neither do I wish to forget how terrible this is, as powerless as I am, being cognisant of these atrocities represents at least some kind of reaction.[129]

Fairy-story red apples cling to the almost bare trees in glorious abundance, shining like jewels lit by the low-slung sun. Early cropping trees, of which my apple tree is one, fared badly this year due to the late April snow, but the trees on lower ground do not seem to have suffered too badly. Most of the autumn apples seem to go to waste, which seems a shame, but the birds need and rely on them. I am, therefore, surprised to see something strange lying on the ground; odd bundles are spaced out under the apple trees, and I cannot make out what they are until I get closer and see that they are large, clear plastic bags filled with red apples. Several ancient, rickety ladders are perched precariously against the trees in the orchard, but there is no one in sight. It must be Mittagszeit – lunch time.

I see the old man who is normally tending his garden; he has clambered up the steep hill at the side of his house despite his age, which is considerable, and is urgently hammering in a makeshift, rough-hewn fence post, the sound echoes loudly through the valley. I fear for him as he must also descend the steep hillside to safety, but he is used to walking on such terrain. I wave, and he waves back smiling, raising his hat and nodding to me.

There is fresh snow on Koralpe and small pockets of snow along the whole range. The Saualm has a crest of blue-white snow, set off by a picture-postcard blue sky. I anticipated that it would be very beautiful to complete the walk in autumn, but the day outdoes itself, the colours are so rich: the leaves of the gilded birch trees are of topazy-nut, and the ruby-red of the vinegar tree leaves sings out. The light has a quality which is only found at this time of year: after the summer solstice in June the position of the sun in the sky is lower, and both light and colour are different; it is not only poets and artists who see this golden light. I have now walked in all four of the seasons and in many different light conditions, and I can safely say that there is no light like autumn light; it is completely magical.

At the highest point of the walk I sight a yellowhammer, an apt bird to see at this golden time of year.[130] I manage to use my binoculars competently and get a very clear sighting: I notice the forked tail first and then the beautiful yellow, lime-green breast, and can identify too that this is a female. It's already 4 pm when I take a break, sit in the sun and drink the rest of my coffee. I used to think that completing the walk in four hours or less was one of my main goals; I see this as ridiculous now. I walk. I look. I see. I hear. I live in the present moment. I sit and enjoy the quietness until a quad bike roars past me and wakes me from my reminiscence.

I drank too much water before I left, and was caught short. This high up, I rarely if ever see anyone, but just in case, I dash down a little grassy track to a wooded area and find a large tree. Almost immediately, I see a handsome teenager and his attractive mother coming into view. I jump up and pull a muscle in my thigh, but I manage to stride nonchalantly out of the woods as if I was merely hiking from that direction, and pause to photograph a patch of very beautiful coral-orange fungi. I am quite impressed with my lack of panic. I shout 'Grüssgott' to them, possibly a little too loudly, and they pass on by, smiling knowingly.

I find my bench and sit and eat my pitta bread and hummus in near silence, with only the odd bellow from a cow feeding in the nearby barn, or the occasional strange piercing call from the two buzzards flying high. The sun has not stopped shining all day. I sit transfixed and enjoy the warmth on my face. Scanning the landscape, I can see spiky pine trees in the distance, silhouetted against the white filmy lightness that surrounds the Karawanken mountains. I see for the first time new delights: a single cow in the distance standing on an impossibly green velvet field with its own dark shadow, so vivid as to be mesmerising. I can see my few silver-grey hairs reflected in my phone screen as I write this, but I am not unhappy about them. It is the years that I have lived that have taught me how to sit quietly and find beauty in the shadow of a cow standing on cool grass, or the sight of the silhouettes of pine trees in the far distance.

As I pass the house of the man with the most impressive woodpile collection in Austria, I note that his cottage is obscured by a small copse of October-yellow birch trees. Wispy blue-grey smoke puffs out of the chimney, and there is that distinctive aroma that comes only from a newly-laid fire, the loveliest pipe tobacco mixed with the smell of aged pine wood. The backdrop to this is the dying light of the day, pink and blue across the mountains with white clouds spread across like peaked meringue. These are the last golden sun rays of the day; I watch as they fade behind snow-capped peaks. A wonderful finish to a splendid October walk. It suddenly becomes cold, so I put on my hat and gloves and head for home. One of the quietest and calmest walks to date.

46

verdigris

30ᵀᴴ october

When I awake, my muscles are stiff and sore from the long working hours on the house and even longer hours in the garden, but I feel fitter and the adverse effects from the long days of physical labour are short lived. I flex my muscles and stretch and soon feel better.

I want to walk early, so I prepare a quick breakfast of

scrambled eggs and hot coffee. As it is Allerheiligen (All Saints' Day) tomorrow, we treat ourselves to a slice of Allerheiligen Striezel bread – a plaited brioche-like, sweet bread, rich with butter and decorated with flaked almonds. The plaited form represents a plaited head of hair, apparently because at one time it was not unusual for Catholic women to cut their hair as a symbol of mourning. All Saints' Day was invented when it became impossible to dedicate the time needed to celebrate every single death day of the many saints. It is a national holiday, and here in Bad Sankt Leonhard, at 1 pm precisely, the churchyards are full. People come from near and far, and the usually near-empty roads are filled with parents, grandparents and children, walking slowly, but not silently or sadly, to the graveyard. Some men are dressed in the traditional Carinthian or Steiermark dress – either a long dark brown jacket or a dark grey jacket with green epaulettes, worn with dark trousers. Some women wear a Dirndl, a traditional costume worn only in Austria, South Tyrol and Bavaria; a tight-waisted, cleavage-enhancing dress, which is based on the traditional clothing of an Alpine peasant. Other people, however, dress in smart informal clothes, and even jeans and leather jackets seem to be acceptable apparel. Each person finds their family grave and stands beside it, the local brass band plays, and as in Bad Sankt Leonhard the churchyard is spread over two locations and separated by a meadow, and both the music and the priest's words are relayed via a Tannoy system. The list of the people who have died in the last year is read out, there are prayers, and the priest walks amongst the graves followed by choir boys, the leader of whom carries a large cross while holy water is sprinkled onto the graves by the priest. I have attended three of these ceremonies so far, and on all occasions the sun has shone and it has been almost warm. Katie remembers that as a child the ground was always thick with snow. After the priest departs each family lights at least one candle, and in the evening, when the light fails, the churchyards are a mass of flickering flames burning red, as many of the church candles are encased in red glass jars. These red, flickering flames burning brightly in the cold of the evening is an awe-inspiring sight and very moving. This Catholic holy day helps in preparing those who attend for their own eventual demise. I appreciate the day, for this yearly contact with death normalises it in a useful way. We can't avoid it and as the Prince of Denmark says:

> Hamlet: *There's a special providence in the fall of a sparrow. If it be now, 'tis not to come. If it be not to come, it will be now. If it be not now, yet it will come—the readiness is all.*[131]

* * *

With a slice of Allerheiligen Striezel packed into my rucksack, I get away at 10.45 am, but as the clocks have just changed, I have gained an hour. We are now on the fateful descent to Christmas, but the weather holds fast, and it is a gorgeous, sunny, cold day - only 3.5° C. But perhaps I will be lucky, and it will reach 10.5° today. The yellow lime tree leaves by Leonhardikirche church have all fallen; the tree is now a huge black globular skeleton, set against the white high spire of the church. The golden birch leaves have also now mostly gone, but the darker more orange-yellow sycamores leaves are in full glory.

It is Sunday, so it is very quiet and peaceful; I prefer to walk on a Sunday, but it is not always possible. I find it more relaxing as here there is still a marked difference between a work day and Sunday, the day of rest. Walking on Sundays feels right. Ridges of cloud and mist streak the sky, which is divided into three layers. Altostratus clouds float directly above the Koralpe and above these is a delicate section of curling cirrus, while above these is a pale baby-blue cloud-free sky. Soon it becomes dull and overcast with dark rain clouds looming, and I fear that it might be a gloomier walk because of this, but at the first bench stop, a blue sky once again appears and the sun, although hiding, is there. There is no breeze at all. There is a sense of calm. The occasional bellowing cow or whinnying horse breaks the silence, and the sound of one dry leaf as it hits other leaves as it falls to the ground is surprisingly loud.

I allow myself time to sit and look for a few minutes. Now that it is colder I have once again brought a flask of coffee to drink; it tastes better than it ever does at home. I look around me, and at my feet, I can see a tapestry of wild chive flowers in a delicate shade of mauve. Yellow hawkweed, which last year I would have found indistinguishable from dandelion flowers, is still blooming, and despite a series of early morning hard frosts, their seed heads are still standing proud.

Moving on, I study the verge. A tri-coloured Verbascum is a mixture of life and death: the bottom of its stem is still bright green, but the top has been bitten by frost and is brown and dying, three little yellow flowers with red centres struggling on in the middle section. Tiny young self-seeded pine trees are green and healthy, contrasting with crispy, brown, curled-up bracken, which looks exactly as if it has been burnt at its edges. The daisies are so fresh that they still have a pink-tinged newness.

Out of the corner of my eye, a tiny red glow flares up and high on the bank I see a wild strawberry plant that is still thriving. I scale up and retrieve the few sweet, delicious berries. I venture down a path that I have never been down before, shaded over by broadleaf trees. It is dark and gloomy, but there are gnarled, knotted rotting tree stumps and beech roots, groaning with a bright verdigris of moss and lichen. By diverging from the path I usually take, I accidentally stumble into Peter Wohlleben's world, the one he describes so eloquently in his book *The Hidden Life of Trees* (2015).

Suddenly I am away from the commercial pine forests and cultivated crop fields. I peer at the bank, and I can see the tiny filaments of the exposed roots of trees, which are used by the tree to carry messages via a fungal network warning of impending disasters – a pest infestation, for example. I am in a place that certainly looks very different to the tidy and ordered world I usually walk through. In his book, Peter Wohlleben explains that in the world of commercial forestry communications between trees have been ruptured because the fungal networks don't exist in the cultivated intensive world of farming and logging. In ancient forests trees of the same species are related to each and co-dependent. They are in constant communication and continually support each other; even seemingly dead tree stumps continue to be protected, fed and communicated with.

Perhaps these gnarled roots are warning each other about my presence. Is this why we find woods and ancient forests spooky and creepy? At some subconscious level maybe we feel spooked because we feel that we are outsiders in the symbiotically, connected world that plants and trees belong to, and from which we are excluded. With the mist and fog swirling around me I do feel a little unnerved, but perhaps the Brothers Grimm, Arthur Conan Doyle, JRR Tolkien or Stephen King have contributed to my current emotions too. Perhaps these writers, and others like them, were writing what they instinctively felt. Long before Wohlleben's book it seems that at a basic level we have always known that to enter a forest was to enter a magical world of speaking trees and potential danger. Our innate awareness of the forest's ability to communicate may explain why so many of them are associated with places of spiritually and worship. After all the Ancient Greeks believed that the rustling of the leaves in an oak tree was the voice of Zeus, so this idea is as old as thought. Moreover, the great eighteenth-century nature writer Théodore Rousseau 'heard the voices of the trees' and 'wanted to talk with them' to put his 'finger on the secret of their majesty.'[132]

An open gate at the end of the path lures me on, and I pause to look down on a declining landscape as a momentary mist rolls in under a row of aureate hazel leaves. I retrace my steps, continuing to admire the minute detail of this new world I have found. If I have learnt nothing else over the past ten months, I now truly know that looking and seeing are different things and this is a skill which I am happy to continue to develop.

* * *

The few leaves that are left on the apple tree are honey-yellow now. I pluck one to take home and dry as a memento of my year of walking. As I move into a more open area, I enjoy the sun which shines off and on, obscured by a sky which is a beautiful study in cloud formations. There are duvet-down clouds, nimbus cumulus and a superb example of a lenticular cloud, the kind of cloud that because of its oval disc-like shape mistakenly convinces people that they have seen an unidentified flying object.

At the highest point, I survey the surrounding mountains: the new season snow has not appeared on either the Koralpe or the Zirbitzkogel, but the Saualm has had enough snow to make a few small snowmen. The Karawanken range is shrouded in haze and lies like a blue-blanket backdrop behind the scene, which is still amber, orange, yellow and green but is declining into the grey of early winter. At the house with the frescoes, I see dark nettle leaves with purple flowers and tiny cream, yellow and purple wild pansies nestling under a very old and twisted Lavanttal banana apple tree. At my rest stop bench, I can't hear anything other than the distant rumble of a jet plane far away, but I cannot see it. After a few moments I recognise the gentle sound of the exhaling breath of cows feeding in their stall. I can both see and smell the musky sweet aroma of a new and very large heap of compost; it steams, the heat rising as it is heated by the sun.

The tranquil scene is relaxing, and I close my eyes and drowse for a few minutes. When I awake, I am encouraged to press on, as due to the changing of the clocks the sky already has an end of the day look. The road is lined with golden-yellow leaved birch trees which descends to Schiefling and is surrounded by vivid green perfectly-manicured fields so that every hump and contour of the land is revealed. Lines of perfectly-mown grass stretch out before me. The verges have been left long: lupin and dandelion seeds will be able to fall to provide next year's bounty, but until then we must brave the winter and learn to love the darker evenings. We will eat our stored winter vegetables with their trapped sunlight inside, perhaps with a dark glass of red wine, the fire and candles lit. Cosy. Warm. Safe.

47

BELL

5ᵀᴴ NOVEMBER

It is a dull day, but if I am lucky, the temperatures might climb above freezing. I can hardly believe they will, because early this morning the land was bound tightly in early frost and fog. I am a little reluctant to go, and consequently ill-prepared, and I have to turn back after ten minutes because it's much colder than I expected. Returning for a thicker coat, I also search out my hat and gloves.

The day becomes ever duller as the shroud of grey cloud

thickens. The trees are now almost bare of their recent golden ornamentation. Such is the progression of the days as we turn towards winter, and I feel a painful pang of nostalgia for the warmth of the summer and the beauty of autumn. I have to work much harder to see the intrinsic splendour of the land. I look for colour and see golden apples still clinging to the bare branches of the small apple trees and in the drabness of November, even without sunshine, the colours shine out. I see an elderly woman striding along, and she is a festival of colour – a yellow walking stick, a bright blue headscarf, a red woollen scarf around her neck, a sage green jacket, a skirt adorned with a diamond pattern in red and black, and olive green wellington boots. She marches past a long row of multi-coloured beehives. As I climb, I see that the larger fruit trees still have green leaves and the sycamore and larch trees are still golden. I've never really looked closely at a larch branch: the needles radiate out from a central button, like a slightly cranky windmill. Moss on north-facing tree trunks also catches my eye, a thick and luxuriant dark green. I reach the shrine, with its brightly-painted image of Saint Laurence holding the instrument of his torture and martyrdom – a griddle on which he was burnt to death – and shudder at the cruelty that man is sometimes capable of.

High up on a bank a single Canterbury bell flower winks at me, its petals a deep and gorgeous purple. I usually don't take much notice of these blooms because they are so ubiquitous, but in the much more subdued monochromatic landscape, this pretty flower provides a welcome splash of colour. The Canterbury bell is only one in a large family of more than three hundred varieties, all taking their names from the Latin campanula, meaning tower of bells.[133] Canterbury bells are native to Southern Europe but were introduced to British gardeners in 1597 when John Norton published John Gerard's *Herball or Generall Historie of Plantes*.

The book ran to nearly 1,500 pages and included woodcut prints of many of the plants. Gerard's epic accomplishment seems all the more impressive because he spent his whole life living in London, in a tenement with no garden of his own. Gerard's lack of a garden makes me think about the absence of flora today compared with its abundance in summer, when there are so many varieties to see that I couldn't possibly have listed them all.

I began the walk last December, and as December moved into January, I often trudged along in similar conditions to today. The walks started much as a symphony would, beginning quietly and then swelling into the main movement. The central section, representing fecund summer, with the orchestra at full capacity, strings swelling and wind instruments providing colour and harmony, flowers bursting into bloom and crops yielding their abundance, the percussion being provided by chirping crickets and cowbells. Now the seasons are declining into the slow adagio of late autumn and they will soon reach the final coda of a silent white winter. All the movements of the symphony are equally important and all enjoyable in varying degrees.

This analogy makes me feel much more satisfied: of course, I cannot expect to see colour and beauty on every walk. When I stop for coffee my breath vaporizes; I watch the breath clouds pass from me and into the atmosphere and I feel as it mingles into the surroundings that I am not simply a transient being passing through; I am now part of the landscape. I close my eyes to enjoy the distant sound of the mountain stream as it rushes on its downhill journey.

It's Saturday, so it is very quiet and so far I have not seen any farm workers or tractors. A few cows and sheep remain in the fields, but they are much stiller now; presumably they are preserving their energy. The conditions begin to yield other pleasures: the lack of tree canopy reveals the mountain stream to me, the spumy water rushing past me not more than a hundred feet away but normally hidden. Not only purple Canterbury bells flower still, there are also pretty nettle flowers to enjoy. The Koralpe is completely shrouded in thick rain clouds; I cannot see the summit, but the rain streaks through the distant clouds like a watercolour wash. As I reach the apple tree, a light rain begins to fall on me too, but after a few moments it ceases, the clouds part and a ray of sunshine appears. The bright sky and pale sun calms my mind.

48

AMMIL

❦

9ᵀᴴ NOVEMBER

It is only 2.7°C, and it feels bitter. Yesterday there was considerable snowfall on high ground, but we have little or none here. I go outside and begin clearing the drive of snow. I start to sweep up all the tinkly fragments of ice, so that our driveway doesn't become an ice rink and freeze solid. Katie comes out to tell me some fateful news: she has heard on the radio that Donald

Trump has, against all hope, won the US election. I log in to my computer to find that a good friend of mine, a distraught American citizen, has sent me W.H. Auden's poem entitled *1st September 1939*. One of the stanzas reads:

All I have is a voice
To undo the folded lie,
The romantic lie in the brain
Of the sensual man-in-the-street
And the lie of Authority
Whose buildings grope the sky:
There is no such thing as the State
And no one exists alone;
Hunger allows no choice
To the citizen or the police;
We must love one another or die.

But we do not love one another. It seems that we have learnt very little in the past seventy-seven years. I feel utterly depressed. On the 23 June, the day of the EU Referendum in the UK, which was also by coincidence a day of walking for me, I felt nervous and worried that the 'Leave' contingency would prevail, so the result wasn't a complete shock. Despite that terrible turn of events, I did not expect a Trump win. In both the UK and the US hate and greed seem to have been stirred into a pot full of misplaced yearnings for a return to an antediluvian past. There seems little or no awareness of the turmoils of history. The result is a poisonous concoction that has been imbibed and to which we must now try to find an antidote.

* * *

There is snow in Reichenfels, and directly above our house the small village of Kliening is divided into two: the side nearest our home is green and lush, then in a straight line beyond there has been a fresh fall of snow. It is a visual illustration of the election in the US, or the Leave and Remain voters in the UK, an unhappy, divided land. I am so downhearted that I do not leave until nearly one o'clock and then I have to drag myself out of the house. But as the sky is now a vivid blue and the sun is shining continually, I feel a little heartened.

I walk unthinkingly. At about 3,000 feet above sea level, I see that a covering of snow embellishes the pine trees from the night's snowfall, but only the topmost branches have been affected. As I rise higher, I look up to see that I will eventually reach trees completely cloaked in snow. I quicken the pace. My body is glowing with warmth, but my face feels cold, and I pull my scarf around me. It seems like I am walking in falling snow, but it is just a whiffle of wind which is blowing snow from the high tree branches above me. It drifts lazily down, caught in the sun's rays, and this gladdens my soul, but only a very little.

It becomes cold, and I feel the damp air encircling me, so I move on quickly. As I round the corner to catch my first glimpse of the Koralpe in the far distance, I see that it is shrouded in grey cloud and therefore invisible, but a bright patch of grey-blue sky opens to reveal a dazzling spot-lit gash of stunningly beautiful, pristine snow-covered hills in the distance. In a clearing between the hills stands a platoon of pine trees standing perfectly erect, like stoic Russian soldiers from a bygone era, motionless and disciplined, their snow-cloaks of no consequence to them. Around the trees is virgin snow, so they look exactly like well-drilled soldiers standing to attention on a marked-out parade ground, a testament to the precise and accurate work that the foresters oversee.

I am thrilled to see that the apple tree is laced with snow, as I love to look at dark trunks lined with white snow. I look at it for many moments, fully appreciating it. As I leave, I climb higher, and look down upon a thousand pine trees all sugared with snow. I stand in awe at this beauty. Closer to my field of vision, red apples still cling to nearby trees against the black silhouettes of their trunks and the branches laced with pure white. The whole landscape has a fairy tale, mythic quality.

I see a decaying sunflower head, hanging limply from a wire fence. I pluck it and take it for my collection of found objects. For me it symbolises both the fear and the hope I feel: I fear that the world is becoming yet more polarised and forgetful of the lessons of history, but I must have confidence in the future; even this dead flowerhead has seeds which I will plant so that it can become a new yellow, hopeful sunflower.

On my descent I am only thinking of returning home, and cannot concentrate fully on anything. But then I happen to glance casually over to an ugly drain which drips water perpetually and see that the water drips have created a large finger-like collection of tumbling ice; I walk over to take a closer look. Kneeling, I find the most beautiful miniature ice sculptures, each casing of ice entrapping a single vivid green occupant – a lone blade of grass or leaf. I am very heartened by these sights, and even though the ground is wet I spend as long as the cold conditions will allow, taking up my camera and losing myself in the act of focusing on these miraculous sculptures. Water splashes onto my lens, and it is many minutes before I get even a few photographs that are clearly in focus. In Devon, they have a term for the thin film of ice that lacquers leaves, twigs and grass blades when a freeze follows a partial thaw - ammil. The word is derived from the old English word 'ammel', which is the old version of the word enamel[134]. In looking at these blades of grass and shamrock-like leaves wrapped in ice, I am witnessing a living dictionary incarnation of a nearly lost word from a world not yet quite lost. I have never seen anything like it before. Such a phenomenon appears more readily on high ground, and I live in the hope that I will see something as beautiful as this again, especially as it has been created from something as ugly as a plastic water pipe. I needed this today. It goes some way to improve my mood. The walk has restored my sense of perspective; it was so beautiful as to seem dreamlike.

On the final stretch home, I pass a row of immense dark green pine trees. I am still above the snow line, so they still have their thick coats of snow; their bright orange pine cones sing out in the colourless landscape. Walking beside these vast trees is like walking through a medieval tapestry. All I need now is a roaring fire, and today I definitely need a very large glass of mulled wine.

49

MIST

20ᵀᴴ November

It is overcast and misty. I find it hard to motivate myself. But it is a not unpleasant 8.8° C, and according to the weather forecast, it will become sunny. My spirits are lifted as soon as I round the corner to climb up the Erzbergstrasse: I am met by half a dozen great tits feeding voraciously from a feeder in the churchyard. Twenty or more very healthy-looking specimens fly hither and thither, standing out starkly on the now almost bare trees. The barrenness of the landscape is much alleviated by the glimpses of their yellow and black plumage, and in the quietness of winter, their twitterings cannot be ignored. Several magpies take flight noisily. Three jackdaws fly past me to perch on the nearby telephone wires. A patch of blue sky in the distance encourages me further on my way.

The path is lined by tall orange and black snow markers which are put out by the Gemeinde in case there is a heavy snowfall, as they help both walkers and the occasional driver to know where the road ends; often there is a sheer drop at the edges of the route. These bright markers clearly show that winter will soon be upon us. As I rise and walk through the pine woods the mist begins to close in again and all around me I can see, feel and sense moisture and decay: stones thick with dark green moss, leaf-less branches with black, frostbitten stalks, larch needles lying in thick layers on the ground. The place where I saw the beautiful delicate ice sculptures is carefully covered now by cut pine branches, to prevent further freezing and save the water pipe from cracking. But November has been unusually warm, so there is still some new life. Young, pale green bracken leaves spread their glow nestling alongside virile copper-rust autumn bracken, but these delicate new leaves will not survive the low temperatures.

I hear and see a dissimulation of blackcaps chirping noisily and lifting themselves into the air like a squadron of fighter planes.[135] They rise from a patch of lilac trees, their purple candle-like blooms long gone. Both sexes have a neat coloured cap to the head, black in the male and reddish-brown in the female. I have been able to see some at close quarters, as we have had the pleasure of having blackcaps in our garden over the past few days. We tried to put out all kinds of food but we finally bought peanuts and within minutes – there must be a bush telegraph – we had blue tits, great tits, blackcaps and even a crested tit constantly flitting backwards and forwards, carrying half-peanuts away with them. We have thrown out old apples that we have not managed to overwinter, and every morning two or three female blackbirds feed on them. As they land they invariably flick up their long, elegant tails, most likely to warn other birds off – blackbirds are nothing if not territorial.

* * *

The apple tree, and those in the orchards around, especially those with that still have their golden and red fruit, are besieged by a rash of redwings, feasting very noisily.[136] They resemble a female blackbird or a thrush but breed more exclusively in woodland and scrub, so I have rarely seen them. I last saw a flock of them when I was on holiday in Wales; I had no idea what I was looking at and had to ask a local farmer. My father often talked about how when he was very young and new to birdwatching in the late 1930s the fields around Banstead in Surrey were filled with fieldfares and redwings; both were a ubiquitous sight. I know that he also spotted redwings when he was in Austria in the late 1940s. Luckily for me they are fairly easy to recognise, being large (nearly ten inches in length) with prominent reddish flanks and speckled breasts similar to thrushes, to which they are related.

A fat-chested male bullfinch sits sedately and quietly, bobbing around on the branch above the field entirely undisturbed by the noisy fieldfares.

The mountain stream is spumy white and hisses loudly, swelled by melting snow and rain. Rewarded for my long climb through the melancholy pine wood, I am met by the Koralpe highlighted against a band of blue sky, ornamented with snow. As I reach the highest point at 2.30 pm, the sky begins to turn to gold in the west and the sun starts gradually to slip away. For a few long minutes I look back at the Karawanken range again, but now it is utterly transformed as a sea of mist surrounds it. The scene looks exactly like one dreamt up by a Hollywood special effects team. Or perhaps I am looking through a window into Asia? The misty crown of the Karawanken range evokes one of Katsushika Hokusai's woodblocks of Mount Fuji.[137] I have never seen them look so beautiful or so unlike themselves.

* * *

We have a friend staying here and visiting us from England, so today I allow myself to cheat a little and just a few hundred yards before I reach the last stage of the walk Katie and our friend collect me by car. We visit a tiny little inn in the forest, which was once a water mill for the grinding of flour. It's charming, smoky inside and very busy. All the seats are taken, and the tables are full to bursting. It's utterly unspoilt by time and progress. A warm and cosy end to a day filled with stunning beauty but at times tinged with melancholy by sadness for the loss of summer.

50
DOG

27ᵀᴴ November

We have friends staying with us from Berlin, and they are not keen to attempt the whole of my walk but would like to experience some of it. It's a pleasant 8.5° C, but the sky is a mass of cloud, early morning mist is still rising, and black rain clouds are evident. I prime them to be quiet as we round the corner to pass by the Leonhardkirche, as I hope we will see goldfinches. We are not disappointed. We approach slowly and catch a glimpse of a charm of them, but soon they rise and fly away with that distinctive dipping motion, singing their broken glass song as they go.

We move on past the church, and the bells begin to toll noon very loudly, while the clouds part to reveal a milky white sun which shines momentarily but brightly on us. This meteorological event is of epic proportions and seems to be cosmically fantastic to my walking partners – it is as if I have I orchestrated it especially for them. Despite the intermittent sunshine, it is warm and mild for November. Baby lambs only a few days old frolic and feed, looking around in amazement at this strange new world. One is entirely black apart from a tiny patch of white on his head; it resembles a yokeless fried egg.

My companions leave me just after I round the first bend and before the climb becomes too steep. I bid them farewell, breathe in some clean, fresh air and set off as a solitary walker. I am gregarious and talkative by nature, but since I have begun to walk alone I have acquired a great appreciation for quiet and solitude; this is a very new skill for me. Walking with companions is about sharing my knowledge, much of it new-found, and wanting them to love the views and the sights as much as I do. It brings its own pleasures, but it is not possible to be attentive to new sights on such occasions.

As soon as I am alone, I look around me to see what today can bring. I immediately see a puffball mushroom lying at the roadside; it must have tumbled down from the bank. I spend a happy few moments pressing the side of it with my foot and watching the dark brown-black spores puff out. It's hard not to smile at nature when it is this inventive and clever.

I climb to where I can usually catch my first glimpse of the Koralpe, but I am met instead by thick fog which has descended very quickly. I can hear cowbells, but cannot see any cows. I quicken my pace and reach the apple tree in record time, but fearing more fog and possibly rain I double back and take a slightly shorter route back to Bad Sankt Leonhard, a path I took once before in thick snow at Katie's urging. It is the first Sunday in Advent, so it seems apt to be taking a path which will pass by the little yellow chapel.

I enjoy my diversion very much, and I am rewarded when as the day dims the sky clears and the leafless trees are silhouetted against a white sky with a thin blue and orange banner of light above Schiefling. By taking this shortcut, I have a new view of a familiar scene to appreciate. I can look down on the church in Schiefling and admire the paths I have previously taken. But when I reach the little yellow chapel, the magic is no longer there: since I passed by last time it has become dwarfed by a new and enormous barn, and there is a strong odour in the air. It is filled with battery chickens; I am not at all thrilled by this. I am saddened that they are not being reared organically and allowed to range freely – there is no shortage of space here.

I am musing on this so much that I am caught off guard when a gorgeous black and tan dog bounds up to me and nearly knocks me over. He is such a happy beast, with a smiling face and I think an equally happy soul. One look at him and I find it impossible to be unhappy. He chews on my coat strings and bites the fingers of my gloved hands affectionately, all the while dancing around me madly. I move on, but he follows me for about ten minutes, so I decide to take his photograph. When I take my camera out, he poses, preparing himself for the picture, looking directly into the lens and puffing out his chest – he is a real professional. Eventually I hear his owner calling him, and reluctantly I send him back home, having to speak to him firmly in German. This encounter reminds me of all the dogs that I have had in my life and how much I loved every one of them. A dog would have been a great companion on this project, but also a great distraction.

After the dog departs, a wren lands nearby and hops along the fence, following me as I ascend the hill and noisily chirruping all the way to up. In German, the wren is called der Zaunkönig, the King of the Fence, and this is apt indeed.[138] In almost all the sightings I have made of the little wren he has been nestling in a hedge or atop a fence, frequently making a riotous noise. Then, as wrens tend to do, he suddenly disappears into a crevice. The wonderfully descriptive scientific name for the wren is taken from the Greek word 'troglodytes' or cave dweller, because the wren rootles about on the ground and dives under things to find insects and spiders. Much as I would like to have a dog by my side I know that this would be the death of such sightings. The wren is now very close to me, and he trills a little in greeting and hops away again.

I arrive at the apple tree, but today it is merely a ghostly, black outline, only just visible through a sea of November fog, which has descended suddenly and very quickly. There is not a trace of the view I was admiring only moments before.

Luckily the fog lifts and I admire the view for the next half an hour of walking, soaking it in until it descends once again. It continues to rise and fall for the rest of the day. I notice during the last part of the walk that the sunflower field has been ploughed and hardly any traces of the golden-yellow beauty of the summer blooms remains. The monochrome landscape of winter will soon be upon us.

On the pull up the hill towards home that there are posters urging people to vote in the upcoming elections. One poster features a man sporting a beard of grey stubble and dressed in a simple pale blue shirt, with an open collar, he is wearing Lederhosen. He looks out across open fields, with his hands hooked into his pockets; this man is Van der Bellen. He is standing against the far right candidate Norbert Hofer. Van der Bellen's family were members of the Russian nobility, but formerly of Dutch ancestry. His family suffered greatly under Stalin's punitive regimes, becoming refugees when they eventually fled Russia. I hope beyond hope that he will be elected, as he is a politician who understands the blight of conflict on the modern-day world, leading to the recent rise in the need for people to flee their homelands. I have heard him speak and he is measured and calm; this too would be welcome in a year that has proved to be so shocking and disturbing. I can only stand by and watch, as I am not allowed to vote here. I feel as if there is a cold stone lying in the pit of my stomach. I hope that Van der Bellen can sail against the rising tide of right-wing political thought taking shape in Europe and further afield. After the twin agonies of Brexit and the shocking recent election of Trump earlier this month, I am hoping against all hope that the moderate candidate Van der Bellen will be successful and will be elected as the new Austrian President.[139]

The last of the daylight dwindles as a large black crow flies noiselessly past me past the fast-flowing river.

51
DILAPIDATION

4ᵀᴴ December

It was a freezing -7.7° C overnight, so we awake to a frosty, foggy, misty morning and old snow lies thinly on the ground. The sun makes its first appearance at about 10 o'clock - a very welcoming sight. By the time I leave at 10.20 am it's a much more acceptable 1°. I pass the Leonhardikirche and the immense lime tree, and stop as I always do to admire the millions of leaves on the tree. No matter what colour they are they have such beauty, but I especially love the yellow ones of autumn. Today I have to admire the tree's skeleton, as it is entirely leafless, and the deep grooves of the cracked bark. I steal a few moments to pace out the circumference of the tree base; I estimate that it is roughly 32 feet in diameter.

I turn once more to face the sun, and a flutter of sparrows fills the bare frames of the apple trees, chirruping and gossiping as they search for food. The orchard is still thick with yellowing lime-green apples - a delicious morning snack for birds. A great tit pecks at one, then swoops away impatiently. I count a further eight great tits on the wild elderberry trees by the stream. At first they sit happily waiting for me to pass, but they become nervous and zip away to a safer distance. The path has fractured into rivulets, worn by the random passage of the white mare that criss-crosses the paddock day after day. At the river bank crystals of ice cling to the fringes of grass that overhang these ley lines; I have never seen the river so low, with the right side of the riverbed showing through, a rocky, sandy, dusty brown-grey, and a mere trickle of water running by the left bank only.

The vast summer meadow, today a gradually-turning-winter-frosted brown, is a military parade ground of molehills – the RSM (Regimental Sergeant Mole) has obviously been cracking his whip. The hover of crows that line the alder caw loudly, laughing down on the scene, their airborne freedom mocking the underground captivity of the moles. The only colour in the farm courtyard as I pass through is an enormous spray of bright pink chrysanthemums with sunny yellow centres overhanging the path. A cat meows at the farm door, and an elderly gentleman opens the door a little. I see only the brim of his hat through the crack in the door, and then a hand pops out to beckon the furry friend inside.

The sky is white and blue above the church in Schiefling. I reach a wooded area and hear a mournful call: two birds fly past me. I raise my binoculars and see first a pinky-red breast, then a jet black cap, a soft grey back, a white rump, a jaunty upward-curving white wing stripe, a black tail, and then as he turns that savage-looking bill. It is a magnificently-coloured bullfinch and his slightly less colourful mate. They are very close to me, rootling in the low branches of the pine forest for food.

As I emerge from the trees, the vista opens up. Through the open gate I can see the mountains and the old dilapidated barn with its fading frescoes, both bathed in sunlight. On the north elevation of the barn I see something glinting; there is a perfect row of stiletto daggers of ice running along the whole length of the building. It is only the sun's declining angle that allows me to see them. They are about ten inches long. I move in and stand directly under the eaves; lit by the sun, these ice sculptures are almost golden.

I walk around the building and step over a large puddle which is crusted over with pure white ice. A self-seeded sapling – now a quite impressive tree – is growing out from a barbed wire fence, its lacy outline backlit against the sun. The windows of the barn, most without glass, are blind, but those with glass are merely short-sighted, pearly with frost. The lintel over a large double window has collapsed, and the shutters hang limply as the crumbling stonework can no longer support them. It's a mystery, but the building's dilapidation only serves to enhance its beauty.

As I approach the apple tree, I hear what I think must be a strong gust of wind, but it is a dissimulation of at least forty blackcaps arriving. As they do not see me until the last moment, I have time to see them clearly, and I manage to hide so that I can observe them for a while. Spooked at last, they all lift off as one, flying away to descend on another tree, feasting in a frenzy on its apple crop.

One bird sits proudly on a high branch, and I watch him

for some moments. A green woodpecker calls and flies over me towards the Karawanken mountain range, which is lit by an apricot sorbet blister of light. Oval clouds appear to be hanging motionless above like something dreamt up by a renaissance artist, unreal, mystical even. A whisper of grey cirrus clouds curl feather-like towards the sun and eventually obscures the orange sky. It is late, and I hurry to arrive home before darkness sets in.

52

FROST

6ᵀᴴ December

It was again -7.2° C overnight, so it is freezing but very sunny and beautiful. I don't want to miss the bright white frost, so I make a good, early start. I am already out of the door at 9.15, and it is a perfect morning. A very bright sun lights up a pale blue sky. Great tits, chirping merrily, bright yellow and black dabs against the bare trees, dance and feed by the side of the stream. The fields are the colour of the delicate underside of a sage leaf, laced with a layer of icy frost which spreads a veil over the grass. Every tree is a scarecrow laced with ice. The fields in the distance below the

Koralpe are gently contoured, and a straight road runs through the undulating scene. A row of thirty or more trees bordering the road are silhouetted against the bright sunlight, their shadows made tall and slender, casting a row of perfectly regular giant outlines on the frosty pale green grass backdrop. They look flat, like two-dimensional lithographic illustrations or a row of artists' brushes, just waiting to be taken up. Perhaps an artist could render the beauty of the scene, although the light changes from moment to moment, so fast that it would be impossible to capture quickly on paper; even a photograph could not do it justice.

The white rendered church in Schiefling is bathed in a winter-white light; with its tall spire and slate grey roof, it is precisely the building that an artist would add to enhance the scene. The views are unrecognisable from any other walk I have undertaken, and in an hour it will be different again.

I decide to walk the slightly shorter route which takes me up Steinbruchweg. It is rather beautiful, as the path runs along a mountain brook. There are tall pine trees, so the walk is green and lush in places. The brook is bubbling away very noisily as it tumbles down the hillside over rocks and boulders. This is a more shaded area because of the overhanging trees and no direct sunshine can hit the water directly, but some small shafts of light break through and catch every tiny icicle that clings to the bank. They shine with an almost LED brightness, creating pinpoints of light: one, two, three, four, five in random patterns. Even a talented lighting designer would struggle to recreate this effect. I usually struggle to climb this hill, but in my search for the icicle lights, I soon find that although I am out of breath, I have reached the top effortlessly.

The sky is of a pale hue, it is hazy, and I cannot see the Karawanken mountain range, but I see the Koralpe, which has no snow save for one strip on the northern side, which is merely a single line of perfect snow for skiing, created by a snow-making machine. The sky is almost without clouds, save for some delicate cirrus streaks. The grass is still mostly green, but in places, the signs of the hard frosts that we have had recently are beginning to show. I see one small patch of hawkweed, a few straggly buttercups and a tall spray of purple Canterbury bells struggling on. They all provide a splash of welcome colour in the now much more subdued, monochromatic landscape.

I see a field of four young cows - they have not had any young as their udders have not formed. They have short, straight horns and are alert and very interested in me. They gather in a neat line and stare at me quizzically, their furry ears backlit by the sun. As I turn a steep and sharp corner I am greeted by yet more cows, this time with calves feeding at the teat.

I reach the crossroads and then the apple tree, unremarkable in its dormant early winter state. I descend the path, leaving the tree behind, and in the curve of the road, bare red willow stems stand out, looking far lovelier now than in their apparent summer clothing. Sitting quietly aloft is a yellowhammer. The burgundy-red of the branches beautifully sets off the bright yellow-green of the bird. This is a male: he has a bright yellow head, a streaked brown back, a chestnut rump and yellow underparts. He sits very still and bright against the blue of the sky. I move in slowly until I am directly under the tree, but still he sits. It is then that he begins to sing – not the tuneful, lyrical song of a robin or a blackbird, but a thoughtful burst of the song is rising slightly up the scale with a short pause of about six seconds in between. It is such a delicate and quiet sound that it demands a great deal of concentration to listen to it. He is a rare thing of beauty on a most beautiful day. Eventually he flies away, and the spell is broken.

53
Lace

8TH DECEMBER

It is a very sunny 7.7°C, which surprises me – it was a freezing -7.5 °C overnight. I leave at 11 am and all is quiet, for today is a bank holiday. The Immaculate Conception is being celebrated. I had to look this up because I believed that is was concerned with the Virgin birth of Jesus, but I was wrong - the Immaculate Conception deals with the thorny problem of the conception of the Blessed Virgin Mary herself. According to the teaching of the Catholic Church, Mary was conceived not by normal biological means in the womb of her mother, Saint Anne, but by God who acted upon her soul to make it 'immaculate' and free from Original Sin. One can see how, as the Mother of Christ, it is crucial that Mary be free from sin, the sin that arose from the fall of man and stemmed from Adam and Eve's rebellion in the Garden of Eden. Specifically, it is the sin of disobedience, caused by the consuming of the fruit from the tree of knowledge – the knowledge of good and evil.

Traditionally the forbidden fruit is thought to have been an apple, although the fruit is not named in the Bible. Once again, I think that my accidental choice of an apple tree as one of the main foci of this project has more philosophical weight than I at first considered. From the Judgement of Paris to the Book of Genesis, the (golden) apple, more than any other fruit, is the symbol of knowledge and temptation. In Norse mythology, the goddess Iðunn keeps apples that grant eternal youthfulness, so the apple may also represent immortality. In fact, in the Garden of Eden, there were two trees, the Tree of Knowledge and the Tree of Life. Adam was expelled from the garden because God feared he might also eat from the Tree of Life and thus live forever.[140] So the apple is a symbol of both knowledge and immortality.

This Bank Holiday has become more secular here: in all the major cities in Austria many people take advantage of an extra free day to do their Christmas shopping, but here and in most rural areas church attendance is more usual. But as it is now approaching lunch time and church is over for today, it is nearly silent, and there is not a soul around; everyone is enjoying the calm of a holiday day. Pausing to listen, all I can hear are birds chirruping all around me. There is activity and noise everywhere, and as I walk on, bird after bird lifts and takes flight. A blackbird ground feeding amongst copper leaves rises angrily and gives an alarm call as it departs. Chaffinches and great tits rise and take flight by the dozen.

It is then that I hear the strange trill sound of a crested tit; I have never seen one before, and it takes me a moment to realise what I am seeing.[141] They are very rare in the British Isles, although they are sometimes found in Scotland, but even there they are restricted to the ancient pinewoods of Inverness and Strathspey. The crested tit is happiest and widespread where conifers and deciduous woodland grow. I can see a long line of conifers, and the path is inclining, so I am level with the mid to top branches of the trees. Very close by there is a male who is having a rest and pausing for a few moments on a low branch; he is almost within reach of me. He is a charming little fellow, about four inches in length, and very small (crested tits weigh only 0.3-0.5 ounces.) The plumage on his back is a greyish brown and his wings and head are mainly white, but he has a distinctive black eye-stripe. Most striking of all is his little punk hairdo, a distinct crest which is dotted black and white. Although related to the blue and great tits, the crested tit does not enjoy anything like the same strength of numbers; it is a vulnerable and protected species. If I see nothing more of beauty today, I will be more than happy. He flies higher up into the branches, and I lose sight of him, but he calls and back comes a response from a mate, I listen to their conversation for a while.

I am once again almost too warm in my thick coat. Although patches of frost remain in shady areas, I find some sunscreen from my pocket and apply it; last time I walked my cheeks became quite sunburnt, so this time I am prepared. I see a family sitting on their veranda enjoying a meal together, and they wave and smile. Their three cats are sunbathing lazily in a patch of sunshine on the driveway, and in an exact echo of the felines, three sheep lie in the same formation in the nearby field. There is less haze today, and the sky is once again pale blue with mackerel clouds which dot the horizon. I get hotter and hotter as I climb, as there is not even a breath of wind.

I see something move, and right before me is a greater spotted woodpecker.[142] He starts to knock at a tall pine but is disturbed by a passing tractor. I am thrilled to see this large and brightly-coloured bird; his plumage is pied black and white with red on his lower belly. I know it is a male as he has a distinctive red patch on the back of his head. He shimmies around the tree, exactly like a child playing hide and seek, placing himself away from me and away from danger. I sit on a tree stump for a few minutes, hoping I will get another peek.

As I wait, I enjoy the heat from the sun. I feel very spoilt when, waiting for the woodpecker to reappear, I spot a nuthatch.[143] I have only seen two before. My first was in North Wales, where I had gone on holiday in an attempt to do some walking, but it had rained so much that I was forced to sit inside and watch nature from within. It was then that I made my sighting – there he was feeding from a garden bird table. My second sighting was in the first autumn I arrived in Austria, when I began to explore the area for the first time. I walked to the beautiful, craggy 14th century Gomarn ruin that lies high on a hill above the town of Bad Sankt Leonhard. Adjacent to the ruin is a path lined on each side by slender silver birch trees, which many birds call home. I was not even paying close attention, but I could not miss the stunning yet muted colours of the little bird when it came into my eye-line – another nuthatch sighting.

The Eurasian nuthatch is a very distinctive bird, with an oddly large head, short tail and powerful bill and feet, a gorgeous grey-blue on its upper parts (the sort of colour that Farrow and Ball would call Manor House Grey), a lovely chestnut red on its breast and an Adam Ant black eye stripe, a dashing and distinctive bird.

Nuthatches scale up and down tree trunks with jerky movements: they are the only bird to descend headfirst down a trunk. It is this movement that makes them easy to spot, especially in trees denuded of leaves. Its English name comes from its habit of wedging a large food item in a crevice and then hacking at it using its strong bill. Nuthatches are very resourceful and hide seeds, or snails, into crannies and nooks in trees, sometimes even covering them with moss or bark. They also hide their nest holes with mud to protect the young inside from larger birds. It is perhaps not coincidental that greater spotted woodpeckers predate young chicks, usually preferring the smaller members of the tit family, but I dare say that a nuthatch chick would serve just as well; perhaps I am now watching two potential adversaries just a few tree hops from one another. Both birds are beautiful, but I am also reminded that nature is red in tooth and claw.

I walk on and crest the hill, to see that the moon is a perfect half-sphere hanging low in a perfect blue sky surrounded by soft curling clouds. I can see that the Koralpe is bare, sans snow, and for the first time in a while, I can see the extended length of the whole range before me. The alternating rounded and sharp peaks are very prominent. Above them hangs a single line of white clouds, as if drawn in by hand, and below them a blue-white line of mist; the scene is awe-inspiring. I spend much of my time while walking contemplating beauty, but I think today the view is sublime. When Edmund Burke wrote his now famous *Philosophical Enquiry* in 1757, he was amongst the first thinkers to connect the Sublime with experiences of awe, terror and danger, distinguishing Sublime from the merely Beautiful. For Burke, the Beautiful is a scene of perfection, well-formed and aesthetically pleasing, but to encounter the Sublime is to be overwhelmed and to feel that what we are confronting has the power to destroy us.

We have become so accustomed in the 21st century to

a preference for the Sublime over the Beautiful that we think little of it. The preference for a quick climb up Mount Everest before lunch or abseiling down a raging, craggy waterfall before breakfast is considered to be un-noteworthy. Before I moved to Austria, I had minimal experience of the Sublime, experiencing it only theoretically through the paintings of John Martin and Caspar David Friedrich, but I had a print of Friedrich's *Wanderer above the Sea of Fog* (1817) hanging by a window in my last house, and I was captivated by it. It was only when I first visited Austria that I had any idea of how the Sublime felt.[144]

My knowledge hitherto was purely intellectual. Mountains, even when viewed from a distance, have a magnificence that is beyond all possibility of calculation, and I often stand awed by the scene before me. My presence, just a small dot in the landscape, makes me aware of the sublime beauty all around me. I am humbled by it. I have also come to believe that for me anyway there is no better antidote against stress and mental strain; no better medicine is available.

I am reaching the last few miles of today's walk, so I fill my lungs with cold, fresh air and descend from the high altitudes to the lower path by the river. I note that the ice on the weir has frozen into a silent sculpture of thick white pleats, the ice formations all equally spaced as if by design, as ornate as the lace on a Victorian wedding dress. I have often seen the weir water frozen into clumps, but this has artistry, symmetry and poetry woven right into it.

54

EXTRACTION

14ᵀᴴ December

We have just returned from a short trip to Vienna, to deliver Christmas presents to friends. Vienna is a gorgeous city, but the hustle and bustle of the metropolis are enjoyable only in small quantities. I feel very much in need of my walk today. It is sunny, and a surprisingly warm 6.6 ° C. I manage to leave before the clock strikes noon. Several great tits are skimming around the silver birch and pine trees by the church. More join in, and I watch their shadows on the surface of the road.

Suddenly I hear the clear crystal sound of a single trumpet player playing a mournful tune. I turn and look through the old iron gate and into the churchyard: a funeral is taking place. The trumpet player's simple, plaintive melody rings out in the cold, clear December air. I look on discreetly; the player controls his playing beautifully, reducing the volume in the final phrase to a quiet pianissimo. The mourners stand with heads bowed. Two minutes of silence follows. I feel the bittersweet pain of the witnessing the end of a life, sad for the mourners and naturally fearful of my own mortality.

I feel that after witnessing the funeral, the proximity of death will undoubtedly inform this walk one way or another. I hear a noisy crow squawking, and my mind thinks of carrion. Death and dying always seem closer in the winter months; everywhere there is evidence of things dying back. In summer life is full and prolific and ever increasing, but the winter speaks of decay and diminution. My eyes alight on a small piece of wood, slender and tapering at the bottom, and on top a knuckle making the whole resemble a handcrafted wooden nail. It looks exactly like a nail that might be used to nail down a coffin lid. Or is it a wedge of wood to hold a simple lock in place? Or was it formed by nature? I think of all the potential past histories of the piece of wood; it does not bother me that I do not and cannot know the right answer. I photograph a bracken leaf, one half brown, one half green – life in death and death in life.

I move from the dark shadow of the forest to the bright sunshine of an open area with stunning views across the valley, from cold into warmth. It would be easy to be morose, but a small patch of seed heads backlit by the sun and swaying gently in the breeze delights me and restores my sense of perspective. I have changed, and my reason for being now is not to be defined by my profession, by working, but by living and seeing: by extracting from life every drop of beauty, to seek the essence of life much as a perfumier does. I want to siphon off beauty and pour it into my life.

By way of a perfect example, as I cross the bridge over a mountain stream, the sun shines brightly through the tall, slender pine trees and alights on four red, jewel-like wild berries. I photograph them, taking time to admire their perfect oval beauty. A few moments later the earth has revolved, and the sun no longer shines on them. In that fraction of time, I was there, and I mined the moment.

At the highest point, I pause to survey the scenery and most especially the sky, a symphony of blue-grey and white. Tiny white ovulate Magritte-like clouds dot the sky in the most opportune places, floating magically over the brooding outline of the Karawanken mountain range. A golden sun appears, too bright to look at.

Large circular roughly cut pine trunks surround the apple tree, the beginnings of a fence. They are not attractive, but I hope the finished barrier will in time soften and mellow. I loved the old, worn lichen-encrusted dilapidated fence, but all things pass. The sloping field under the apple tree is partly in the sun and partly in the shade, and long shadows fall across the field, cast by towering spruce trees that form a giant-like barrier between farms. From nowhere eight large deer appear. They are running, but seemingly at a slow pace. They are both majestic and mysterious, and as quickly as they appeared they melt into the dark green folds of the forest of pine.

The day is growing cold; I quicken my pace and make up time. The light begins to fade, and the sky turns first crimson and then gold. I pass the church once more and bow my head in respect to the recently deceased. When I return home Katie tells me that the funeral was for a local man, very well known to my new family in Austria, in fact, they all remember him as a small boy. He was only in his early 60s. This knowledge adds one more note of mournful poignancy to the day.

55

stone

ψ

I leave at 11.30 a.m., it is now a pleasant 5° C and sunny with blue skies, but it was a freezing -6° C overnight. As soon as I step out I see a spectacular green woodpecker, that beautiful inimitable green. He is fixed as if carved, completely motionless, resting about a third of the way up a telegraph pole. I am sure that a tree might more easily provide a meal, but he waits patiently and after a few moments he obviously does find a grub or two, as he begins to eat. Spooked, he suddenly takes flight and sounds his alarm call very loudly. A kestrel comes into view and circles overhead for some moments. The kestrel is not much bigger than the woodpecker, so I'm surprised to see him so rattled. A very exciting start to my walk.

It's much harder to walk when it's colder. One feels obliged to wear, or carry, a thick coat, gloves and hat, as it always becomes colder when walking up to high areas. But when exertion raises the body temperature, internal fugs and overheating become the problem. Although it's a cold day with a light breeze, there is plenty of sun, which makes the world seem a much nicer place. I long to walk in snow again and enjoy the majesty of nature clothed in white, but I must take whatever comes. A family – parents, grandparents, two boys and three dogs – pass me by. The two boys are mock sword fighting with sticks which immediately break on impact. They laugh good-naturedly and carry on walking. We exchange a glance and smile at each other. I always feel a kinship with walkers, regardless of their age.

Once again I take the slightly alternate route via Steinbruchweg. I notice for the first time the beautiful green of the rocks: it is not lichen or a moss as I thought, but the green is embedded in the rock. There is not much water flow, so I climb down into the bed of the river to take a closer look. The delicate hues of the stones are very welcome in a landscape otherwise devoid of colour: green epidote, rich in silicate minerals, calcium, manganese and aluminium, sometimes called pistacite because of its pistachio green colour. It reminds me immediately of the bright green woodpecker I saw at the beginning of the walk this morning.

A large slab of dazzlingly white marble, with all its associations of luxury and glamour fretted within its surface, lies nearby. Mellow, yellowish quartzite stone appeals to me especially; it has piezoelectric qualities and is used to control the frequencies of radio transmitters. I have a personal interest in this, as there is no medium I love more than radio. In all the various houses I grew up in there were radios in every room; my father was a fanatic for BBC Radio Three. In my teenage years I was entirely sure that I would become a radio announcer and practised in my bedroom for hours on end, imitating the clipped accents of radio announcers or presenting my own roadshow. This dream was finally fulfilled when I moved to Devon and was asked to present my own radio show. I was not happy in Devon, yet on Thursday evenings I would enter the dimly lit cool of the studio and play vintage classics, or my guests, all actors or artists, would talk about their latest endeavours, successes or setbacks. It was the part of the week I most looked forward to.

Nestling next to the quartzite is a cold grey-blue schist, the complex, folded patterns revealing the extreme temperature and pressure conditions under which the rock was formed. My favourite, an orthogneiss with speckles of black amphibole, looks like it was designed by Mary Quant.

A walker I meet fairly often passes me by and stops to ask me why I am standing in the bed of the brook; she seems rather alarmed. I explain that I am looking at the stones and admiring their colours, and she holds her palms out in astonishment and walks away laughing, wishing me fun and good luck. She shakes her head, probably thinking 'crazy English.'

* * *

I sit on a bench for a few moments and all is quiet, but presently a very noisy little wren appears and begins to hop about in the overgrown bank, not minding me at all. A happy companion. The Koralpe is very clear today and I feel I could reach out and touch it. It has a zigzag streak of man-made white – the Christmas skiing season is underway. The Karawanken are a misty, majestical dark blue against a light blue sky and above them hangs a series of silky creamy stratus clouds.

The apple tree is now almost completely enclosed behind its new fence, as the farmer seems keen to finish it before Christmas; only a few posts were in place just a few days ago, but now three slender young pine tree trunks have been fixed horizontally to the stubby supports. It looks raw and new, but it will mellow in time. What the fence lacks in beauty it makes up for in utility. I will never be able to look at the tree again without its wooden prison. The field below the tree will be used for livestock, so I see that it is necessary. But all the same, I cannot help but feel a little sad about this. It is no longer free.

I enjoy a sunless walk back, and as the day darkens the trees make filigree patterns against the sky. There are huge mistletoe baubles hanging high in the trees which tower above me. In the distance the sky begins to improve, as it often does at the close of the day, and starts to glow a Turkish-delight pink beginning on the horizon. A small patch of duck-egg blue grows, bleeds into and overtakes the vast slate-grey of the sky which has accompanied me most of the way, hanging over me pendulously and threatening rain for at least the past hour. I feel very tiny in the landscape; this is a humbling experience.

The day dies and it begins to get cold, but I wait to see the trees blacken, becoming silhouettes against the failing light. A crimson slit appears in the sky momentarily, then spreads and dies. Darkness finally descends.

I have seen alchemy at work once more.

56

Burne-Jones

22ND December

It is the anniversary of my first walk today; I am much heartened by this and begin at a very decent 10.55 am, celebrating inwardly as I go. Temperatures plummeted to -7.5° C overnight, and there was a tremendous hoar frost. I amble so that I can admire every ice crystal and ghostly white cobweb. It is not long before the sun begins to melt the ice and I am showered with a constant thistledown shower of soft sleet as I walk under trees and high bushes. I stand in it for several minutes looking up into the downy frost rain. It is better than walking in falling snow as there is no danger, only beauty.

There is a superabundance of great tits, dotting from tree to tree, calling and feeding. I watch as a blue tit flies onto a fir branch and sits motionless in a halo of frost and ice; he does not move at all. This is the closest I have ever been to a wild bird. I can see his breast rising and falling as he breathes and hold my breath too, so as not to break the spell.

I take the slightly shorter route and ascend Steinbruchweg. The brook is noisy and is running fast and furiously. A myriad of stalactite and stalagmite icicles cling to rocks and vegetation; like so many Tyrolean Swarovski jewels, a better example of silver alchemy I cannot imagine. The weeds that line the path are cloaked in pure white ice, so much so that they resemble a crop of shimmering white shiitake mushrooms. The barbed wire is also laced with ice-covered animal hair and the various seed heads that cling to the wire look as menacing as the barbs they cloak, but the ice barbs dissolve at the slightest touch.

A briar of high, dense and very tangled bramble and wild roses with pearl-frost rose-hips tumbles over a fence, the red hips standing out starkly in the blanched landscape. Seeing these tumbling brambles and roses I am immediately transported to Buscot Park, the Oxford home of Lord Faringdon, and to a cold and frosty day in 1992. I was on a pilgrimage to see *The Legend of the Briar Rose* by Edward Burne-Jones, my favourite Pre-Raphaelite artist. I was then new to Burne-Jones and the Pre-Raphaelites and was enthralled by their work. I have never lost my love of the fantastic, romantic worlds they conjured up. My passion for their work was further enhanced when I was eventually able to work on the restoration of a series of Burne-Jones cartoons during my time as a Keeper of Art at Torre

Abbey in Devon. The Abbey owns seven of a series of nine pencil cartoons known collectively as 'The Planets', preparatory drawings for stained glass windows.

I shall never forget walking into the saloon at Buscot Park and seeing the Burne-Jones panels for the first time. The principal characters in this visual re-telling of the Sleeping Beauty fairy tale are all superbly rendered and Burne-Jones' skill in representing the human form is legendary. But what I remember most is the care he had taken over the accurate representation of the roses and brambles that encircle the castle and encage the sleeping princess. They are painstakingly recreated. This led me to research this more fully, and I was not surprised to discover that while Burne-Jones was working on the four panels, he worked from nature, forbidding his gardeners to touch certain areas of the garden in his home, The Grange, and allowing a 'tangled profusion of gorse, ferns, cow parsley, wildflowers and brambles [to grow].'[145]

I look closely at the tangle before me and realise that Burne-Jones' attention to detail was even more impressive than I believed it to be twenty-four years ago. In the Briar Wood panel a wall of tangled roses forms a complex backdrop behind a group of recumbent, sleeping soldiers lying at the feet of a cliché knight in shining armour. The roses seem to have life precisely because Burne-Jones studied the forms in nature. By studying them he could see that branches do not grow haphazardly and randomly; they have a fractal structure which repeats itself uniformly as it grows. As the Fractal Foundation explains: 'A fractal is a never-ending pattern [...] infinitely complex [and] self-similar across different scales. They are created by repeating a simple process over and over in an ongoing feedback loop.'[146]

I leave the tangle of roses with a batch of photographs of frosty briars, having gained an entirely new appreciation of the mathematics of nature. I look up at the Koralpe, Saualm and Zirbitzkogel and note that they have only a pocket handkerchief of snow at their peaks; the snows of winter have not yet arrived. The sun shines brightly, there is a haze of mist, and the pale sky is streaked with delicate clouds; I am fortunate that the weather has been so kind to me. I can see the farmer who owns the apple tree in the distance, and I watch as he hammers in another fence post. Suddenly and without ceremony, he downs his tools, and he and his tractor go off for lunch. The Austrians, quite rightly, are very punctilious about lunch, and everything stops for the taking of the midday meal. There would have to be a major crisis or emergency to prevent its taking place. I do not stop and rest for long today. Lunch seems like an excellent idea, but I have no provisions with me.

I am nearing the end of the walk when I round the bend in the path and there standing very close to me is a herd of deer. They neither see me nor sense my presence. I try to raise my camera, but I realise that I would undoubtedly frighten them, so I stand quietly in the shadow of a tree and watch them grazing. I return home full of the excitement of being reminded of one of my favourite artists, and having seen the deer I am, at last, feeling festive. I suggest that we walk into the town and visit the temporary Christmas Glühwein Bar, which is nothing more than a small pine hut, surrounded by hay bales and tall tables to set drinks on, but the fire baskets are filled with glowing logs, and candles make it romantic. It is just cold enough to feel that Christmas is indeed only a few days away, but not too cold to stand about in the town square.

I admire the huge Christmas tree in the town square, which reaches up and above the roof line and is tastefully decorated with large creamy-white light bulbs. Next to the tree is a life-size Nativity scene, complete with life-size figures: Joseph, Mary,

Wise Men, a fat Ox, and a skinny Ass all carved from wood and hand painted. They stand around the crib gazing lovingly into it, but oddly the manger is empty. I am puzzled by this, so over our hot mulled wine I ask Katie if she happens to know why. There is not only a story but one that, of course, involves Katie directly. On a visit here a few years before we moved here, Katie and her niece were doing precisely what we are doing now; drinking hot spicy Glühwein in the town square. Aided by two or three mugs of the sweet, hot liquid perhaps, they concluded that it was very odd to place Jesus in the manger before he was born on the 25th December, so they resolved to make an appointment to see the priest the following day. He was delighted to be asked to comment on this crucial matter and readily agreed to meet with them. The meeting did not go quite as expected for the Priest. The exact details of what was said regarding the finer points of theology are lost to history, but Katie and her niece were obviously victorious because Bad Sankt Leonhard now has, throughout the whole of Advent, possibly the only Jesus-less manger in Europe. Baby Jesus arrives secretly without ceremony in the night of the 23rd December, as in Austria the main celebrations take place on Heiligabend – Christmas Eve – so he is there in plenty of time for his birth on Christmas Day. Who places him there we do not know.

57
TEXTURE

❧

26ᵀᴴ December

It is a freezing and frosty morning, but as midday approaches, it rises to an almost balmy 9 ° C and is warm and sunny with not a breath of wind. At the weir by the river, the water is gushing very noisily, swelled by ice melt. Large broken slabs of thick ice litter the bed of the river, creating a mosaic of jagged triangles; they must have been disturbed by rapid water flow, as they all point up to the sky. In between these slabs, the sun dances on the water. I have to shade my eyes against the dazzle.

It is Stefanitag, and within twenty minutes I have already met eleven walkers, all out on this fine holiday. Stefanitag commemorates St. Stephen, whose name day is celebrated on December 26. Saint Stephen is one of the first martyrs in the history of Christianity, and one of the seven Deacons of the early church in Jerusalem. He was stoned to death because, despite a prohibition, he continued to spread Christian doctrine.

In Austria, it is a public holiday because St. Stephen is an important saint here, as evidenced by the naming of St. Stephen's Cathedral in Vienna. It is seen as an opportunity to visit relatives, to exercise or to attend more public celebrations. The Stadtkapelle – the city brass band – in nearby Wolfsberg are holding a special Stefanitag matinee performance today, as they have been doing since 1947. It's a cheerful event offering a varied musical menu ranging from Artie Shaw to Bernstein to South American music. The band members wear banana yellow jackets and are incredibly enthusiastic.

I was most surprised when we visited the local shops over the Christmas period and found that the giving and accepting of gifts is reversed: it is customary here for shop owners to provide their customers with gifts. It seems that echoes of the feudal system in Britain remain and linger, whereas here there is a more pragmatic approach to Christmas giving: gifts here reward loyal customers for their business, not their faithful service.

Boxing Day has become little more than a day of relaxing and overindulging, and most people remain at home. Some perhaps go for a long walk, or those brave souls that live near the coast might attempt a Boxing Day swim. Usually it's an event involving lots of Santa costumes, near nudity or Union Jack swimming trunks, and very little actual swimming. I was invited to take part in the Boxing Day swim in Torquay in the first year I lived there, but fortunately, I had already accepted an invitation to be somewhere less cold and considerably less wet.

Soon I leave the holiday walkers behind, and spot two pale grey collared doves; they take flight, making a sound as they lift into flight like an unoiled door creaking open. The sky is now pale blue and there are a few flicks of pale near gossamer-like stratus clouds over the Koralpe, which has a small welt of snow on the north-east side. A filmy lightness pervades; the weather is decidedly unseasonal. If it were not for the unusual number of aeroplane vapour trails which indicate that people are jetting to and from distant places, it would seem like an ordinary day in early autumn perhaps, not a few days after Christmas in a country which is known for its harsh winters. It is so warm that my sunglasses steam up as I rise and the effort of walking makes me glow with heat.

I meet no other walkers and no one works the land, but I do meet an elderly woman, walking slowly with the aid of two walking sticks. She is dressed in traditional, or typical, Austrian garb, a jacket of navy blue with green epaulettes and metal buttons. She catches my eye and wants to know who I am, and why I am daft enough to be walking here alone on Stefinatag. I manage to speak to her in German (without pause, hesitation or lapsing into English) for a full two minutes. I even use a few words I learned only a few days ago. I am glad to be forced to speak, although I still find it difficult. I make to leave, and she calls me back: can you tell me, she says, is there still lots of fog in England? No, I say, not any more. I am often asked about the fog in England, and occasionally Jack the Ripper is asked after too. It's strange how some clichés take a very long time to dwindle. She looks very relieved and thanks me for the information.

As I climb the last part of the walk, it becomes even more deathly quiet: there is not a single animal, wild or domesticated, anywhere to be seen. I have the whole of the mountains, the hills, the trees, and the open sky to myself. I cannot remember a more enjoyable Boxing Day. I trundle along almost absentmindedly, feeling relaxed and untroubled.

As I approach the tree, I glance up to the sky and realise that it has become an expanse of mackerel clouds. There is no need to hurry, so when I see a large, round, soft hay bale, which I presume must be 'gay hay' as it is wrapped in pink plastic, I rest in its bosom for a long moment, watching the clouds moving, forming and changing shape. The alarm call of a low-flying blackbird alerts me to the presence of something or someone, and within moments a Lycra-clad cyclist whistles past me at high speed, accelerating fast. He nods hello and is gone, vanishing into the distance.

I find more signs of life: the twenty or so gorgeous russet-red gold to pure white hens that are a constant presence near the apple tree have been temporarily moved to the other side of the farmyard. They now have uninterrupted views of the Koralpe and Karawanken mountains. There can be no better position, but they grub about in their usual manner thoroughly unimpressed, even though they must have one of the best views in chicken history.

* * *

I am aware that my project is nearing its end, and there is one sense that I have used much less than the others: touch. I approach this task as I did when I was first learning to appreciate and understand classical music. I taught myself to ignore the melody line and listen to the bass line, or, perhaps, just the percussion section, and eventually, I could, if I concentrated very hard, single out the weird, odd woodwind toots and fluffs from the whole; it became a hobby of mine. So I deliberately ignore the big picture and the open view of the horizon, and focus on the minutiae.

I stoop to feel a patch of low growing juniper: it is scratchy and prickly, I didn't expect this. I find a blackbird's feather: it is soft and warm to the touch. I brush the feathers against the grain, which makes the feather look tatty and ill-tempered, so I stroke it back again so that it looks tidy and it looks much happier. I place my hand on a stone that has been in the shade; it is entirely smooth and ice cold. A fence post sprouts a rash of sage-green lichen; it's so dry that it turns to powder in my hands, while another damper patch rolls into a ball like a shy woodlouse. A tatty, nut-brown beech leaf crumbles in my hands with a cracking sound. In contrast, I find a curled up sycamore leaf, hollowed into a dry crevice, it is the colour of a dried tobacco leaf, its stalk rising into the air, its rib cage arched, and it is not crisp and brittle as I expect, but soft like vellum. I stroke the bark of one of my favourite silver birch trees, closing my eyes to enjoy its diamond pattern sequencing of rough and smooth. A small red furry sumac cone, from the Vinegar tree, has the feel and shape of a field vole. A sprig of dry, hairy yellow-green lichen is attached to a nibble of a branch, which has a different sage and dark green lichen fighting for space on the same fragment of wood. An oblong of dried bark glistens: black sap has oozed and set, and the iridescent algae that were once living on it have become fixed in place; nature's enamelling process. A tree stump has been used to hold barbed wire in place, and a host of moss has taken up residence. I stroke it, avoiding the cruel spurs.

A year ago I would not have done any of this; it just would not have occurred to me. It's a relief to have found enough calmness to appreciate such things and to allow myself the time to savour them.

58
CRUCIFIXION

✧

29ᵀᴴ DECEMBER

A disappointing dandruff of snow fell in the night, but not enough to be picturesque. Due to the immense amount of gardening we managed to achieve, the reparations on the house and some unexpected teaching work in the UK, it was impossible for me to walk every week across the whole of the year, so in order to complete all the walks in the given time frame, I am having to walk two a week. I admit that I am a little tired when I leave at 11 am. The sun is a blazing pale golden orb suspended in a sky of pale sea blue, slightly lighter at the horizon but a marginally darker blue above. There is not a single cloud anywhere to be seen, not even in the far distance. It is only 0.5°C, and there is a stiff breeze, which almost immediately becomes a cold wind. I see an elderly gentleman sweeping the few fallen snowflakes from his driveway, not even enough to fill a small shovel. He is wearing a grey felt trilby-like hat, bound round with a rope, and a feather tucked into this traditional Carinthian hat. He looks up and confidently says 'Grüssgott', a greeting which I return. People are out and about visiting friends and family or on their way to the local shops, but as many people are at work, there are fewer walkers out today.

The tiny stream that flows into the river is thick with ice. In the dusting of new snow, I can clearly see animal footprints. I imagine a wild beast, but they are most likely those of a domestic dog. As I stoop to look more closely, I hear the piercing screech of a bird of prey; a buzzard circles and at one point is flying directly above me. Whenever I see such a magnificent bird I am overawed and often tearful, and today is no exception. As he circles ever closer, the clear blue sky is the perfect backdrop to see him. He is flying over the field that was a few months ago a sea of sunny sunflowers but is now brown, ploughed and bare. He effortlessly glides away and with a few flaps of his wings leaves without diving for prey.

I sit for a while and listen to the wind whistling through the trees. Curled brown leaves skitter across the surface of the path and make a surprisingly loud sound. The sun still shines and the sky is still one mass of blue, but I am not too hot today; if anything I am underdressed and a little cold.

I am well aware that the best way to stay warm is to keep

moving, so I do not delay. As I round the bend, I am pleased to see that the Zirbitzkogel has a good thick covering of snow, but the Koralpe has just a disappointing light dusting. As I near the apple tree it becomes windy and cold. Just before I reach it, a hundred sparrows lift as one into the air from the nearby farm; the owners are obviously bird lovers – they have many bird feeders. I see more animal tracks in the snow and fancy myself a great pioneer tracker in the outback, but realise that I have no idea what they are and cannot tell the difference between a bear and a deer, although I do know that they don't belong to a Yorkshire terrier.

I am at the highest and therefore coldest part of the walk, and I suddenly feel freezing cold. I have miles to go, so I hasten my way back home. As I leave the apple tree the vista opens up. The delicate tracery of a naked birch is clearly outlined, so I glance up to take in its full beauty. I watch for a few moments as a blue tit lands on a snow-covered pine branch and takes a snow bath, making tiny showers of snow fall from the tree.

I am not religious, but at this time of year it is difficult to be completely immune to the iconography of the season, so when I see two sticks that have quite accidentally fallen across one another to form a perfect cross, I immediately think about the Crucifixion and invest these two pieces of wood with a meaning far beyond the reality of two fallen twigs lying on a patch of snow. It is a reaction brought about by cultural conditioning – I cannot help seeing them as something mystical. Nonsense it may be, but such is the power of the imagination. Despite my protestations, I am a product, or perhaps even a victim, of my upbringing.

As the light fades, I realise that I have strolled more than hiked today, but I don't hurry. I remind myself to look up – as a new birdwatcher this is something I must remember to do. I am rewarded by the sight of a parliament of fifty or more rooks lined up on the telegraph wires; as they fly into land, they perch with military exactness, each sitting precisely the same distance from the next. They all face the same way, seemingly thoughtful and end-of-the-day-quiet, happy merely to survey the world. I have always underestimated, ignored or perhaps even faintly disliked the Corvidae bird family, the crow, rook, raven, jackdaw and magpie, though I have always liked the jay, I am unashamedly drawn to its exquisite colours. I remember that I once learned a poem about rooks by heart to gain a Sunday school prize. At the time I paid no attention to its ornithological veracity and hardly knew a rook from a blackbird, but I remember enjoying it merely for the poet's ability to knit a skein of words together. I recall the poem now; it comes back to me after a few attempts. In truth, it would be a strange child who could understand the depths of such a poem:

> *There, where the rusty iron lies*
> *The Rooks are cawing all the day.*
> *Perhaps no man, until he dies,*
> *Will understand them, what they say.*
> *The evening makes the sky like clay.*
> *The slow wind waits for night to rise.*
> *The world is half content. But they*
> *Still trouble all the trees with cries,*
> *That know, and cannot put away,*
> *The yearning to the soul that flies*
> *From day to night, from night to day.*[147]

The sky moves from clay to caliginous and my penultimate walk is over.

59
Free

1ST January

It is the last day of the fifty-second week of 2016 and it happens to have fallen on the 1st January, which means that I am completing my project in the year of my fifty-second birthday, which seems apt.

I procrastinate, eating breakfast and drinking coffee while listening once again to my favourite Christmas songs. I do not begin until it is quite late – well after lunch. Today I admit to a certain lethargy and tiredness and a longing for long days filled with sunshine and flora. As it is the first day of a new year I allow myself to begin the countdown to spring and look forward to the long, hot days of summer: days filled with flowers, new things to grow and eat and all of life throbbing noisily. Fortunately, the temperature has risen to nearly 4.4°C, increasing from a very chilly overnight temperature of only -8.3°C. It is also incredibly bright and sunny, with another completely blue cloudless sky, a slightly paler blue than in recent days but still stunningly beautiful. The sun is bleached out but shining like a vast and powerful torch, casting long shadows which fall across the now brown-green grass making it seem less dull and lifeless.

Within minutes I have to remove my jacket, as it is very warm in the sun and there is not even a hint of a breeze. The sun makes a huge difference to my mood. There is no doubt that walking in the winter is harder and more of a struggle, especially when the sun does not appear; then it feels like an endurance, and the longing for spring and summer is ever present. My heart always leaps for joy when a new day dawns and the landscape is white, the snow muffles sound and all is dreamlike, but such days come all too rarely.

The stream has evidence of old decaying ice, a fresh ice layer and a covering of new snow which dazzles in the New Year's Day sunshine. It seems almost deathly quiet – until I adjust to the quietness, when I hear a crow squawking and a magpie rattling. I hear a tiny sound of rustling and see a small bird flitting from branch to branch, a chubby male chaffinch. Blackbirds hover at the base of the old apple trees whose branches have hung heavy with fruit for many months. The sleek black birds peck away at rotten and half-rotten apple cores. I encounter a zephyr of long-tailed tits but being shy, they soon take flight. I hear the faint sound of several great tits; these birds especially have been my constant companions on this walk.

As I climb I reach areas glowing with recent snow still fresh in places, and it glares in the New Year's Day sunshine. It is much colder now, and I have to struggle back into my jacket and thick gloves. The sun becomes amber and bright, and I see standing only a few hundred yards from the apple tree an old stone pillar which supports a rickety gate. Topaz light falls directly on to the honey-coloured stone, and I see a date highlighted on it: 1835. It is deeply etched into the surface, but I have never seen this before. In some arcane way, the knowledge of this date further connects me to the people who helped forge this landscape, and I like the fact that I am only seeing this now on my last walk. If I walked this walk a thousand times, I would always see something new.

This idea makes me feel light and elated, and I remember my first walk, so heavy with unnecessary worry, and how blind I was to almost everything in front of me. Walking the same walk repeatedly within the confines of a looped, closed circuit has paradoxically freed my mind and released my soul; walking not into myself, but out of myself.

With beautiful circularity, I immediately notice as I reach the apple tree for the last time that the farmer has placed the last remaining pieces of the new fence in place. For the first time, the tree is completely entrapped behind its new fence. As the walk and my time in Austria have passed, I have become more and more free, and by a strange coincidence, the tree has become more and more captive. I feel a bittersweet rush of emotions. My task is complete, and my happiness is tinged with both relief and sadness.

As the sun sinks in the sky I glance back towards the view I have come to love so much. There are only a few moments left before the sun disappears behind the Zirbitzkogel. Just before it fades away the whole scene is suffused in a golden light, and my shadow is large against a backdrop of green firs.

I will leave nothing but my shadow behind, but through the magic of the ambulatory process I have walked myself into alchemy, and I am forever changed. For the first time I think that I truly not only understand but can truly appreciate what Ralph Waldo Emerson was trying to elucidate in 1836 when he wrote: 'Not the sun or the summer alone, but every hour and season yields its tribute of delight; for every hour and change corresponds to and authorises a different state of mind, from breathless noon to grimmest midnight.'[148]

60

ALCHEMY

Almost as soon as I began writing my book, I referred to it as either my apple book or by its then title *A Shadow Falls across an Apple Tree in Austria*. I didn't like the title, but I kept it all the same. Luckily, a good friend reminded me that the word 'shadow' had negative connotations and advised me to consider changing it completely. During the editing and revising process I let the problem rest in my subconscious to see if something would present itself. The word alchemy kept coming into my mind, so I re-checked the Oxford English Dictionary's definition of the word: 'the medieval forerunner of chemistry, concerned with the transmutation of matter, in particular with attempts to convert base metals into gold or find a universal elixir.' I knew that the walk had been transmutational for me; after all, at the beginning of the process I had felt heavy, like base metal, and I was weighed down with worry, but through the weeks and months, I started to feel lighter and brighter. Besides, my unexpected collaboration with Katie, a goldsmith and artist, further cemented this idea. So my new title, *Walking into Alchemy*, was born. As I had only ever heard of chemical alchemy, I did not consider that the word might have other connotations, but when I was running more fact checking, I discovered that there is also something called 'spiritual alchemy'. I had never heard of it, but this initiated another journey of discovery. I was amazed to learn that in spiritual alchemy the idea is to quest (I do love the word quest), not for the material, not for gold, but for personal renewal. Contact with the natural world is often seen to be of central importance, and such a pursuit often follows a period of depression or other adversity.

There are seven stages in both chemical and spiritual alchemy. The first is called 'calcination'. In chemical alchemy, the material to be transformed is first burnt and turned into ash. In spiritual alchemy, breaking attachments to worldly possessions is the first goal; I instinctively knew that I had to unshackle myself from debt and from possessions that I could not afford to keep. The packing up of my life in England and lifting the burden of my mortgage were the first step, and I immediately felt that a great weight was lifted from me.

The next stage is dissolution. In chemical alchemy, this involves taking the ashes from the calcination process and dissolving them in water. In spiritual alchemy, it's a releasing of the structures and the systems that define our perceptions of ourselves. This I found very hard; I have always been embarrassed by my inability to fit in and to conform. I desperately wanted to give up my nine to five job and pursue a creative role for myself, but lacked the courage to do so. I was, it seemed, always defining myself using the wrong criterion.

After this comes separation: in chemical alchemy, the elements from dissolution are separated and filtered. In spiritual alchemy, the conscious mind has to give way to the unconscious mind; this is difficult because painful memories re-surface and have to be reconsidered. Unexpectedly, the walks gave me time alone and made me think, and I had no option but to filter out the bad and separate the good. After a few months, this enabled me to re-evaluate my emotions and memories. I was also able to create new narratives, and I began to see connections with things I had long forgotten to remember: favourite passages of music and paintings, while thankfully, my love of Shakespeare returned.

In the procedure called 'conjunction', the chemical alchemist creates a new substance from the separated elements. In spiritual terms, the unconscious and the conscious must now come together. Having been acutely aware of the social structures at play in the world, and in so many ways bound by them, I began to feel more able to prevent them from having ultimate influence over me, and I have continued to feel this since I completed the walks.

For me, the most challenging part of the procedure has been my reappraisal of politics, war and religion — those three essential aspects of life which we are actively dissuaded from discussing in everyday life. It took me many months, and during my hours of walking, I constantly thought about world issues. Walking in the year of Brexit and the rise of Trump made this perhaps inevitable, but it also afforded me an opportunity to think about and analyse my personal view of the events.

In the fifth step, fermentation occurs by adding bacteria and other living organisms to the substance to continue its breakdown. The equivalent here is that suffering and adversity begin to come together, and the conscious and the unconscious, now newly united, can recognise and appreciate the beautiful.

Distillation in chemical alchemy occurs when solutions are heated and condensed in order to purify them; this is the most crucial step in spiritual alchemy, because purification is achieved through various forms of contemplation or meditation. I could not have contemplated so much and meditated on life so deeply had I not removed myself from my daily life and immersed myself in nature.

The ultimate goal of the chemical alchemist is to coagulate and crystallise the initial substance into a solid state in order to produce the infamous Philosopher's Stone and gain the ability to turn base metals into gold. In spiritual alchemy, it is the bringing together of dualities, an awareness that the inner world and the outer world are not different but reflections of each other. I feel that I now reflect the person I am, perhaps the person I always wanted to be. I feel less as if I want and need to hide and obfuscate; I still often hide behind humour, but I am now able to do this in a much more controlled manner.[149]

Finally, I chose the walk quite randomly, from the many that had been laid out by the local town council. The Q3 route officially begins in the centre of the town of Bad Sankt Leonhard, at the Paracelsus well (Q stands for Quelle or spring). Paracelsus (1493/4-1541) was a chemical alchemist and a physician. In defiance of the ideology of his time, he argued that the body is a chemical system and that balance and good health can only be achieved if it is in harmony with its environment. Over the intervening years, chemical and spiritual alchemy have become diverging, even competing, ideologies; it need not be so. Especially when one remembers that the Philosopher's Stone was also often referred to as the Elixir of Life, a potion that when drunk could cure all diseases and offer not only youthfulness but eternal life.

Therefore, of all the walks I could have chosen it seems more than serendipitous that I quite randomly selected the one that springs from the well that bears Paracelsus' name. Additionally, it is comfortingly mysterious to me that an apple tree, that species which for many centuries has been seen as a symbol of both knowledge and immortality, also attracted my attention.

61
KINTSUGI

22ND DECEMBER 2018

Today it is the 22nd December 2018, the anniversary of my first walk in 2016. Although I have returned to the walk, sometimes with friends and sometimes alone, on some days it seems to me now to be no more than a dream – did I really do it? I feel that I need to mark the anniversary, so I forget about wrapping presents and putting up decorations, and at dawn I slip out of the house to re-live the experience one more time and in real time, rather than as just a memory. I am fortunate; I walk into a world rimed in a crisp hoarfrost, and there is a pale lemon sun just rising over the Koralpe which illuminates white blades of grass and dried seedpods which are now filigree skeletons.

The sky is divided into three bands: mist, then clear sky and then more mist at the top. In the section in between, I glimpse ice-furred pine trees and fresh snow on high peaks. Crows caw and the stream, thick with ice on the surface, is beginning to thaw, so I can hear the gentle trickle of meltwater which provides a delicate percussion under the distant clang of the church bells. In the field where the white mare usually trots a new woodpile has popped up, and sitting atop this is a perfect wooden sleigh; I don't think Saint Nick will be able to find it there though.

I remember to glance into the sunflower field, the one I discovered in August 2016; it's so easy to pass it by without looking through the curtain of trees. Most of the sunflower crop was harvested long ago in the summer, but there are fifty or so tall, elegant blooms still standing. Withered now and no longer yellow, and with their heads slightly bowed, they are ghostly spectres of their former selves. Their decrepitude is made even more pronounced by the hue of morning frost which clings to them. They stand out like a huge musical score written across the sky; it must be plain chant as the notes vary very little.

I sing the notes quietly into the still, cold air. Then I stand amongst them, and although weedy and spindly they still tower above me. Their golden glory may be lost, but they are still magnificent; rarely have I seen anything so seemingly without life looking so beautiful. But, of course, they are not dead. Their seeds still feed the birds, and some will fall to the earth and from these, new blooms will come again next summer.

As I am leaving, I glance back and see in a distant field three pale yellow llamas standing stock still and staring at me. I don't think they enjoyed my singing at all.

I walk on into a whitish-green world of frost. There is no view as the fog is so dense, but through the mist the sun shines, so it is not alarming or depressing but thrilling, I slightly lose track of the footpath, so I am able to discover the walk anew. But I am very cold, the mist is damp, and I don't remember ever being this chilled on the walk before. I have to get out my trusty Pac-a-mac and my extra gloves and scarf and walk much faster to raise my body temperature.

At the entrance to the field where the copse once stood there is a festival of broken gates and collapsing barbed wire, all coated in sugared spiders' webs and ice crystals. I glance behind me and see that the sky has cleared to blue, and the Zirbitzkogel stands proud of the fog, a shining white isosceles triangle of pure white new snow. I pass through the farmyard where in October 2016 I ate chestnuts with the owners, and see that someone has decorated the small Scots pine with shiny, red baubles. Sparrows ignore them, but a magpie looks on admiringly. I think there might be one less bauble by sunset.

The climb to Schiefling is as hard as ever, but at least the effort makes me warm. I reach the church and hear a strange sound like the clicking of a manual lawnmower: impossible, surely? I look around and then realise that it's the church bell mechanism grinding and whirring high up in the tower. Suddenly the bells clang alarmingly and very loudly; this encourages me into the churchyard. I unwrap my flask of coffee from its double layer of tea cosy and foil (note to self – I must buy a flask that keeps drinks warm) and steam rises from it as I drink. A young boy passes me; he is wearing thick winter clothes, but he has no gloves. He blows on his hands and shouts 'Hallo' to me. I shout back, 'Frohe Weihnachten' (Happy Christmas) and he nods and smiles back. The bells cease, but the whirring continues. I move on, not wishing to lose my warm glow.

After two more hours of walking the fog clears to reveal a pale blue sky, and the backdrop of enormous spruce trees is dripping with tawny-gold pine cones. At last the sun shines down on me, and it is warm and comforting. Perhaps inevitably I view the clearing of the fog and mist to reveal a calm, undramatic sky as a metaphor for my new life. It is not full of drama or pain, two things that I was perhaps guilty of 'enjoying' – in a strange way these things can make one feel very alive. My life is calm and reasonably ordered. I no longer move from crisis to crisis, I no longer work with people who feed off the excitement of fire-fighting problems when they arise instead of solving them in advance through proper planning. I feel I have moved on, but I don't want to forget the past, because I have learnt a great many things along the way. As the 13th century Persian poet Rumi implores us to do in his poem Childhood Friends, we must:

Keep looking at the bandaged place.
That's where the light enters you.[150]

I see myself as a piece of Japanese pottery that has been repaired using the kintsugi method, the Japanese art of restoring broken ceramics with a lacquer of gold or silver. The Japanese word Kintsugi (金継ぎ) means 'connected by gold or repaired by gold.' The story of Kintsugi, as an art form, is said to have begun in the 15th century when the Japanese military commander Ashikaga Yoshimasa broke one of his favourite Chinese tea bowls. The broken pieces were gathered up and sent for repair, but when the restored bowl was returned Yoshimasa was appalled by the hideous restoration, which had been completed using ugly, thick metal staples. The commander urged Japanese craftsmen to come up with a more aesthetic method of reconstruction. The subsequent Kintsugi approach, which emphasises rather than hides the damage, illustrates a crucial difference between Eastern and Western philosophy. Kintsugi embraces the breakage, treating it as an essential part of the object's history and it is the repair which allows the beauty of imperfection to shine out. A broken pot is not something to be discarded, but once repaired it is considered to be more precious than it was when it was whole and perfect. After restoration, the cracks and fissures stand out and the cracks now filled with gold or silver are the most prominent feature. The entire story of the history of the object is apparent.

Valuable things get broken, and over time we inevitably make mistakes and have failures, and tragedies and disasters befall us. But they are part of us, and perhaps eventually they improve us. To look even more closely, the Japanese letter 金 (kin) means gold and the letter 継 (tsugi) means inherit, succeed, patch and graft – as in the grafting of a tree. Therefore, 金継ぎ (kintsugi) also conveys within it the idea that we inherit from the past, and we can acknowledge that in the present and pass it onto the future. For me, the repaired fractures filled with gold can also be seen as a metaphor for the walk itself, and more – there are so many golden footpaths running through and across the land, and they are all just waiting to be discovered.[151]

* * *

I round the bend to approach the apple tree with my heart beating fast, as I always worry that one day it might have been felled. I know I would be heartbroken. But it is there in all its leafless glory. I know its shape and form, and it's like seeing an old and beloved friend again. I take a moment to look once more at the wonderful view. Then I remember that I must hurry, it will soon be Christmas and I have much to do. Yes, it will soon be Christmas, I am not dreading it, and I feel well; this is a very nice realisation.

Furthermore, I feel settled in myself, and I am settled here. This project has helped me in so many ways – I now understand more about the local topography, and it has given me a sense of place. But even more importantly, I have met people, and I have made friends. I have achieved this partly through giving readings about my book as it developed. It also helped me to get work as an English trainer. In the past few months, I have, with help, established a customer base, and I now teach several groups in our little town. Unexpectedly I was asked to teach a group of children, something I would never have volunteered to do, but it is a real joy. Just a few days ago I organised a little Christmas concert for the parents to attend and I felt full of pride for the children that I teach. I am a fully paid-up member of the community, and without taking the time to heal myself, I wouldn't have been able to take on these new challenges.

We all need to find our own ways to achieve this. My way was a walk in the hills in a small town in Austria. I hope, that you too can find your path.

APPENDIX

WALKING INTO ALCHEMY – THE ROUTE

The walk begins just below the St Leonhard's Church, which is referred to throughout as the Leonhardikirche. The walk is waymarked Q3 and officially begins in the spa town of Bad Sankt Leonhard.

Co-ordinates 46.9620° N, 14.7950° E.

From the town, which is 2342 feet above sea level, the walk rises a further 1507 feet to a total of 3848 feet.

In total it is about 14 miles (if you begin in the town centre).

The walk takes the walker in a north-easterly direction.

The apple tree co-ordinates are: N 46° 57.342 E014° 50.306 (Erzberg).

The walk (Q3) begins in the centre of Bad Sankt Leonhard at the Paracelsus well. From there turn right into the main street, the Hauptplatz, in the general direction of Wolfsberg. Go past the shops and banks and head towards the church with a spire which you will see on your left. Opposite the Spar Supermarket, which will be on your right, turn left up towards the church into Erzbergstrasse. Climb up further towards the church; you will also see a huge lime tree. Directly before the tree and just before the church there are two turnings to the right. One runs alongside a high stone wall, which climbs steeply – do not take this road, as the walk is a circular one and will bring you back to the church at the end of your walk. Take the first turning right, Lindenweg opposite the Lindenbaum (lime tree). Lindenweg is a straight, narrow road which declines a little towards the end, where it becomes a pedestrian-only path. You will pass houses on your right and see the Leonhardikirche (church) on your left.

When Lindenweg ends, it leads down towards a public footpath, an orchard on the right and hazelnut trees and a stream on your left. Take this path to the main road to join the Klagenfurterstrasse (you will need to walk along the verge for a short distance). Just before the roundabout, you will see a turning to your left; there are a few houses on the left and a paddock on the right. After a short distance bear right onto a grass path to walk alongside the Lavant river and across a wide, flat meadow. The path narrows as it passes close to the river on the right and crop fields to the left (look out for sunflowers in summer peering at you from behind the trees).

You will walk through a small copse; there is also a bench here. Follow the path, cross a small road (Steinbruchweg) and keep going. After a short while you will pass through a farmyard (if you are lucky you may be offered a schnapps or some roasted chestnuts by the owners of the farm, as I have been). Keep left and climb slightly, then find the straight path between woodpiles on your left and cow stalls on your right. There will be another bench on your left, which affords lovely views of the hills, and a small cargo train is very likely to trundle past in the distance too, a memory of the trains that once brought people from far afield to take the spa waters.

Follow the path until you meet the road and the village of Mauterndorf.[152] Turn onto the road to your left; you will begin to climb and pass fields of maize, and after about five minutes you will cross over a stream, over a small bridge which has attractive red railings. A steep climb will take you to the church in Schiefling, which is always open during the day and is well worth visiting.[153]

When you pass the church, you must bear left past a modern marble fountain and straight on, passing inns and hotels left and right. Keep left again, and again the road rises steeply. After another half a mile you will see a house on your right selling honey. There is a charming mural of a young Austrian boy in Lederhosen and feathered hat, set at a jaunty angle, on the side elevation. Shortly after this, you will enter a stretch of pine woods, and then as you rise, you will pass a house that has a superb collection of woodpiles. Rise still further until you meet a left curve in the road, and here a gap at the end of some railings is a great vantage point to see the Koralpe and Karawanken mountains. Follow the road, remembering to look around you as the views are stunning now.

After fifteen minutes or so you will reach a bench; you may find this a good place to take a break. You are now at almost the highest part of the walk. Sitting on the bench here in winter snow can fall softly, and in summer hundreds of swallows and swifts dart around madly. A lovely stretch through tall pine trees then follows, and the vista will open up to reveal another stunning view of the Karawanken mountain range as you descend.

After you cross a cattle grid, you will see a house on your right which is empty; it has two wonderful historical murals which are noteworthy. The road then sweeps down to the right and after you have passed by some farm buildings you will see the apple tree at last. Carry on to pass through the Liedl Villa, where many goldfinches and sparrows are likely to alight as you pass. The road drops down now steadily. You will hear the mountain stream rushing past, and at the crossroads you need to follow the road left to pass across the bridge and over the stream. Descend through the curves of the road, admire the tall pines and you will again see farms. As you follow this road, you will see that the view suddenly opens up to show pine trees climbing steeply as the ground rises in the distance.

Keep descending to the final curve in the road over the mountain stream to reach more farms and houses. You will see a shrine to St Laurence on your left, and just beyond this, a gap in the trees affords a superb view of the town of Bad Sankt Leonhard. From here it is but a short distance to the Leonhardikirche. Pass the church and follow the road as it bears sharply left and back to Erzbergerstrasse and the town once again.

ABOUT THE AUTHOR

Amelia Marriette left school to work for her parents in the family business, a delicatessen, after which she obtained work at the Ministry of Defence (Royal Signals and Radar Establishment – RSRE) in Malvern, Worcestershire, training to become a computer operator working in radar simulation. Having completed her first degree in Humanities through the Open University, she resigned from her post at the Ministry of Defence to read for an MA in Shakespeare Studies at the Shakespeare Institute, Stratford-upon-Avon (University of Birmingham). A part-time job at the Royal Shakespeare Company (RSC) in Stratford-upon-Avon led to an unexpected opportunity to work with the curator and the RSC museum collections, and this led to a further qualification at St. Andrew's University to obtain a post-graduate diploma in Museum and Gallery Studies. This in turn led to work at the Holst Birthplace Museum in Cheltenham, where Amelia was employed as the curator. Her last post in this field was as the Keeper of Art at Torre Abbey in Torquay. While in Devon Amelia also presented Amelia's Culture Show on Riviera FM radio. A new relationship and redundancy led to an opportunity to begin anew, and Amelia relocated to the Carinthian Region of Southern Austria in June 2015.

As well as focusing on her writing, Amelia is also an English trainer and lecturer in Shakespeare Studies in Austria and the UK. Amelia has written several pieces for the stage and has a continuing relationship with Malvern Theatre Players, who have performed all of her work. Her comedy about the printing of Shakespeare's First Folio called *Nay, Remember Me!*, first performed as part of the Royal Shakespeare Company's Fringe Festival in 2001, was published by Lazy Bee Scripts in December 2018. *Walking into Alchemy* is her first work of non-fiction.

Amelia also has one academic writing credit to her name: a chapter in Shakespeare, Film and Fin de Siècle, Macmillan (2000), 'Urban Dystopias: Re-approaching Christine Edzard's As You Like It.'

Amelia Marriette walking the *Walking into Alchemy* route in 2016.
Carinthia, Southern Austria.
Photo Credit: Dennis Eason, 2016.

POSTSCrIPT

Since finishing the project, Amelia revisits the walk regularly. Having made a connection with the local language institute Sprich Dich Frei, she occasionally accompanies students, trainers or local journalists who wish to enjoy the walk in return for a donation which goes to assist local refugee groups. This idea was borne out of the fact that the walk passes a large hotel which is now used as a home for refugees, acting as a constant reminder of this world problem. It therefore seems appropriate to use the walk to help raise funds and awareness of this issue.[154]

Endnotes

1   http://www.bad-st-leonhard-i-lav.at/Die_Geschichte_des_Heilbades

2   Paracelsus was born in Einsiedeln in Switzerland, under the name Philippus Aureolus Theophrastus Bombastus von Hohenheim. He was a philosopher, physician, botanist, astrologer, and general occultist.

3   https://preblauer.at/die-geschichte/

4   The Castle of Otranto was written by Horace Walpole in 1764; it is generally regarded as the first gothic novel.

5   https://greyartgallery.nyu.edu/exhibition/british-art-111301-012602/clouds/

6   The Black Death was a medieval pandemic that swept through Asia and Europe. It reached Europe in the late 1340s, killing an estimated 25 million people. https://www.nationalgeographic.com/science/health-and-human-body/human-diseases/the-plague/

7   Stefan Karner, Bad Sankt Leonhard in Alten Ansichten, Europaische Bibliothek, 1987, p. 21.

8   During the first decades of the 13th century, Gothic sculpture became more innovative. Statues became more animated - a slouching from the hips with the weight on one leg became known as Gothic sway.

9   Founded in 1925, the SS or "Schutzstaffel," which translates as "Protective Echelon," initially served as the Nazi Party leader Adolf Hitler's (1889-1945) personal bodyguards. Later the SS became one of the most powerful and feared organizations in all of Nazi Germany. https://www.history.com/topics/world-war-ii/ss

10   Letter from Paul Nash to Margaret Nash written from France while on commission to make drawings at the Front as a war artist, 13 November 1917. http://www.tate.org.uk/art/archive/items/tga-8313-1-1-162/

11   Lunaria annua, a plant with disc-shaped seedpods which are known as silicles.

12   Malus domestica, white Klarapfel – clear apple – an old dessert variety. It is an early fruiting variety, being ready to harvest in mid to late July.

13   Horace, Satires - a collection of satirical poems written by the Roman poet, Horace. Composed in dactylic hexameters, the Satires explore the secrets of human happiness and literary perfection. Published probably in 35 BCE and at the latest, by 33 BCE, the first book of Satires represents Horace's first published work.

14   Carduelis carduelis, the European goldfinch is a small passerine bird in the finch family. It is native to Europe, North Africa and western Asia, but it has been introduced to other areas including Australia, New Zealand and Uruguay.

15   Herbert Friedmann, The Symbolic Goldfinch: Its History and Significance in European Devotional Art, Pantheon Books, 1946.

16   Reg Herschy, Freedom at Midnight: Austria: 1938-55 A Story of the Traumatic Years of Occupation, The Self-Publishing Association Ltd, (1989), p. 13-14.

17   Daphne was my father's first wife, and the mother of my half-sister Ann and my half-brother Dennis. Daphne and my father married in 1947. Daphne died of cancer in 1960.

18   Parus major, the great tit- a passerine bird, part of the tit family Paridae.

19   Alcedo atthis, the Kingfisher, is of the family of small to medium-sized Coraciiformes order.

20   The study followed the birds for ninety days, recording 66,184 visits to the feeders. http://www.sciencemag.org/news/2015/11/birds-would-rather-go-hungry-leave-their-mate-behind

21   Kenneth Grahame's children's book Wind in the Willows was published by Methuen in 1908.

22   Cumulus is Latin for heaped and humilis is Latin for humble.

23   Field for the British Isles, was exhibited at Torre Abbey, Torquay, Devon in 2009. http://www.antonygormley.com/show/item-view/id/2152/type/solo#p2

24   Event Horizon by Antony Gormley, 2007.

25   Blind Light by Antony Gormley was first exhibited at the Hayward Gallery in 2007. http://www.antonygormley.com/show/item-view/id/2259#p9

26   J.M.W Turner painted Rain, Steam and Speed: The Great Western Railway in 1844.

27   Rain, Speed, Steam, By J. M. W. Turner - National Gallery, London.

28   Galanthus nivalis, the snowdrop or common snowdrop is the best-known and most widespread of the 20 species in its genus, Galanthus.

29   Tussilago farfara, the coltsfoot is part of the daisy family Asteraceae, native to both Europe and parts of western and central Asia.

30   Primula vulgaris, the primrose or common primrose is a species of flowering plant in the family Primulaceae, native to western and southern Europe (from the Faroe Islands and Norway south to Portugal, and east to Germany, Ukraine, the Crimea, and the Balkans), northwest Africa (Algeria), and southwest Asia (Turkey east to Iran).

31   William Shakespeare, Hamlet, (1.3.48-52), Ophelia to her brother, Laertes.

32   https://schoolgardening.rhs.org.uk/Resources/Info-Sheet/Flowers-in-Shake-speare-s-Plays

33   Bellis perennis, the common daisy, lawn daisy or English daisy is a common European species of daisy, a member of the Asteraceae family.

34   https://www.birdwatching.co.uk/birdspecies/2017/11/3/long-tailed-tit

35   Regulus regulus, the goldcrest is a very small passerine bird in the king-let family. Goldcrests are widespread throughout much of Europe, but they can be found in the Himalayas and Japan. Goldcrests migrate from Scandinavia and the near-Continent in the autumn to warmer climes.

36   Regulus ignicapillus, the firecrest is a very small passerine bird in the king-let family. It breeds in most of temperate Europe and north western Africa. It is partially migratory, with birds from central Europe wintering to the south and west of their breeding range.

37   Tilia grandifolia - Large-Leaved Lime Tree - a deciduous tree from the Lin-den (Tilia) family. The specimen in Bad Sankt Leonhard was put under Naturdenkmal protection in 1955.

38   Pieter Bruegel the Elder - Hunters in the Snow, (Winter), 1565 - Kunsthistorisches Museum, Vienna.

39   William Shakespeare, Hamlet, (1.3.9-40).

40   Petasites, butterbur, or coltsfoot is a genus of flowering plants in the sunflower family Asteraceae.

41   Gonepteryx rhamni - the common Brimstone, a butterfly of the family Pieridae.

42   Aglais io - the peacock butterfly, a colourful butterfly, found in Europe and temperate Asia as far east as Japan.

43   Erithacus rubecula, The European robin, known simply as the Robin or Robin Redbreast, a small insectivorous passerine bird.

44   The Autumn Robin, John Clare, 1820.

45   Tristan Gooley, Walker's Guide to Outdoor Clues and Signs, (Sceptre, 2014), page 11.

46   Crepuscular rays are rays of sunlight that appear to radiate from the point in the sky where the sun is located — referring to rays that shine through the openings in clouds or between mountains.

47   Crocus vernus, or spring crocus, is a species in the family Iridaceae, native to the Alps, the Pyrenees and the Balkans.

48   /www.brown.edu/Departments/Joukowsky_Institute/courses/mediterraneanbronzeage/files/3620616.pdf

49   Motacilla cinerea - the grey wagtail - is a member of the wagtail family, Motacillidae, measuring around 18–19 cm overall length. The species looks somewhat similar to the yellow wagtail but has the yellow on its underside restricted to the throat and vent.

50   Pyrrhula pyrrhul, Eurasian Bullfinch, Common Bullfinch or Bullfinch, a small passerine bird in the finch family, Fringillidae.

51   Fringilla montifringilla, Brambling, a small passerine bird also a member of the finch family Fringillidae. It is also known as the mountain finch.

52   Turdus merula, the blackbird, a species of thrush.

53   Myosotis palustris from the Boraginaceae family. Forget-me-nots are also known as scorpion grasses. The common name "forget-me-not" was borrowed from the German Vergissmeinnicht, and first used in English in 1398 AD during the reign of King Henry IV.

54   Corydalis Cava, or Hollow Larkspur, is a member of the Papaveraceae family, native to the temperate Northern Hemisphere and the high mountains of tropical eastern Africa. They grow in the Himalayas, with at least 357 species in China.

55   Euphorbia amygdaloides or wood spurge is a species of flowering plant in the family Euphorbiaceae. Found in woodland in Europe, Turkey and the Caucasus.

56   Anemone nemorosa, the wood anemone, is an early-spring flowering plant in the buttercup family Ranunculaceae, which is native to Europe.

57   Taraxacum officinalis, the dandelion, is in the family Asteracaea. They are native to Eurasia and North America, but propagate in Europe as wildflowers.

58   Violaceae, pansy from the violet family.

59   Lamium album, white nettle or white dead-nettle, is member of the family Lamiaceae, native throughout Europe and Asia, growing in a variety of habitats from open grassland to woodland.

60   Chastleton House has one of the fines Long Galleries in the UK: https://www.britainexpress.com/counties/oxfordshire/houses/Chastleton.htm

61   Falco tinnunculus, the Common Kestrel or Windhover, a species belonging to the falcon family Falconidae.

62   Potentilla crantzii, or alpine cinquefoil, a flowering plant in the rose family, Rosaceae.

63   Citrus maxima, pomelo, is the largest citrus fruit from the Rutaceae family. It is a natural (non-hybrid) citrus fruit, native to South and Southeast Asia

64   http://www.living-in-germany.net/the-ice-saints/

65   Royal Horticultural Society website: https://www.rhs.org.uk/Advice/Profile?PID=1012

66   Ben Shephard, The Long Road Home, (Bodley Head, 2010), p.46.

67   Roundup© was invented by the organic chemist, John E. Franz. Franz discovered the herbicide glyphosate while working at Monsanto Company in 1970. https://en.wikipedia.org/wiki/John_E._Franz

68   Chambers Concise Dictionary, G.W. Davidson, M.A. Seaton, J. Simpson (Editors), W & R Chambers, 1988 edition, p. 1134

69   Raphael, The Alba Madonna, 1510. National Gallery of Art, Washington D.C.

70   Aegopodium podagraria, or common greed, is a perennial herbaceous plant from the Umbelliferae, (Apiaceae) family.

71   Glechoma hederacea, or gill-over-the-ground, catsfoot, or field balm, is from the Lamiaceae family and is related to mint.

72   Centaurium, or Feverfew, God hyssop, Lauri herb, from the Gentian family (Gentianaceae).

73   Ranunculus acris, or wild ranunculus is in the buttercup family – Ranunculaceae.

74   "The best moments in our lives are not the passive, receptive, relaxing times… The best moments usually occur if a person's body or mind is stretched to its limits in a voluntary effort to accomplish something difficult and worthwhile". https://positivepsychologyprogram.com/mihaly-csikszentmihalyi-father-of-flow/

75 With over 2,500 species in more than 90 genera, the rose family Rosaceae, which includes among its number: apples, pears, quinces, medlars, loquats, almonds, peaches, apricots, plums, cherries, strawberries, blackberries, raspberries. https://www.britannica.com/topic/list-of-plants-in-the-family-Rosaceae-2001612

76 See for example Eric Ravilious's, Mount Caburn, 1935. http://www.the-athenaeum.org/art/detail.php?ID=246073

77 Robert Macfarlane, Landmarks, Penguin Books, 2015, Glossary VII, Fields and Ploughing, page 258.

78 Pilosella officinarum, or mouse-ear hawkweed, a yellow-flowered species of flowering plant in the daisy family Asteraceae, native to Europe and northern Asia.

79 Argyranthemum, marguerite, marguerite daisy, or ox-eye daisy, is a genus of flowering plants belonging to the Asteraceae family.

80 Leonardo Pisano, or Leonardo Fibonacci (born C. 1170, Pisa?—died after 1240), was a medieval Italian mathematician who wrote Liber Abaci in 1202 (The Book of the Abacus"). The first European work on Indian and Arabian mathematic. In the nineteenth-century the term Fibonacci sequence was coined by the French mathematician Edouard Lucas, at this time scientists began to discover such sequences in nature; for example, in the spirals of sunflower heads, in pine cones and in ferns. https://www.britannica.com/biography/Leonardo-Pisano

81 Armoracia rusticana, horseradish, is a perennial plant of the Brassicaceae family, which also includes mustard, wasabi, broccoli and cabbage.

82 The piece was composed by the Estonian composer in 1977, a year after Benjamin Britten's death on the 4th December 1976.

83 William Shakespeare, king Lear, Act Four, Scene One.

84 Cordelia's silence is one of the most powerful dramatic devices that Shakespeare ever employed and the word 'nothing' appears in the play thirty-four times.

85 Phoenicurus ochruros, black redstart or black redtail. A small passerine bird, an Old World flycatcher (Muscicapidae).

86 Cirsium dissectum, meadow thistle, is an erect perennial herb, yet another member of the Asteraceae family.

87 Trifolium, from the Latin, tres «three» + folium «leaf», clover or trefoil, consisting of about 300 species in the lequminous pea family Fabaceae.

88 Silene dioica, known as red campion, an herbaceous flowering plant in the family Caryophyllaceae.

89   Lathyrus pratensis or meadow pea or meadow vetchling, is a perennial legume.

90   Stachys palustris, marsh woundwort, a perennial plant and a member of the mint or deadnettle family (Lamiaceae).

91   https://monicawilde.com/marsh-woundwort-medicinal-use/

92   Andrew Gurr, Rebuilding Shakespeare's Globe (Weidenfeld and Nicolson Ltd, 1989), p. 64

93   https://www.poetryfoundation.org/poems/44272/the-road-not-taken

94   Robert Macfarlane, Landmarks, Penguin Books, 2015, page 207. Soodle: to walk in a slow and leisurely manner, stroll, saunter. A word coined by the poet John Clare and included in Macfarlane's Glossary V.

95   https://www.google.at/search?q=Breeding%2520Cattle%-2520from%2520+Austria+_eng.pdf&spell=1&sa=X&ved=2ahUKEwi3lZD-1qvbaAhUCaFAKHa5pCUAQBSgAegQIABAn&biw=1242&bih=579

96   Fra Angelico, Annunciation, Fresco, (circa 1450), the Convent of San Marco, Florence.

97   Campanula medium, Canterbury bells or bell flower. An annual or biennial plant of the genus Campanula, belonging to the family Campanulaceae.

98   Symphytum (genus) - Comfrey is a common name.

99   Vanessa cardui, or painted ladies, in the family Nymphalidae.

100   Sleeping Hermaphroditus at the National Museum in Rome, mid-second century AD Roman copy.

101   Verbascum densiflorum, mullein, a plant species in the genus Verbascum.

102   Campanula medium, Canterbury bells or bell flower. An annual of biennial plant biennial plant of the genus Campanula, belonging to the family Campanulaceae.

103   Geranium pratense, meadow crane's-bill or meadow geranium is a hardy flowering perennial plant in the genus Geranium and a member of the family Geraniaceae.

104   Both Mark Forsyth, The Horologicon: A Day's Jaunt through the Lost Words of the English Language, (Penguin Books, 2013), page 23. It is from Forsyth that I also found the wonderful lost word 'dewbediamonded'.

105   Haze-fire, a luminous morning mist through which the dawn sun is shining, Robert Macfarlane, Landmarks, Penguin Books, 2015, page 40.

106   Theridiidae, cobweb weavers or combfooted spiders. Theridiids are sedentary and typically construct an irregular web with sticky strands attached to the substrate. The strands break when prey touches the line, pulling the prey toward the centre of the web.

107   Samuel Taylor Coleridge, Biographia Literaria, (London, 1817), pp. 95-96.

108   William Shakespeare, Henry V, Act 1, Prologue

109   Angelica sylvestris – sylvestris meaning to grow in woodland, from which the English word 'sylvan' also comes.

110   Buteo buteo, or common buzzard. A medium-to-large bird of prey whose range covers most of Europe and extends into Asia.

111   Robert Macfarlane, Landmarks, Penguin Books, 2015, page 49.

112   Claude Monet, The Artist's Garden at Vétheuil, 1880.

113   Phoenicurus phoenicurus, the common redstart, is a small passerine in the redstart genus Phoenicurus.

114   Colias croceus, the clouded yellow, is a medium-sized butterfly in the Pieridae family.

115   Trifolium pratense, red clover, a herbaceous species belonging to the bean Fabaceae family, native to Europe, Western Asia and northwest Africa.

116   Rachel Carson, Silent Spring, (Penguin Books Ltd, Harmondsworth, 1977), p. 24.

117   Dr W.E. Shewell-Cooper, A Gardener's Diary, (English Universities Press Limited, London, 1953), p. 63.

118   https://www.sciencedaily.com/releases/2015/04/150408090342.htm

119   Pieris rapae, small cabbage white, a butterfly species of the whites-and-yellows family Pieridae.

120   Euonymous latifolius, common names include spindle, spindle tree, burning-bush, strawberry-bush. Native to East Asia, extending to the Himalayas, but also seen in Europe, Australasia, North America, and Madagascar.

121   Raphael, Portrait of a Cardinal, circa 1510. Prado Museum, Madrid.

122   Carlina acaulis, or dwarf silver thistle, or Charlemagne thistle. It is native to the alpine regions of central and southern Europe.

123   Poecile palustris, the marsh tit, is a passerine bird in the tit family Paridae and genus Poecile, closely related to the willow tit.

124   Rhus typhina, the staghorn sumac, is a species of flowering plant in the family Anacardiaceae, native to eastern North America, but is widely cultivated as an ornamental specimen throughout the temperate world.

125   https://en.wikipedia.org/wiki/1920_Carinthian_plebiscite

126   Paul Nash, We are Making a New World, 1918.

127   Thomas Gainsborough, Rocky Wooded Landscape with Rustic Lovers, Herdsman, and Cows, 1771-1774

128   Leslie Parris, The Tate Gallery, Landscape in Britain, c. 1750-1850, Tate Gallery, 1973, p. 38. Gainsborough writing to his musician friend William Jackson (undated).

129   According to the Syrian Center for Policy Research, an independent Syrian research organization, the death toll from the conflict as of February 2016 was 470,000. The spread and intensification of fighting has led to a dire humanitarian crisis, with 6.1 million internally displaced people and 4.8 million seeking refuge abroad, according to the UN Office for the Coordination of Humanitarian Affairs. https://www.hrw.org/world-report/2017/country-chapters/syria

130   Emberiza citronella, the yellowhammer, is a passerine bird in the bunting family. It is native to Eurasia but has been introduced into New Zealand, Australia, the Falkland Islands and South Africa.

131   William Shakespeare, Hamlet, (5.2.165-168), Marcellus after he has seen the Ghost of Old Hamlet, Hamlet's murdered father.

132   Quote from a talk between Théodore. Rousseau and Alfred Sensier, 1850's; as cited in Barbizon days, Millet-Corot-Rousseau-Barye by Charles Sprague Smith, A. Wessels Company, New York, July 1902, p. 147.

133   Campanula medium, Canterbury bells or bell flower. An annual of biennial plant biennial plant of the genus Campanula, belonging to the family Campanulaceae.

134   Robert Macfarlane, Landmarks, (Penguin Books, 2015) Glossary I: Flatlands, page 40.

135   Sylvia atricapilla, the Eurasian blackcap, is a common and widespread warbler.

136   Turdus pilaris iliacus, or redwing is a member of the thrush family Turdidae.

137   Katsushika Hokusai, Cushion Pine at Aoyama from his iconic Thirty-six Views of Mount Fuji, which includes the internationally famous and iconic print The Great Wave off Kanagawa. (1826-1833).

138   The Eurasian wren (Troglodytes troglodytes) is a very small bird, and the only member of the wren family Troglodytidae found in Eurasia and Africa.

139   Van der Bellen had previously won against Norbert Hofer, a member of
        the Freedom Party of Austria, and was sworn into office on 1ˢᵗ July 2016, but
        the results of the second round of voting were annulled by the Constitutional
        Court of Austria due to absentee votes being counted too early. The election
        was re-held and Van der Bellen was once again victorious. On 4ᵗʰ December
        2016, he was elected, but with only 54% of the vote.

140   King James Bible, Genesis 3:22, Cambridge University Press, Cameo Reference
        Bible, 1998, page 4.

141   Lophophanes cristatus, the European crested tit, or simply crested tit, a
        passerine bird in the tit family Paridae.

142   Dendrocopos major, the great spotted woodpecker is a medium-sized wood-
        pecker, part of the family Picidae, a group of near-passerine birds.

143   Sitta europaea, or Eurasian nuthatch, a small passerine bird.

144   Caspar David Friedrich, Wanderer above the Sea of Fog, 1817.

145   Quoted in Jan Reynolds, Birket Foster, B.T. Batsford, 1984, page 106.

146   https://fractalfoundation.org/resources/what-are-fractals/

147   Charles Hamilton Sorley, from The Poems and Selected Letters of Charles
        Hamilton Sorley, edited by Hilda D. Spear, Blackness Press, 1978.

148   Ralph Waldo Emerson, Nature, James Munroe and Company, (1836), p. 143.

149   https://labyrinthos.co/blogs/learn-tarot-with-labyrinthos-academy/the-sev-
        en-stages-of-alchemical-transformation-a-spiritual-metaphor-infographic

150   The Essential Rumi, translated by Coleman Barks and John Moyne, Castle
        Books, 1997, p. 140.

151   It was a visit the Maidstone Museum in Kent that introduced me to the
        Kintsugi method: https://museum.maidstone.gov.uk/kintsugi-revealing-beau-
        ty-broken/

152   There is an inn on your right, but if you visit it will take you out of your way a
        little. It closes on a Tuesday.

153   The largest hotel in Schiefling is not open to the public any more, as it has
        been converted and put to good use as a home for those fleeing war-torn Syria
        and the Middle East, but there are two other inns where refreshments may be
        purchased: Simmerlwirt and the newly restored Schöllerwirt.

154   Sprich Dich Frei (which translates as you can speak freely) was established by
        Myriam Robveille in 2008, Myriam is also involved with an NGO called Mitein-
        ander (which means - with each other) which organises training in German for
        refugees who now live in the local area, regardless of their creed or religion.

Manufactured by Amazon.ca
Bolton, ON